THE
QUEEN OF THE
RING

THE QUEEN OF
THE RING

Sex, Muscles, Diamonds,
and the Making of
an American Legend

Jeff Leen

Atlantic Monthly Press
New York

Published simultaneously in Canada
Printed in the United States of America

FIRST EDITION

ISBN-13: 978-0-8021-1882-0

Atlantic Monthly Press
an imprint of Grove/Atlantic, Inc.
841 Broadway
New York, NY 10003

Distributed by Publishers Group West

www.groveatlantic.com

09 10 11 12 13   10 9 8 7 6 5 4 3 2 1

To the memory of Ethel Leen

Contents

CONTENTS

You realize that a man can take a train and never reach his destination, that a man has no destination at the end of the road, but that he merely has a starting place on the road—which is Home.

—Jack Kerouac

1

The Match of the Century

On August 20, 1954, as America slipped into the conservatism of the Eisenhower era, a professional wrestling match unlike any other took place in Atlanta, Georgia. To begin with, two women were wrestling for the world championship. The opponents, the champion Mildred Burke and the challenger June Byers, were widely considered to be the two best female wrestlers in an era when wrestling skill still mattered. Bitter rivals, they once had worked closely together for the same manager, a man known as Diamond Billy Wolfe, who had been the husband of Burke and the lover of Byers. But this was no catfight over a man. It was a business dispute, pure and simple, aimed at settling the question of who would run women's wrestling throughout the nation.

Most astonishing was the character of the match itself. In an age when every other pro bout was a faked exhibition designed to fool spectators, Burke and Byers planned to wrestle for real, to conduct what was known inside the game as a "shooting match." Pro wrestling had been fixed for years, and by the 1950s the ring action had become more and more florid in its fakery, but the ability of wrestlers to "shoot" still set them apart. Shooting ability protected champions from opponents who might think of deviating from the script and pulling a double cross in the ring in a bid to steal the title. In the past, when powerful promoters could not agree on who should be champion, they let their wrestlers shoot for the title. But that had not happened in decades.

So Burke and Byers would shoot, with no time limit. The first woman to win two falls by pin or submission would receive the championship belt and effective control of the business. Since the public was never told outright that wrestling was staged, it would likewise not now be told that this match was for real. Only the wrestling cognoscenti would know; this match was for their benefit, not the fans. The Atlanta bout was not merely an aberration; it was one of those moments that in later years can be seen as a signpost for the passing of an era. The fading epoch would come to be known as the Golden Age of Wrestling, a period when television and the strong interest of women fans won for wrestling its highest place thus far on the American scene. Female wrestlers had their own place in this renaissance of their sport; wrestling's golden age had been a time when women built like gymnasts had donned tights, laced up boots, and filled wrestling arenas as equals to men.

Mildred Burke had put the women there. More than just a champion, Millie Burke had pioneered women's wrestling as a viable arena attraction in America. She was its Babe Ruth and its Jackie Robinson. At her peak she earned $50,000 a year, as much as Joe DiMaggio and more than twice that of the legendary golfer Mildred "Babe" Didrikson Zaharias, who was widely considered the greatest female athlete of the century. A Baptist girl from Kansas who followed an improbable dream, Burke had emerged during the depths of the Great Depression alongside two other hardscrabble underdogs, the spectacular colt Seabiscuit and the Cinderella Man, boxer James J. Braddock. She began by wrestling men in carnivals, pitting a preternatural balance and command of leverage against local pride and male muscle in dried-up Dust Bowl towns throughout the Midwest. When she was starting out, she was so fast in the ring they called her the Kansas Cyclone. She was a small woman, petite, only five feet, two inches tall, and 120 pounds in the beginning, but she had a bull neck and fourteen-inch biceps in an age when women didn't have biceps. "Muscles" had been another of her early nicknames. Her legs were so muscular and stout that they vaguely conjured up the image of a centaur: a human torso atop the trunk and legs of a horse. Despite the muscles and her lack of conventional beauty, many men found her extremely attractive. Her pinup calendar, which featured her flexing her biceps and posing in a revealing zebra-stripped two-piece swimsuit and high heels, had found a happy home in newsrooms across the country.

Those who paid to see her could tell she was an obvious master of "scientific" wrestling. She expertly employed the most painful and punishing holds of the day: the wristlock, the step-over toehold, the body slam, the body scissors, the head scissors. When she drop-kicked an opponent in New Jersey the crowd gasped; they didn't think a woman could do that. What she had envisioned and then created was something no one had seen before: a female champion who was both feminine and strong, beautiful and powerful, combining the physique of an athlete with the sex appeal of a bathing beauty and the glamour of a movie star. "Sure, when I'm on the mat, I'm tough as a picnic egg," she told a reporter in the early days in her flat, slightly nasal midwestern accent that always made even the most outrageous pronouncements sound merely matter-of-fact. "But when I'm dressed for the street or home, you won't find anybody who would take me for a wrestler. I'm still all woman and twenty-six inches around the waist."

Against all odds, she had broken the barriers to give women's matches a place as the main event on wrestling cards with men. Millie Burke had wrestled before thousands from Los Angeles to Boston, from

Miami to Mexico City, from Portland, Oregon, to Portland, Maine. In Havana, the Cuban president himself had welcomed her to his marble-lined palace. In Washington, she had basked in the adoring attention of senators. In Manhattan, she had performed eighty body-bridge exercises on the desk of Robert L. Ripley, who enshrined her in his *Ripley's Believe It or Not*. She had been written up in *Time* and *Life* and by hundreds of newspaper hacks across the land. Leading a life lit by flashbulbs, she went out into the night draped in diamonds and furs and the finest silk dresses. More than all that, she had come along when the entire industry of pro wrestling was in a precarious position, rocked by scandals brought on by newspaper exposés of fixed matches and fake champions. With her speed and skill and style, Millie Burke had helped save the sport and send it on to its greatest heights in the new age of television. Yet now it was she who was in the precarious position.

On the eve of the Atlanta match, Burke was unusually quiet as she sat in the dank locker room at the city auditorium, an aging redbrick structure at the corner of Courtland and Gilmer streets. She had just turned thirty-nine, and time and her trade had coarsened her features and added twenty pounds, most of it muscle, to her frame. By her side was her twenty-year-old son, Joe, the one constant in her life. He noticed immediately that something was wrong. His mother had always been loose and joking before her matches, the picture of confidence. She had learned early that wrestling was mostly mental, and she had armored her mind against panic, controlling her emotions, sensing the fear in others and using it to her advantage. Now it was she who felt the fear and it made her tight. She was hurting and the stakes had never been so high. Her son became fearful too. He thought of all of her injuries and for the first time he was afraid she might lose.

She shouldn't be here. Throughout her career she had been a physical marvel but now she was a near wreck, a patchwork of pain and wounds. In twenty years in the ring, she had dislocated both thumbs, broken ribs, torn up both knees. Three years earlier, she had narrowly escaped death in a spectacular automobile accident; five of her ribs had been snapped near the spine. The convalescence she needed had been cut short, for she was not just a champion and an icon but also a business and there was money to be made. Her neck and ribs were never free of residual pain. Her long-standing weak point, a gimpy right knee that occasionally slipped out of joint, had been reinjured in a recent match; bloody fluid had been drawn but the swelling and soreness remained. She should have postponed the match but her circumstances and the pride that had driven her from the beginning wouldn't allow it.

Local dignitaries came into her dressing room, as they often did before a big match. The chief of police arrived to wish her well. Burke told him that Joe was now her driver and the boy needed a license. Could the chief help? You come by my office tomorrow, Joe. I'll fix you up. That had been the kind of life she had lived for nearly two decades.

The wrestling card would begin at 8:30 p.m. Burke and Byers would be working the co–main event on a bill that included a passel of colorful pachyderms: Buffalo Boy Zimm, Chief Big Heart, Bowery Boy Jack Steele, and El Toro. But the women's match was the one everyone wanted to see.

"All eyes of the wrestling world will be watching the ladies' title match in which Mildred Burke, the present queen, will meet Miss June Byers, title contender," the *Atlanta Journal* article announced. "Most Important Match of the Year Scheduled for Atlanta," the wrestling programs headlined. "National Wrestling Alliance members, promoters and wrestling officials from all over the United States are making plans to attend."

The hype left out the fact that Burke was hurt.

"These two clever girl wrestlers are both in tip-top condition and both have plenty of experience behind them. The match promises to be one of the hardest fought contests of the season as both are equally determined to win and each is confident in her own mind she can defeat the other. The girls have asked that the match be a two-out-of-three-fall affair, with no time limit. There must be a winner."

A "grudge match," it was called. That wasn't hype.

Millie Burke's grudge was not with June Byers; it was with Byers's manager, the emperor of the women's wrestling business, Diamond Billy Wolfe. Once he had been Burke's manager as well as her husband. Billy Wolfe was an American archetype, the lone man who builds an empire through vision, courage, ruthlessness, and the general greasing of palms. He had been the brain behind Burke's wrestling brawn, a fast-talking, fast-thinking carnival barker of a businessman whose steely toughness powered her rise. "She's my prize package," he told a newspaper reporter in the early days. "She's got balance and a sense of timing. And did you feel her muscles? Let the gentleman feel you, Millie. What biceps for a dame, huh? And feel that muscle under the shoulder. Not only that, but Millie's got magnetism like an actress or a lady preacher. When she comes out into the ring, everybody takes to her." Her muscles and his mind had made the industry of women's professional wrestling in America. They both gloried in the money they made and used it to cover themselves with precious gems. But the male peacock outdid the female. He sported diamonds on his belt buckle, watch fob, cuff links, and stickpin. He had four diamond rings, including one with a ten-carat stone. "His diamonds make him shine like a chandelier in a gay '90s dining room—$60,000 worth," a *Washington Post* columnist noted.

At their height, Wolfe and Burke had thirty women wrestling for them and filling arenas across the country. A ladies' man surrounded by female flesh and more than willing to partake, Wolfe slept his way through almost half of them, but Burke didn't care. Theirs had always been a business relationship rather than a loving matrimonial bond, a mutual dependency based on pure pragmatism. She wanted only to be champion, and she was willing to do whatever it took. Then it all came apart. It turned into a legal and financial fight, a war of money, for the business they had created. The last battle of the war would be of muscle and blood and bone, two women for one championship to settle it all.

June Byers entered the ring, and then the call came for Burke. The champion always went last. Millie Burke walked out of the dressing room, Joe trailing her. Like Byers, she wore full makeup—rouge, eye shadow, and lipstick—looking her best. Her auburn hair was dressed in a careful marcelled wave. The hair would be tossed and the makeup smeared and sweated off within minutes of action in the ring, but that first impression on the crowd meant everything.

Tonight, as she nearly always did, Millie wore wrestling tights of brilliant white satin, a one-piece swimsuit that had been reinforced with elastic for industrial use in the ring. At a time when most wrestlers donned drab black togs, she had been the first to regularly wear white. People had protested; it was obscene, it made her look naked. She didn't care. With her innate sense of ring style she knew that the white reflected the harsh descending light back into the crowd, making her sparkle like a diamond. Her deep tan contrasted nicely with the white satin. Her matching white wrestling boots, size five, were custom-made using the finest soft leathers at Barney's, a little shop in downtown LA, for sixty dollars—a month's wage for a workingman when she started buying them back during the Depression. Her robe was the crowning gesture. Again she chose white, satin and silk, trimmed in ermine and encrusted over every inch with rhinestones. It was worth every ounce of the physical effort it took to wear it. "When the powerful ring lights hit those rhinestones, it was a shimmering symphony," she later wrote in an autobiography that has never been published. Around her waist, to complete the effect, hung her most prized possession: her championship belt. It weighed fifteen pounds and was said to be twenty-four-carat gold with four sapphires, six amethysts, and a seven-carat diamond. She had held the title so long her cameo had been inserted into it.

Before her were a cone of white light and a small square of white canvas cut against a roaring, darkened circle of humanity, thousands disgorging emotion in waves of sound. "Wrestling partakes of the nature of the great solar spectacles, Greek drama and bullfights," a French philosopher would write a few years later. "In both, a light without shadow generates an emotion without reserve." The arena was a smoky, airless place, a swirl of heat and noise. A segregated crowd of white faces stared back at her, an audience of adults in suits, hats, and dresses. In her heavy robe and belt Burke climbed into the ring and under the ropes, as she had on a thousand occasions, one leg at a time.

Bouncing on the taut canvas, she eyed Byers and listened as the ring announcer spoke and the crowd quieted. The announcer gave the weights. Burke was stunned by how big and powerful Byers looked. The Texas woman held every physical advantage. She was younger, bigger, stronger, fitter. She was a full five inches taller, and at least twenty pounds heavier, a bundle of rippling muscle. One of the women wrestlers who saw Byers in training later recalled that she "looked like a racehorse," with "a thick back, very tight and high thigh muscles, big muscular arms and neck." Byers was known as one of the meanest and most brutal women in wrestling. She didn't just beat her opponents, she terrorized them, with punches and open-handed slaps against their breastbones that resounded from the ring. Still, Byers was a bit cowed by Burke, who held the mental edge and the advantage in wrestling skill. Years later, Byers would recall her wariness at the sight of the champion: "She had a bouncy, elastic quality about her and her skin looked as if it were bursting with vitality."

The bell sounded. The crowd drew a breath and gaped at the brightness before it. In the cone of drenching vertical light two women rushed forward, bouncing on the balls of their feet.

2

Millie Bliss

Mildred Burke and Billy Wolfe were products of the Midwest, but not of the placid, stereotypically wholesome land that exists mainly in the imaginations of those who believe that all midwesterners are farmers who grew up in loving, churchgoing families. Burke's and Wolfe's Midwest was a darker place existing on the fringes of the farm economy, a dilapidated Depression-haunted landscape of small towns and wide-open spaces, the Midwest of the carny and the outlaw. Burke's birthplace was Coffeyville, Kansas, in the southeastern corner of the state on the Verdigris River near the Oklahoma line. It is still best known for the day in 1892 when five members of the Dalton Gang, hoping to one-up the James Gang, rode in with the unprecedented plan of robbing two banks in the same town at the same time. The Daltons made it into the street with $25,000. They did not make it far. It was *their* hometown, after all, and despite the beards they wore as disguises they were recognized. Fifteen minutes later four Daltons were dead, along with four residents of Coffeyville, which became known around the country as "the town that stopped the Daltons."

By the time Millie Bliss was born there on August 5, 1915, Coffeyville had swelled to a population of 13,000 and had made the transition from frontier railroad-and-cattle nexus to manufacturing center. It was home to an astonishing array of industries: nine glass factories, six brick plants, four foundries, the Missouri Pacific railroad shops, the biggest oil refinery in the state, and more than a dozen other factories and plants, making everything from ice to plows to egg cases. The bustling machine shops had brought the Bliss family to this corner of Kansas.

In her fanciful but illuminating unpublished autobiography, Mildred Burke would describe her father as an itinerant inventor who put the family through cycles of boom and bust. In good times, she wrote, when he came up with viable creations such as a heavy-duty hand soap for mechanics or a nonskid tire chain, they lived well, at one time occupying a big house with twenty-five rooms, including a ballroom on the second floor. In the bad times, when her father's ideas fizzled, the children went to school without socks.

Millie Bliss's childhood was fractured and hard. She was the baby of six children—five girls and one boy—born to Bruce Edward Bliss and his wife, Bertha. The family was crammed into a tiny millworker's house next to the railroad tracks and down the street from a cemetery and the huge Bartlet flour mill on the south side of town. The small, square boxlike frame structure at 1507 Maple Street had one bedroom, a dining room, and a kitchen; the Coffeyville city directory for 1916–17 shows that Millie lived there with her father, her mother, her brother, Louis, and two of her sisters. The family was in constant motion. Just a few years earlier Bruce Bliss had been a butcher in Haw Creek, Missouri. By 1918 he was a traveling salesman for a manufacturing company in Wichita. Two years later he was managing a tire company there. Two of his patents, for his nonskid tire chain and a two-part interlocking tire, date from his time in Wichita. His draft registration indicated that he suffered from kidney, liver, and rheu-

matic trouble. The family moved to Kansas City and then on to Los
Angeles, where during a boom period they owned a small chain of
three restaurants in Glendale. When Millie was eleven, her parents
split up and Bruce Bliss walked out of her life. He would not see his
daughter again until seventeen years later, when he joined thousands
of fans to watch her wrestle as champion.

In 1927 Millie moved with her mother back to Kansas City. It was
just the two of them now. As the older children left to make lives of
their own, the formidable Bertha Bliss became the steadfast rock in
Millie's life, cooking in restaurants to support them and imbuing her
daughter with classic midwestern values. "My mother was a warm-
hearted, loving woman who passed on to me her strong, conservative
moral code," Burke wrote a half century later. "My mother taught
me to look for the best and see the good in others."

Millie was physically small but she was also a natural athlete with
strong legs. She excelled at soccer and running track. And she was
tough. She often played with the boys "because I could take a little
more pushing around than most girls and could hold my own against
them." One time in grade school, when it had been girls against boys
in soccer, the boys started kicking the girls in the shins to make them
quit. Little blue-eyed Millie refused to back down. "I stayed in there
no matter how many times they kicked me in the shins," she wrote.
"I was there or die!"

One thing her mother never talked about was boys. Sex was a
mystery wrapped in ignorance, guilt, and shame. Surrounded by females in a prim and proper Baptist household, Millie grew up with
extremely naive notions about men. "When I first menstruated, I
thought that it was an injury from having a boy playfully jump on my
back from behind while walking home from a movie," she wrote.
Throughout her life men would remain a riddle. Her brother was quiet
and not athletically inclined. His interests were musical and Burke later

claimed he went on to play the pipe organ for the noted Pentecostal evangelist Aimee Semple McPherson and doubled as her chauffeur. The pull of McPherson's Foursquare Gospel Church, its reach magnified by the new invention of radio, drew many adherents from the Midwest to its 5,300-seat Angelus Temple in Los Angeles. Three of Mildred's sisters would become ministers in McPherson's flock. Drawn by a voice, her sisters had found a spiritual path out of devastating poverty; Millie would find her own spiritual path in the corporeal.

At first, Millie's own aspirations were more typical. She wanted to be an interior decorator. She also had another dream, one that she couldn't quite understand, but it thrilled her and filled her with hope. It was always the same: perched on the rim of a large auditorium she peered down a long set of stairs to see a cheering throng below. Suddenly she alighted, flying over the crowd, floating, as if levitated by the applause.

When she was fourteen, the stock market came crashing down over three days in late October 1929 known as Black Thursday, Black Monday, and Black Tuesday. That led to the failure of ten thousand banks and soon millions of people would be out of work and scraping for money. The Great Depression arrived and knocked Millie's already precarious existence one rung nearer to the thin edge of desperation. She dropped out of her freshman year at Manual High School in Kansas City, her formal schooling at an end. She and her fifty-five-year-old mother were forced to move into a boarding home run by a widow and already crowded with thirteen others. Millie took on part-time work as a stenographer while her mother cooked at a hotel.

Burke describes her early work life in Kansas City as a sequence of events out of the *Perils of Pauline*. When she was fifteen, one employer tried to force himself on her as she was taking dictation in his office. She fought him off. "The struggle resulted in the man ejaculating all over himself, whereupon he fled in total embarrassment," she wrote. She was horrified. "I actually thought that I could get pregnant just from his involuntary ejaculation while standing three feet away from me." Overcome with shame, she instantly decided to run away from home. She accepted a ride from a stranger and ended up fighting off another man, this time in a motel room. Only the intervention of the police returned her safely to her home.

In another of the abrupt shifts that defined her early life, Millie next ended up in the town of Black Rock on the Zuni Indian Reservation south of Gallup, New Mexico. For two years she worked as a waitress in a government-run restaurant where her mother cooked. Millie watched war dances and had her picture taken with Indians in full headdress, but a reservation was no place for a teenage girl. Desperate for a new life and still naive, she married a man named Joseph Martin Shaffer, at age seventeen. He was about a dozen years older than her, but little else is known about him today. "I would have married anyone to get off that reservation," she later said.

Mildred and her husband moved back to Kansas City along with her mother. By 1933 the three of them were hard at work trying to make a go of it as proprietors of a small thirty-seat diner they called the B & S Cafe. While her mother cooked, Millie and Shaffer waited on tables and helped in the kitchen. They lived together in an apartment a few doors away. The city was considered to be "wide open," a place of Kansas City steaks and Kansas City jazz, a magnet for musicians attracted by the clubs and workers drawn by the stockyards, the largest in the country after Chicago. The B & S Cafe was located at 1320 East 15th Street in the 18th and Vine district of the city, a historically black neighborhood that was the hotbed for the city's famous jazz as well as speakeasies and spicy barbecue. In the days of public segregation 18th and Vine was a bustling business district for a self-contained community. The area jumped with life and energy under the benevolent eye of the corrupt Pendergast political machine, which tolerated a certain licentiousness. In a few years Charlie Parker would emerge from the ferment to change the face of American music.

That year prohibition was ending, but times had never been tougher; 1932 and 1933 were the trough of the Depression, with unemployment hitting 25 percent, a level nobody had ever seen. Home-cooked meals at the B & S cost 25 cents, the price of a movie ticket. Millie worked twelve hours a day, seven days a week, to make $4 at a time when the average rent was $20 a month and the average income was $1,600 a year. They were subsisting, trying to ride it out. Dust storms coated everything with grit, adding to the grimness throughout the Great Plains.

In her lengthy autobiography Burke mentions only one thing her first husband did for her: he took her to see her first pro wrestling match. It was at the Midway Arena in Kansas City. She later recalled that there were only a handful of women in a crowd of more than a thousand, and when she looked around she was met with hard and hostile stares. But when she looked into the ring she saw a beckoning vision.

Pro wrestling has always been the province of the powerful and the dominant, where imposing physical specimens, stripped to reveal their bodies, triumph in the most naked and open arena. Throughout history the sport has been the domain of the most manly of men, from Milo of Croton, the Olympic champion of ancient Greece who reputedly could kill an ox with his bare hands, to Frank Gotch, an Iowa farm boy who became the first American professional world champion in 1908. For Millie Bliss, a tiny woman who had been treated all of her life as prey, the sight of the muscular men in the ring hit with a liberating force. "Watching these bouts fascinated, absorbed and excited me in a way that I had never known before," she would later recall. "Something deep in my core had been tapped awake."

She was staring at a version of the sport specifically engineered for maximum excitement. By the 1930s wrestling had evolved a great deal from the days of Milo or even Gotch. To the Greeks, wrestling was primarily a contest where men stood upright, gripped each other above the waist, and attempted to throw their opponent to the ground. In the late nineteenth century in America, Irish immigrants and frontiersmen, many of them Civil War veterans who had taken up the sport in the Union army, popularized more freewheeling grappling styles that incorporated ground wrestling and leg holds, like the body scissors, the grapevine, and the head scissors. The sport began in saloons and carnivals and moved up to arenas at the turn of the century. It was an age newly enamored with science, and the matches were glacial contests of so-called scientific wrestling. The action unfolded through precise applications of leverage and force, with muscled behemoths struggling on the mat for imperceptible advantage through marathons that could last five hours or more.

After World War I, however, the public began to tire of the slow, endless matches. "When I began to read sports pages, wrestling was in a state of profound depression, owing to the earnest efforts of a number of wrestlers to defeat each other," the great boxing writer A. J. Liebling later observed. "Conducted honestly, wrestling is the dullest of sports to watch." Time limits were introduced, and so was a new form of wrestling that was fast and furious, full of dramatic reversals and flashy holds such as the flying dropkick and the airplane spin. The wrestlers stayed on their feet for much of the match, at times exchanging punches like boxers. Dramatic buildups presaged the big bouts, and titles were traded back and forth. Sportswriters started calling the sport "rasslin'." It was not just a change in terminology; wrestling had morphed into a form of theater, and it became more popular than ever. It had also become quite fake.

The wrestlers didn't use the words "fake" or "fixed" to describe it. They had a much better word. They called it "worked." A worked match was one where the two wrestlers, by prior consent, engaged in a carefully worked out choreography of spectacular acrobatic maneuvers and bold gestures of pain and retribution. The hero, the virtuous wrestler who fought cleanly and suffered nobly against his opponent, would eventually become known as "babyface." His opponent was the "heel," the dirty-wrestling villain. The buildup to the match was "the program." The object was to generate audience response, or "heat." The dirty secret of wrestling was protected by a code known as "kayfabe," a term that came from the carnivals that served as pro wrestling's birthplace. When civilians were around, wrestlers at all costs maintained the fiction that what they did was real. For the insiders, everything was done to protect the box office. The fans did not want to have to think about whether pro wrestling was real or fake; it was enough for them that the sport provided a consuming drama that immersed its audience in a cauldron of symbolism and emotion. Roland Barthes's philosophical meditation on pro wrestling came decades later, but it captured the essence of why the former carnies who transformed the sport in the 1920s were so successful: "The public is completely uninterested in knowing whether the contest is rigged or not, and rightly so; it abandons itself to the primary virtue of the spectacle, which is to abolish all motives and consequences: what matters is not what it thinks but what it sees."

The leading stars of the "slam-bang" style were Ed "Strangler" Lewis and Jim "the Greek Adonis" Londos. At five feet, ten inches tall and 220 pounds, Lewis was a tank of a man who was impossible for anybody to defeat in a real match. He was built like a gorilla, with a sway back, short legs, a twenty-two-inch neck, and an enormous chest. Even skilled wrestlers were terrified of facing him in anything but a worked match. In the early 1920s Lewis had joined with his manager Billy Sandow and fellow wrestler and trainer Joseph "Toots" Mondt to create and popularize the slam bang style. Lewis himself became so popular that the newspaper hacks enshrined him along with Babe Ruth, Red Grange, Jack Dempsey, Bill Tilden, and Bobby Jones in that first pantheon of American sports superstars, the period known as the golden age of sports.

Jim Londos, who followed Lewis, was something even better, as far as the fans were concerned: the sport's first true sex symbol. Known as the "Man with the Million-Dollar Body," he stood five feet, eight inches tall and weighed a more normal-sized 190 pounds. But he had a sculpted physique with six-pack abs, and his shock of thick dark hair and gleaming white teeth made him look like a movie star. Though nowhere near the wrestler that Lewis was, Londos had real ability and he performed in a faster and more theatrical style that brought in even more fans than Lewis. In 1931 Londos eleven times drew crowds of more than ten thousand to Madison Square Garden. "Whether Londos was the best wrestler of his time is dubious, but he was certainly the best spectacular wrestler," Liebling wrote. Women especially flocked to see Londos, and they were driving wrestling's newfound popularity. "It's the ladies, whose shrill screams reveal how thin is the veneer of civilization over the innate savagery of the human race, who are mainly responsible for lifting wrestling from a dubious barroom-brawl status to a position where it threatens soon to take its place with boxing in the million-dollar-gate class," wrote one feature writer in an article carried in newspapers around the country. A "well-dressed, genteel" college girl went to a match expecting to be bored but instead found herself "on the edge of my seat with intense excitement and interest. Here was no bloody, brutal sport that outraged my sensibilities, but a spectacle crowded with drama—strength pitted against strength—muscle matched against cleverness."

Unlike most of the other women, Millie did not want to be just a wrestling fan; she wanted to be a wrestler. "Immediately I began fantasizing myself in that ring, applying those grips, holds and throws," she later wrote. "A desire and a drive to fill in those fantasies with flesh and blood came surging to life." She loved the drama, the action and the conflict, the rapid changes of fortune that reminded her of a medieval morality play. The clashing of athletic bodies stirred her to her depths. For her, it was a mystical experience, made even more inexplicable by the fact that she had never done any wrestling in her life. Now she thought about it constantly. When she told her husband that she wanted to wrestle he laughed. To mainstream Americans in the 1930s women were still considered to be far too delicate for something like wrestling. The elegant figure skater Sonje Henie was the avatar of women's sports, which were limited to the ice rink, the swimming pool, the golf course, and the tennis court. Magazine articles of the day argued that physical sports were too strenuous for women. "Under prolonged and intense physical strain a girl goes to pieces nervously," Ethel Perrin, a noted instructor of physical education, wrote in the *Saturday Evening Post* in 1928. "She is 'through' mentally before she is completely depleted physically . . . The fact that a girl's nervous resistance cannot hold out under intense physical strain is nature's warning."

Women have wrestled from the beginning, despite the enduring attempts of men to stop them. Around the time Milo of Croton was winning his first great victories in 520 BC, a mixed match between a man and a woman was immortalized on several Attic vases. Atalanta, the strong and beautiful huntress of myth, defeated Peleus, an athlete and hero who was the father of the greatest of all Greek warriors, Achilles. In the *Thousand and One Nights,* a wrestling Arabian princess grappled with men for her hand in marriage. If they lost, they lost their heads; thirty-nine of them decorated the entrance to her palace. In the thirteenth century Marco Polo wrote of another wrestling princess who occupied a magnificent palace in Samarkand and defeated a hundred men who had sought her hand in marriage.

Women wrestlers appeared in numbers in la belle époque at the end of the nineteenth century. In this new age, "physical culture" came into being and a fascination with strength and muscles was unleashed. The famed wrestler and strongman George Hackenschmidt was celebrated for "a body of alabaster beauty, the broadest shoulders, the deepest chest ever seen in the wrestling ring." Strong women arose to display their own bulging muscles. Female wrestlers soon emerged in Russian circuses, Parisian nightclubs, and American saloons. In circus athletic shows, a woman wrestler challenging men in the audience became a regular act. The act moved into variety houses in urban areas. The women wore black tights and spangled leotards, their hair cut short to prevent pulling. In a Victorian era where public bathing was still a rarity, the matches allowed men to stare openly at a woman's body, revealed as it was in contour-hugging fabric. "The erotic component obviously was an important element in such exhibitions," wrote the German author Stefan Nagel in *The Booth,* a history of circuses. "Both men and women demonstrated their perfect body form outlines, strength, free play of muscles, elegance of the movements . . . which manifested not only artistry but rather also provocative sensuality."

In 1891, the *National Police Gazette* sponsored the first U.S. women's wrestling championship in a Bowery tavern. The title would pass through the hands of hulking women such as 165-pound Josie Wahlford and 190-pound Laura Bennett before resting with 138-pound Cora Livingston, who won it in Kansas City in 1914. Livingston was the prototype for Mildred Burke. Like Burke, she was relatively small and managed by a male wrestler who was also her husband. The couple toured the country in carnivals and vaudeville theaters, offering $25 to any woman who could last ten minutes with Cora. Sometimes she would take on men. "The action was spirited and all that, the lady giving the gentleman all he could do to master her," wrote one reporter, who added that "enthusiasm for the skit lost much of its savor" when the customers learned that Livingston was wrestling her husband.

The detractors never went away. "I beheld this vicious-countenanced woman wrestle and tussle in the most ungodly manner," a female correspondent for the Galveston, Texas, *Daily News* wrote after seeing Livingston wrestle in New York City. "My heart sank and I felt weak and sick that a woman could stoop to such performances." John C. Meyers, one of the leading wrestling experts of the day, approved of females as fans but not as wrestlers. "Women are not fit," he wrote in 1931. "Such exhibitions are degrading athletic crimes, should not be permitted, and are a challenge to decency."

Despite her talent, Livingston never transcended the carnivals and the novelty bouts on vaudeville stages. There were not enough women for her to wrestle and there were not enough fans for women's wrestling. The champion who succeeded Livingston, 155-pound Virginia Mercereau, ended up wrestling men. Male middleweight champion Joe Parelli struggled for thirty-seven minutes to pin her. Still, there was little demand for her skills, with mixed matches banned in most places, and she retired in 1930. Other women entered the field. They, too, wrestled men as well as women and drew the occasional crowd. But they were mainly confined to the carnivals and vaudeville houses, and none broke through to achieve sustained success.

The country's mood changed as the Depression deepened. In November 1933 *The Ring* magazine, the premier boxing and wrestling publication in the country, noted that women were wrestling in private matches throughout the country, including "the very heart of Broadway." A few months later a *Ring* writer editorialized in favor of female wrestlers. "Women fought their way to the ringside as fans over a mountain of protest. Undoubtedly, they will eventually succeed in hurdling the present objections and one day crawl between the ropes in public participation."

Millie Bliss was determined to crawl between those ropes. She had more than one reason for doing so. In 1934 her life began to fall apart. Around the time she saw her first wrestling match she became pregnant. Then Joe Shaffer walked out of her life. Once again, it was just her and her mother, with a new baby on the way. They renamed the diner Mom's Café. Not just man but nature itself seemed against them. A drought raged in the Great Plains. That spring an epic thirty-six-hour dust storm blanketed a third of the country, stretching 1,500 miles from Montana to New York City and carrying 350 million tons of sand and grit. In Kansas City it obscured the sun and limited visibility to under a mile. Unemployment still exceeded 20 percent, and business dropped off at the diner. Millie was being squeezed into an impossible spot. The one bright vision was the wrestling ring. "Urgent need for money and constant thinking about how to get it, caused my wrestling fantasies to come boiling up again," she later recalled. "If only I could get to be a lady wrestler, it would be such a novelty that people would crowd into the arenas to see me. Money would be mine in bundles, and I would be able to take good care of my baby." A photograph from the time pictures Millie in her waitress uniform at Mom's, standing forlornly behind a counter lined with small plates bearing triangles of pie. Her mouth is caught in a forced half-smile, her eyes rimmed with dark circles, sad and without hope.

3

Billy Wolfe

One day in the summer of 1934, walking on the streets outside of Mom's, eighteen-year-old Millie Bliss spied two jug-eared, broad-shouldered men gawking at her. She did a slow burn. She was short and pregnant, a walking beer keg with stout piano legs. She figured they thought she looked ridiculous. Through her mounting anger, she recognized the smaller of the two men. He had the badge of a wrestler —cauliflower ears. Years of pounding in the ring had caused the skin and cartilage in the ears to separate, leaving a space where broken blood vessels had leaked fluid that congealed, killing the cartilage and calcifying into rock-hard clumps. The outer skin of the ears, deprived of a healthy blood flow, shriveled up and folded in on itself, giving it the look of the pale vegetable from whence the condition derives its name. The man with the baggy, gnarled ears could have had surgery, but he kept them as proud emblems of his profession. Millie had seen him wrestle in Kansas City in the bouts that had so enthralled her. His name was Billy Wolfe. He was a stocky man, about five feet, seven inches tall, with horned-rimmed glasses, light brown hair, and a ruddy complexion. His ruined ears stuck out from his square skull. She thought he looked "like a taxi with both doors open. His teeth were square, too, and widely separated, giving him the appearance of a Halloween pumpkin when he smiled." He was grinning.

The leering face infuriated her. She turned to the two men, hands on her hips.

"You two are old enough to have seen a pregnant woman before, but you obviously still find it funny. I hope that in my case you get a good look."

She stalked into Mom's, slamming the door.

The men followed her. The larger one apologized. He was Gust Karras, a wrestling promoter based in nearby St. Joseph, Missouri.

"We had just remarked to each other that you had beautiful legs," Karras said. "I hope you'll forgive us."

Karras introduced Billy Wolfe, who did not apologize. Millie made note of that. It was a telling detail that would resonate as the years passed.

By the time Millie Bliss met him Billy Wolfe had gone as far as he was going to go as a wrestler. He was an outstanding grappler but he never grew beyond the light heavyweight ranks, 175 pounds or so, which meant he hadn't had enough size to compete for the really big attention and money. He had neither the brute strength of a Strangler Lewis nor the blinding sex appeal of a Jim Londos. Wolfe's territory was limited to a small area around Kansas City. He had a sore back and he had already turned to the sort of gimmicks that many felt were starting to cheapen pro wrestling, such as getting into the ring with bears and promoting women wrestlers in carnivals.

Like Millie Bliss, Billy Wolfe came from several generations of midwestern stock and grew up poor and on the move. William Harrison Wolfe had been born July 4, 1896, in the small town of Wheaton in southwest Missouri, and he grew up on a farm near Jamesport, in the northwestern part of the state. He had an older brother and two younger sisters. When Billy was young the family moved to Kansas and the census of 1910 shows them living in Phillipsburg, a small town near the Nebraska border. Wolfe's father worked as a rural mail carrier.

The Wolfe boys were drafted during World War I, and it was in the army that Billy found his talent for wrestling. He reportedly won the camp championship while stationed in Kentucky. After the Armistice he settled in Kansas City and became a wrestling instructor at the YMCA. There, he started his pro wrestling career. When he was twenty-five, he married nineteen-year-old Margaret Johnson, known as Mickie. A year later they had a son, George William, and three years after that a daughter, Violet. In the early years of the marriage, Billy Wolfe prospered. By 1923 he was described in newspapers as the middleweight champion of Missouri. Seven years later he got noticed when he lasted forty-six minutes against Charles Fisher, the wrestling coach at the University of Missouri, in a bout in Chillicothe. Wolfe's bear did not fare so well and "was pronounced unfit for a wrestling match as he had begun his winter hibernation and could not be propped up to the point necessary for a mat go."

Wolfe reached the pinnacle of his wrestling career on May 19, 1932. He lost to the light heavyweight champion of the world, one of the leading wrestlers in the country, Charles "Midget" Fischer of Butternut, Wisconsin, at Memorial Hall in Kansas City, a top wrestling venue in the Midwest. Wolfe came close; he won the second fall but Midget Fischer prevailed in the third and deciding one.

Six months later the Chillicothe paper devoted a rare feature story to a wrestler: "Billy Wolf is a paradox. He is one of the best drawing cards for wrestling shows in this part of the country. At the same time, he is one of the most unpopular wrestlers in the game." Wolfe was making a living as a "heel," whipping up the crowd with dirty tactics such as a painful, open-handed slap called the "cupped chest lick."

The crowd loved to hate him, and he became one of the most in-demand wrestlers in northwestern Missouri. "He uses every possible advantage to win a match," promoter Gust Karras explained. "He slaps when he can. He rolls off the mat when he's groggy. He wins most of his matches by beating his opponent into a weakened condition." Wolfe was already displaying the hardheaded, pragmatic outlook that would serve him well later in life. The article said that he had saved his money and bought a house for his family in Kansas City, no small feat for a wrestler during the Depression. Yet he had never allowed his eleven-year-old son, George William, to see him wrestle. "He will never learn the game," Wolfe said. "It's too hard a life." A picture of Wolfe from this time shows a still-handsome thirty-five-year-old man with swept-back hair, rippling muscles in his chest and arms, and very prominent cauliflower ears. The face is sensual and cruel, frozen into hawklike determination. The fierce eyes said it all: I don't care if you like me or even if you respect me, but you will not stand in my way.

That year Wolfe left his wife and took up with Barbara Ware, a big, flashy, good-looking female wrestler of about 150 pounds. The strapping Ware was nearly equal to Wolfe in size. She had appeared on wrestling cards with him in small towns in Missouri since 1932 and had also toured with him in carnival athletic shows, where they both challenged all comers from the audience. "Barbara is another example of the Jekyll-Hyde nature of wrestlers," the local paper noted. "Out of the ring she is as attractive a young lady as you may see. She is quiet spoken. But in the ring she picks 'em up and slams 'em down for wrestling whether it be done by ladies or gentlemen." Ware was in the vanguard of women trying to make a go of it in professional wrestling, and she was beginning to get national attention. She had been mentioned in *Ring* magazine the previous year, and the Associated Press had reported that she had defeated a 130-pound male opponent in six minutes in Topeka. Ware had also held her own against the best of the handful of female wrestlers in the country, including Clara

Mortensen from California and Betty Bushey from Boston; all three women would claim the world title at different times in the 1930s.

After Ware and Wolfe appeared on a card in Chillicothe together on March 2, 1934, the headline in the next day's paper was "Mat Fans Are Happy at Last." Ware had lost her match against a male opponent, but the real news was that Wolfe had been roughed up in a draw. "They have seen Billy Wolfe take a good beating and, as a result, they feel repaid for all the time they have sat through sessions in which Billy tortured his opponents, slapped the wind out of them and then pinned them," the paper reported. The crowd really got its wish in Wolfe's next match. Billy won by knocking out the referee and then kicking his opponent in the stomach. When the referee came to—obviously the match was worked and the whole act was arranged—he awarded the victory to Wolfe. But then the referee socked Wolfe in the jaw and dropped him to the mat. "Pandemonium" broke loose, according to the local paper. The audience rushed the ring and pummeled Wolfe. "Police, wrestlers and others interested in quieter and more select riots did their best to pull enraged fans off of the prostrate Wolfe. Finally Billy was carried to the dressing room. He will live, but will never again be the same man." Despite the hype Wolfe was back wrestling in Chillicothe a week later.

A few weeks after that, Billy Wolfe met Millie Bliss.

He was thirty-seven years old, more than double her age. Behind his thick glasses, his eyes appeared to her to have a sinister glint that was only made worse when he smiled. But he was a wrestler and that fact soon carried the day. He lived on Lydia Avenue a couple of blocks from Mom's. He also operated a small private gym over a garage less than a block away, where he trained wrestlers. "A wrestler with a gym!" she wrote much later. "My wrestling fantasies and my imagination now began breaking into a gallop. He could have looked like a gargoyle and I would have been interested."

At this point the story becomes an account told a hundred times. Both Burke and Wolfe told it repeatedly, to newspaper writers across America. Some of the facts shifted around but the core remained constant. Soon after that meeting on the street, Billy Wolfe became a regular customer at Mom's, and Millie Bliss could hardly believe her good luck. She used her position as a waitress to woo him. He was a big believer in eating the right foods, with his own theories on health. He believed that vinegar was harmful, that carrot juice improved eyesight, that mucous could accumulate in the body and cause problems. To alleviate his sore back Wolfe said his doctors had advised him to eat plenty of raw foods, especially vegetables and salads. He told her it was to help his spine by keeping his system alkaline. She began to ply him with oversized salads. He especially favored the large combination salad, and she took care to make it exactly the way he liked it. He usually came into the café with Barbara Ware. After several weeks of salads Billy seemed in a mellow mood. With Ware sitting next to him, Mildred made her pitch. "I want you to teach me to wrestle," she told him.

Wolfe stared at her, then threw his head back and laughed.

"You?" he said, looking her up and down. "Why, you ain't no bigger than a pint of piss."

He shoved a cigar into his mouth and Ware lit it for him. "What in hell makes you think that you'd make a wrestler?" he continued. "I mean, Christ, look at you. What makes you think you could do it and not get busted to bits?"

"I can't really tell you why," Mildred said, "but I have this feeling inside that I can do it. I want to do it more than anything else in the world. I've been to the matches and I know I can do it."

"Aw, bullshit," he said, waving her away with his cigar and turning back to Barbara Ware.

Now that her dream was out in the open, Mildred was relentless. She kept it up, pestering Wolfe to let her wrestle. Wolfe was equally adamant.

"You're too small, girlie, for this racket," he said.

She was convinced it was fate. He kept brushing her off.

"Even if you were good, who'd pay to see you?"

"Well, give me a chance anyway," she would counter. "Teach me to wrestle."

She threatened to stop making his favorite salad. He was unmoved.

Mildred's campaign with Wolfe had to take a breather when her son, Joe, was born on August 4, 1934, the day before her own nineteenth birthday. She went into labor right at Mom's. "When Joe decided to come into the world, I was actually waiting on tables. The customers in Mom's Café took me to the hospital." The birth had complications; Joe developed problems with a gland in his neck and Mildred had to take him by streetcar to see a specialist in nearby Independence. She kept the baby in a crib in the kitchen at Mom's so she and Bertha could watch him. She couldn't afford a babysitter. The bills were mounting and business was falling at the restaurant. Her desperation deepened, and she eventually went back at Wolfe and with renewed ardor. "Give me a tryout. Can't you see the money to be made?"

Finally, he relented. He agreed to a tryout. In his gym. Against a male wrestler.

What happened next became a central part of the legend of Mildred Burke. In the telling over the years, Millie's opponent grew from 130 pounds to 160, but the rest of the details remained remarkably consistent. On the appointed day, 115-pound Millie emerged from the smelly dressing room at Billy's dingy gym to get her first taste of wrestling. She wore a pair of boy's black sneakers and a modest black one-piece bathing suit. "I could not have been more embarrassed had I been stark naked, so alien was this whole scene," she later recalled.

In front of her was a wrestling ring. On the far side, Wolfe perched on the apron. He smoked one of his ever-present cigars, exhaling a blue fog. In the ring, her opponent waited. He was a wiry and strong eighteen-year-old gym rat known as Gypsy Joe, fit and fast and a full head taller than she was. She didn't know it but the boy had been coached by Billy Wolfe to teach the little waitress a painful lesson. Wolfe had given the boy "a crash course in basic wrestling, with special emphasis on the body slam." Wolfe told Gypsy Joe to "slam her so hard that she'll quit bothering me." He was paying the boy $2, plus another $2 after he wiped up the ring with the little woman. But fate took a hand.

"Slipping across the ring, he immediately picked me up, spun me and proceeded to body slam me—except it didn't quite turn out that way," Burke recalled. Instead of allowing the boy to slam her into the mat, she held on and brought him down with her. "By some deep instinct, some quirk of talent or flash of intuition, when I hit the mat I pulled him down and instantly took the top of him. *The gypsy was flat on his back with me on top of him!*"

She managed to pin the boy, then looked up to see Billy Wolfe "slack-jawed and pop-eyed." His wet cigar clung precariously to his lower lip. Quickly, he snatched it out.

"Wait a minute!" he said. "There's something wrong here. There's something *very* wrong here. Let's try it all over again."

Wolfe huddled with the boy.

For the second fall, Millie instantly appropriated the boy's body slam technique. It was as if his touch had transmitted the knowledge of the hold to her. "I saw how he had picked me up," she later recalled. "I picked up the gypsy boy. Up in the air he went, and then I slammed him down hard. Dust rose in a parching cloud from the impact."

Prone and stunned, he was easy prey for her pin. She rose off the mat in triumph. She had defeated the boy twice in less than a minute. It was as unreal as watching a mongoose take down a king cobra.

The cigar had dropped from Billy Wolfe's mouth.

In the culture of pro wrestling, a child of the carnival and a cousin of the long con, deception is rife and determining facts is a fraught business. But the story of Millie Bliss and Gypsy Joe has the ring of truth, if for nothing else than Mildred and Billy retold it so consistently over so many years. Burke said that she ran into Gypsy Joe years later in Omaha, Nebraska, when she was world champion. She didn't recognize him. He identified himself and asked for a rematch. "That might have been all right, but I looked at this guy and he wasn't the same little gypsy boy that I trimmed in KC," she later recalled. "My gypsy had grown. He now weighed two hundred pounds and every pound of it was muscle. I just grinned, patted his arm and left fast."

In the weeks following the match with Gypsy Joe, Wolfe put Millie into serious training. She began lifting weights and doing calisthenics and other exercises. Wolfe also arranged other tests for her, to ensure that her besting of the boy wasn't a fluke. Wolfe matched her against larger women, a couple of them the wives of wrestlers who had picked up things from their husbands. She beat them all. "Every hold, block and release that any of these tryout women knew and tried, I countered as though I had been in the game a lifetime," she later recalled. Over time, she came to believe in reincarnation, and that her prodigious natural talent for wrestling had come from a past life. "An intuitive ability was there to anticipate my opponent's moves. A gift of balance aided me, of which I had no previous awareness. This sense of balance, combined with an eerie confidence that I could not be knocked off my feet, enabled me to deal with much larger women throughout my career. Whatever move was used against me, I learned it immediately. Never did I forget such a move. These gifts were simply there, ready and available for use in the career I had chosen seemingly out of a clear sky."

Six years later Wolfe recounted the story in the *National Police Gazette*.

"I sure had this little girl figured dead wrong," he said. "Geez, I hired a kid and paid him a quarter to get into the ring with Mildred. I said to him, 'You give it to her so good, that she'll never come around here bothering us again.' Well, this little boy gets into the ring and does his level best, but she knocks him out so fast that it leaves me thinking that maybe she's got something there that I didn't see before."

Mainly what he saw was dollar signs.

4

Wrestling Men

As Millie Bliss took up with Billy Wolfe, Barbara Ware departed. The details of their parting are unknown. Ware continued to wrestle and later married a wrestler who became her manager, as Wolfe had been. If Wolfe had been planning to make a long-term business of women's wrestling, Ware would appear to be a far better choice than Millie Bliss. In addition to being an experienced and skillful wrestler, Ware was powerfully built and conventionally beautiful; she looked like a big-boned showgirl. Millie was tiny and boyish; she could pass for a schoolgirl. It seems unlikely that Wolfe would have tossed Ware over for Millie. More likely, Ware and Wolfe had difficulties—perhaps she tired of his wandering eye—and parted ways, leaving Wolfe in need of a replacement wrestler for his carnival athletic show. Millie filled that need.

She also filled another need. A vulnerable young girl-woman, single with a child and forced to grow up fast, she ended up in a romantic relationship with the womanizing veteran wrestler who was beginning to break down at the end of his career. She admitted to growing fond of him. "He could be likable when he chose and when it suited him," she later recalled, in the single grudging sentence in her unpublished autobiography that betrays any trace of positive sentiment toward Wolfe. When he proposed marriage she saw it as the way to nail down her wrestling dream and also secure the future of her son, Joe. Although her mother thought her crazy, Millie took her baby and set off with Billy Wolfe to wrestle in the athletic show he was putting together for a carnival tour in 1935.

For most of the small and even medium-sized towns of the Midwest in the 1930s, carnivals and circuses were still the event that brought in the crowds. In the 1870s the railroads had made it possible for P. T. Barnum to bring onto the road his Grand Traveling Museum, Menagerie, Caravan, and Hippodrome, creating a sensation in an America where no other such form of mass entertainment yet existed. Baseball was in its infancy and football and basketball were half a century or more away from popularity. Radio, movies, and television were figments of future imaginations. Pugilism was at the time largely banned as sheer brutality. Citizens in Barnum's day, even in the bigger cities, could look forward to little more than walking contests, bicycle races, the local horse track, or the freak show with its midgets, giants, armless and legless wonders, bearded ladies, tattooed marvels, fat and thin men and women. And, of course, the animals. In the Midwest, as elsewhere, everybody turned out "to see the elephant." Thus, small traveling carnivals became the primary source of live entertainment for the masses just as wrestling emerged as a professional sport.

By the 1930s athletic shows featuring wrestlers had long been standard at most carnivals and circuses. After the Civil War, a wrestling craze swept New York City, spurred by gamblers and Union army veterans schooled in wrestling and boxing. Fans flocked to see the great William Muldoon, a 250-pounder known as the "Solid Man of Sport" and "the best preserved athlete in the world." In bouts at Henry Hill's Houston Street hall, an infamous saloon in lower

Manhattan, wrestlers like Muldoon performed before audiences that included the influential newspaper publisher James Gordon Bennett, the ingenious inventor Thomas Alva Edison, and, of course, the irrepressible impresario P. T. Barnum himself. The nineteenth-century titans of publicity, light, and spectacle were avid fans of the coming sport, which in turn depended so much on publicity, light, and spectacle. By the early 1880s troupes of wrestlers from the East, Muldoon among them, were riding the rail lines to barnstorm in the middle of the country and beyond. They took to the vaudeville stage or the carnival tent because sports halls and arenas had not yet been conceived.

Muldoon was a big man who promoted health and fitness and he dominated by wrestling in the Greco-Roman style, which actually had been invented in France earlier in the century and required wrestlers to throw their opponents to the ground and refrain from holds below the waist. Alongside Greco-Roman, two more styles gained popularity in the latter half of the century, "collar and elbow," which was brought to the new world by Irish immigrants who established themselves in Vermont, and "catch as catch can," which was derived from an English style called Lancashire mixed with a frontier style called "rough and tumble." Collar and catch were similar in that both styles permitted leg holds and holds below the waist, but catch was faster and rougher than collar, which required wrestlers to begin matches by gripping an opponent's collar bone and elbow. By the turn of the century catch wrestling was the dominant American style.

For the inventive Barnum, whose American Museum of freaks and oddities had once stood a mile down Broadway from Henry Hill's, catch wrestling was the next new thing. Based on speed and a mastery of leverage and holds, catch allowed smaller wrestlers to compete successfully with bigger ones and thus was perfect for the deception that drove carnival profits. The gullible in the audience could be induced to compete with men that looked small or women that looked vulnerable. In the late 1880s Barnum incorporated wrestlers into his new Barnum & Bailey Circus, the "Greatest Show on Earth." The great showman hired the five-foot, six-inch, 150-pound catch wrestling champion Ed Decker from Vermont to issue challenges to the audience, $100 to anyone who could beat the little man and $50 to anyone who could last three minutes. Decker was so good the circus never had to pay a cent. To keep the audience interested, Barnum hired another wrestler and the two pros would trade victories night after night, dressed out in colorful costumes. The rise of the circus wrestler fit in well with Barnum's popularization of the sideshow, the performances set off to the side of the main big-top tent that were meant to entertain customers before the circus began. Soon, athletic shows, known as "at shows," became a feature of the sideshow in every circus and carnival. There were more than thirty traveling circuses in America at the time, and they and the individual barnstormers seeded wrestling through the populace, especially in the small towns of the Midwest. In the early part of the twentieth century the best American wrestlers came from Iowa, Nebraska, and Wisconsin. Though never numerous, female wrestlers were a long-standing part of at shows. "The main feature of this show is a female wrestler, who challenges any of her male onlookers to a match for a consideration worthwhile," a reporter wrote of a carnival touring Kingston, New York, in 1916.

The at shows usually occupied a canvas tent pitched on the midway with the other sideshows. Inside the tent was a regulation ring, twenty by twenty feet, with ropes and a canvas mat. Out front was a small, garishly painted stage called a bally. There, the barker or talker would pepper onlookers with ballyhoo—taunts, enticements, and challenges to any man brave enough to get into the ring with the troupe's wrestlers, men or women. Banners adorned the stage: "No Holds Barred," "This Challenge Is to the World." The very best male wrestlers—Frank Gotch, Strangler Lewis, the "Nebraska Tigerman" John Pesek—had started out in at shows. Those expert wrestlers in the troupe were known as "hookers." The civilians in the audience who challenged them were the "marks." To drum up business after they had run out of marks, the show's promoters would place a wrestler known as a "stick" among the audience. The crowd was always full of town toughs and bullies and the smells were of sawdust and ripe sweat. In the Midwest especially the toughest young men viewed carnival wrestling as a rite of passage.

Before she left for the at show in the spring of 1935 Millie persuaded her mother to sell Mom's and move to California to live with her brother, Louis. Bertha got $200 for the café and Millie told her to keep the money. Millie had Billy while Bertha was now alone. Their preparations complete, Billy, Millie, and Joe drove off for the J. T. Landes Shows in Abilene, Kansas. There Millie expected to become a wrestler and also a bride. After they crossed the state line, Wolfe asked her how much she got from the café sale. Nothing, she told him. He went into a terrible rage. His face changed its shape and color, and the sudden transformation terrified her. It presaged what was to come. "I didn't have even one dollar to my name," Burke wrote. "I was completely in this man's power. The character of our long relationship was actually set at that time—a struggle." He then told her he would not marry her until after they could see if they could make it, in both the business and a personal sense, for one year. If she left him, Wolfe told her, he would see to it that she was jailed for violating the federal Mann Act—crossing state lines for immoral purposes. Naively, Millie believed he could make good on his threat and that she would lose custody of her baby.

With that as a beginning, they set to work in the carnival. The Landes Shows had been traversing the Midwest for decades. Landes advertised itself as the "Largest Motorized Carnival in the Middle West . . . A Tented City of Lights and Sights—Acres of Amusement and Tons of Joy." The attractions included Honest Bill's Circus, a $25,000

"Educated Pony," and aerial acts. The at show didn't merit a mention. In an open-air canvas tent, amid the hurdy-gurdy music and naked lightbulbs, Millie Bliss, in her unglamorous black bathing suit and black boxing shoes, waited night after night while Billy Wolfe barked on the bally, "Twenty-five dollars to anyone who can beat the little lady in ten minutes—pin or submission!" The challengers had to be within twenty pounds of her weight. They had to pin her or force her into submission; if she survived the full ten minutes no money changed hands. The matches were supposed to be for real. And Wolfe paid little attention to the weight limit when there was money to be made. Still, Mildred admired his prowess on the bally board. "Billy Wolfe could certainly work up enthusiasms with his rough-hewn appearance and personal dynamism. He was a good barker." One night during his usual patter Wolfe abruptly changed her last name from Bliss to Burke. He seemed to have special gift for doing things that stunned her. They had discussed giving her a more warlike ring moniker but she thought she should have a say in it. "Bill's standing up there giving a big spiel about this great lady wrestler, and I'm standing down behind the tent ready to come out and he says, 'I now give you Mildred Burke,' and I'm looking around to see who the hell Mildred Burke is," she recalled years later. "He never told me he was going to give me that name. Then I went up the steps and got on the bally board. Why he chose that name, I don't know. He just told me he didn't think Bliss was a good name. He said there was an old saying, 'Ignorance is bliss.' He was right." The name stuck.

The terms of their relationship were set early. Two weeks after they joined the carnival, Millie went to check on Joe between shows and heard Billy having sex in their bed with one of the carnival girls. "He didn't see me, and I didn't interrupt his lovemaking. The effect on me was shattering." This is Burke's account; Wolfe himself never provided one. But his well-worn track as a womanizer gives her words weight.

In the carnival matches Millie struggled to survive and learn her craft. "There wasn't a week went by that I wasn't bruised and battered anew by hometown toughies seeking an easy $25. . . . My elbows and knees were never without abrasions. Rope and canvas burns came almost daily." Nevertheless, she learned how to get through these matches and even to enjoy them. She was often amused by her male challengers and their macho strutting before the matches when they figured they had an easy touch. But she turned out to be a natural at catch wrestling. And catch wrestling, with its emphasis on speed and wrestling holds, allowed a skilled woman to compete with bigger and stronger male opponents. The secret to beating many men, she found, was to get them off their feet and down on the mat, where she could use her strong legs to counter their upper-body strength. By wrestling defensively, she was able to block their moves, and avoid being pinned.

Over the years, about 150 men would accept the challenge. Millie later said she lost only one of these matches, when a collegiate wrestler accidentally kneed her in the stomach and knocked the breath out of her; in another interview, she said she recovered in time to pin the man and was never beaten. In any case, the carnival was her wrestling school. "I wrestled farmers, mechanics, carpenters, and blacksmiths in a bewildering array of body types and wrestling styles," she later wrote. "There was the string bean type, the squat guy who was built like a packing case, and there was the occasional roly-poly. They were pushers, rushers, headlock artists, scissor men, butters, and sluggers. Every single one of them was driven by his own macho thing, and it was vital to all of them not to be beaten by a young girl in front of their hometown people. . . . Whether they knew anything about wrestling or not, I learned from them all. I was placed every day in a ring situation from which that intuitive reaction—always the right move— would deliver me and defeat them."

While she worked as a carnival wrestler, she also took care of her baby. Joe's earliest memories are of his mother wrestling in the carnival. "I remember crawling up the pillows in the back of a trailer looking out the back window at the carnival lights and the tent where she wrestled," he recalled. "I remember looking at it and thinking, 'That's where my mom was.'"

Since deception was always part of the carnival, it was impossible to know what was real and what was faked. Some of the carnival matches clearly were "worked." Decades later Buck Thompson, a lightweight Chillicothe boxer and wrestler, told a local newspaper about his career as a plant to drum up business for Mildred Burke and other female carnival wrestlers. "There weren't many women wrestlers then," Thompson said. "They'd challenge the crowd from the ring for some man to come up and wrestle the woman, and nobody would. I was always the volunteer." Thompson said he would trade falls with the women, trying to build excitement in the audience.

Millie soon became a draw, attracting crowds night after night. In her hometown of Coffeyville, she wrestled and beat a strong and skilled lightweight male wrestler. She then wrestled the man's wife in a match guaranteed to bring a big house because it was so rare to see two women wrestle. But the wife didn't know how to wrestle, and her dead weight and ignorance in the ring proved dangerous. As Millie put the woman in a headlock and prepared to throw her to the mat to end the match, bad luck and bad technique combined to create a bad result. Millie's toe caught on a tear in the canvas, trapping her right leg in an awkward position. Her hapless opponent lost her balance and fell on the outstretched leg with her full weight. "Ligaments popped like champagne corks," Mildred wrote. "You could hear it all over the tent." She managed to pin the woman and finish the match but she was soon in a leg cast and out of commission. She had been a carnival wrestler for only a few months. For Billy Wolfe, she had become another mouth to feed who couldn't pull her weight. He put her to work selling tickets for the other wrestling matches in the show. To attract crowds he put her on the bally board and had her blow into automobile inner tubes until they popped. She also displayed her growing biceps and back muscles, which were starting to ripple into impressive ridges. She was trying hard to make herself useful but she grew increasingly worried that Wolfe would dump her. She knew that her only value to him was commercial.

One day Billy took her and Joe to her sister's place in Kansas City. "This is where you get off, kid," he said. "You're no good to me now." She cried and begged him not to throw her out. He agreed to keep her on long enough to train a woman who could replace her. She wore the cast for three months. When her leg was finally free of it, Millie found that the joint had healed improperly. Now she walked with a bent leg and a limp. Hobbling around, she started training Wilma Gordon, a young, tough Nebraska girl who was their first recruit. One day, working with Wilma and a boy, Millie flipped the boy over her back in a flying mare and her knee suddenly popped back into its socket. "This was like something out of the Bible—a personal miracle. No longer lame, or bent of limb, I stood up straight and free. Right then I knew that I would wrestle again, and that my life's goal would not be denied me."

Soon, she was back in the ring, taking on all comers. Occasionally, women would challenge her, pushing the crowd to a higher state of excitement. One particular match demonstrated Millie's very real wrestling ability. It involved a female giant from a farm in southwestern Missouri who emerged one afternoon to demand a match. Burke remembered her as six feet, three inches tall, with bulging muscles under her dress. Burke recalled shaking with fear before the match. "What a way to end my wrestling career—smashed senseless by this female hulk," she wrote. The big woman was confident. "I've beat all my brothers and every other man I've ever wrestled," she said. "I know I can beat any woman that ever lived."

Forty years later, the woman's daughter wrote an account of the match in a letter to a wrestling magazine. "The robes came off and there was much whistling. My mother looked great even though the two-piece swim suit was too tight for her . . . She towered over Mildred Burke as they closed in on each other and then there was the loud slapping of flesh against flesh." Burke was skillful enough to bring the woman to the mat but did not have the strength to pin her. "She bridged up from my pin just as though I wasn't even on her—as though I was a fly." Millie was tiring and feared she could not last much longer. She needed to solve the woman's strength and fast. When the giantess began to rise off the mat yet again, Millie tapped into her "vast subconscious reservoir of wrestling skill" and responded with a flash of physical intuition. "Throwing my legs up, I hooked her head in a scissor, a crook and a twist," she recalled. "The leverage I had could have snapped the tent pole. I nearly broke her neck." The woman's daughter recalled the sight in cinematic detail: "Miss Burke had my mother's face between her powerful thighs and was really applying the pressure," the daughter wrote. "I can remember vividly in addition to the scissors, Mildred seemed to be almost tearing off the larger woman's arms. They were right above me and I was in tears and shocked as I watched mother's powerful legs trembling, opening and closing and pawing helplessly at the canvas."

Shrieking like a wounded elephant, the giantess immediately gave up. The solution was not to pin the woman but to make her submit, to crush her will and ego. Millie easily beat her for the second fall. "The mental sphere ruled the physical," Burke recalled. "She was beaten mentally before the bell rang for the second tryout."

On another occasion the challenge came from a tough-looking woman with huge hands who confronted Millie on the midway in midafternoon and demanded a match; Millie insisted they wait until evening, when the crowd would be bigger. The woman became enraged and a wild fistfight ensued. Surrounded by a huge—and non-paying crowd—Millie beat the woman bloody. Later the police arrived to warn Millie that the woman was a gangster's moll. She had sent a threat: "Someday, somewhere, you are going to get your head blowed off by a shotgun."

Near the end of that first carnival season, at the 1935 Kansas state fair in WaKeeney, Millie was introduced to the crowd at a racetrack grandstand. Dressed in her tights and boots, she received a thunderous ovation. As she walked off one of the jockeys leaped on her back. The crowd erupted again. She reacted instantly, reversing the jockey's hold and throwing him to the ground. Then, for good measure, she sat on him as the crowd roared. The angry jockey seized the microphone and issued a challenge—his entire winnings at the racetrack that day, $700, against the $25 Billy Wolfe usually put up: a one-fall match against the "so-called lady wrestler."

Millie accepted and that night they squared off at the carnival tent. It took her no more than thirty seconds to put him on his back and take his $700. The humiliated jockey was left sitting long-faced as the crowd filed out. Millie felt sorry for him and told Wolfe to give him back half of his money. "Even though I was making the rough business of wrestling my profession, I never really lost a softness of heart," she later wrote. Wolfe, hard of head and heart, refused.

The business cemented them but Wolfe continued his dalliances. One of the women he was sleeping with was another of the recruits to his female wrestling troupe, Mae Weston, who was the sister of Wilma Gordon, his first recruit. Despite this, Weston and Burke would go on to become lifelong friends; it was an indication of how little she cared about the affections of her erstwhile husband. Weston was not the only woman Wolfe was sleeping with. One night, Burke later wrote, she discovered that Billy had beaten Joe because the boy's crying had interrupted Wolfe's lovemaking with one of his carnival paramours. Millie took Joe and left the carnival on foot, hitchhiking down the road. She said she got a ride from a man who tried to force himself on her. She fought him off and was left by the side of the road again with her child. She had little choice but to walk to a gas station and call for Wolfe. He came and got her. She warned him never to harm Joe again. "I'll wait until you're asleep and I'll cut your head off your body."

At the end of 1935, with their first carnival season behind them, Millie and Billy took the next step. They began matching Millie against men in small arenas. The goal was to escape the carnival and wrestle in reputable venues. Nobody cared about carnival wrestling but getting Burke into an arena match against a male opponent was another matter entirely. Bans against mixed wrestling in public arenas between men and women, considered to be the last taboo in the sport, were even more pervasive than prohibitions against women wrestlers. The regulation of wrestling was so haphazard and poorly enforced, however, that promoters in individual towns, generally small ones in the rural Midwest and West far from the Eastern big cities, had been able to match women against men in sporadic bouts. Ware and Virginia Mercereau had both wrestled men, but neither had been able to make a living out of it because of the difficulty of getting matches and opponents. In Burke's account, she approached promoter Gust Karras and asked him if he would promote a match if she could find a male opponent. He agreed, in part because the wrestling business as a whole was in bad shape. Burke said she then took out ads and wrote letters to small-town newspapers seeking an opponent: "CHALLENGE any man my own weight, 121 pounds, to wrestling bout. Mildred Burke."

On February 13, 1936, a very cold night with heavy snowdrifts, she made her debut in an arena match against a man in the small town of Bethany in northwestern Missouri. The bout was part of a card promoted by Karras at the K.P. castle, a brick structure in a castle design that originally had been built for the Knights of Pythias. "A special event will find Miss Mildred Burk wrestling Cliff Johnson," the Bethany *Republican-Clipper* reported, misspelling her new name in one of the first of the more than one thousand articles that would be written about her. The castle off the town's main square accommodated two hundred in reserved ringside seats at seventy-five cents apiece. About a hundred people braved the weather to watch. Billy Wolfe also wrestled on the card. His match, which opened the evening, was an unexciting draw. But Millie made a mark, and this time the newspaper spelled her name correctly. "Miss Mildred Burke of Kansas City proved that women can 'wrestle' as well as men," the paper noted. "She displayed actual ability in outclassing Cliff Johnson, applying real holds and showing a knowledge of how to break holds placed upon her. She dumped Johnson in seven minutes, using a head hold and reverse hammerlock."

She wrestled in Bethany again in March 1936 against Buck Thompson, who had worked as a stick with Burke in the carnival the previous year. This time Wolfe was not on the card. Forty-seven years later, Thompson recalled his matches with Burke for the local paper. "Mildred Burke was a good rassler," he was quoted as saying. "Once I got a headlock on her right away and I said to the referee . . . 'I've got her.' And right then she flipped my feet out from under me and dropped me on my back on the floor. Knocked the air out of me. She was a good rassler, but I never lost to her."

She repeated her challenge in Leavenworth, Kansas, and drew a big crowd. Billy Wolfe saw all the people and "his eyes flashed like cash register tags as he took in the pressing throng with dollars in their fists," she later wrote. Before the match, Billy went to see her opponent and learned the man planned to wrestle encased neck to ankles in red underwear. He had been told by other wrestlers not to let his skin touch Burke's, so he figured that decency demanded a full-body covering. Wolfe said, "How the hell can you wrestle someone without touching their body?" The man changed into more appropriate gear and Millie beat him with a body slam and pin in six minutes.

In April 1936 she had another match in Bethany that she would always later describe as her first arena match against a man. Given the memorable nature of the proceedings, it is perhaps understandable that she forgot about her earlier matches with Johnson and Thompson. In Burke's account, that first match came about after she issued her challenge and the sports editor for the Bethany newspaper put it on the front page. A 150-pound dishwasher in a local café who had been a high school wrestler accepted. The people of Bethany jammed the town's arena, which Burke described as an old wooden structure that resembled a big barn. She said it held about three hundred and dozens more ascended ladders to look into the windows on the sides. Wolfe did not attend; he had his own match that day, in another town. At match time someone else was missing: her opponent. A deputy sheriff departed to locate him. He was still at the coffee shop, washing dishes. He had lost his nerve. He told the deputy his wife would never forgive him if he lost to a woman before the local crowd. The deputy wasn't worried about one woman; he wanted to avoid a riot. He brought the dishwasher back to the match in the squad car, with red lights blazing and siren blaring.

In the ring, the man was a nervous wreck. He still refused to wrestle. "I can't rassle her," he said. "I don't have no trunks."

"Yes, you do," Millie said. She was wearing a dark one-piece bathing suit covered with heavy woolen trunks, a nod to modesty. She stepped out of the trunks and handed them to the man. He had no more excuses.

The man didn't realize it, but Burke was far more afraid of losing than he was. Burke was risking her dream, her "whole life's goal." But she was pure bravado before the match started. As they awaited the match she managed a word with her opponent. She told him she would make him look good before she pinned him if he didn't pull anything funny or too rough. "That way, your wife won't be mad at you," she said. The jittery man seemed grateful. "Really?" he said. "Thanks a lot. You're a swell gal."

In the ring, both wrestlers trembled with nervous excitement. The howling crowd made Millie go weak in the knees. But she looked across the ring at her opponent, half dazed in his corner, and felt he was already finished. The arena hushed at the opening bell. The wrestlers came together in the center of the ring. The struggle was hard-fought and even. The crowd roared with every shift. After eight minutes Mildred picked the man up, slammed him, and pinned him. The crowd exploded and applause rained down on the wrestlers as they made their way back to the dressing room. It continued for a long while, then subsided as the male wrestlers came out for the main event. "The emotional letdown after the man vs. woman match was too great," Burke recalled. "That was what they had come to see."

What actually happened matched Mildred's account but for a few key details. The headline in the local paper confirmed that Burke's match against Carl Hunter "Sort of Steals Show." It would not be the last time that her efforts in the ring took the spotlight off the male wrestlers. "Miss Burke, called '120 pounds of wrestling dynamite,' had appeared here before to show her ability, and had challenged anybody of her weight," the paper said. "Hunter, who works in a Bethany café, was persuaded to become her opponent but at the last was a little bashful about this business of wrestling a girl and might not have shown up had not Sheriff W. H. Webb gone to the café to coax him to come along."

The ring action didn't quite jibe with Burke's description. For one thing, as the local newspaper clearly points out, she lost the match. "Hunter is not an experienced grappler, but is strong," the paper noted. "He wrestled cleanly but seriously to defeat Miss Burke, who is fast and evasive. After about eight minutes Miss Burke kicked Hunter's feet from under him, but when he fell he dropped on her head. She was somewhat dazed, and he pinned her shoulders down. Afterward, she showed a big lump on her forehead."

Two weeks later she and Wolfe were back in Abilene, the city where they had begun on the carnival circuit, and she asked him to make good on his promise to marry her. Now he readily agreed. She was his star. Mildred Shaffer née Bliss and William H. Wolfe were married with no wedding party to witness it by a probate judge on April 24, 1936. She was twenty and he was thirty-nine. "There was no question of my being in love with Billy Wolfe," she would later recall. "He had become physically and sexually repulsive to me." But she saw him more than ever as her security.

Her most important match to date occurred in the much bigger northwestern Missouri town of Chillicothe, against "a 160-pound ex-boxer who was well-known around that part of the state." This opponent was most likely Buck Thompson, who was an ex-boxer well known in Chillicothe and later said he had wrestled Burke three times in the town. But he was just 126 pounds. Again, given the outcome of the match, it is perhaps understandable that he grew in size over the years in Millie's memory. She portrayed the bout, against a much bigger opponent in a much bigger arena, as a risky next step to boost her career. "I had penguins in my stomach, and by bout time, I felt as though they were playing ice hockey," she wrote. "We went hard at it, and despite his edge in weight, my carnival experience gave me the better of the match. I was able to block just about everything he tried to do." With the ten-minute time limit closing in, the frustrated man picked her up for a body slam. She knew how to break the impact on the mat, and in midair she shifted and braced herself accordingly. But her opponent slammed her straight down on her head in a pile driver, an illegal hold outlawed because it was an easy way to break a wrestler's neck. The impact momentarily knocked her out and she sprawled helplessly on the mat.

Figuring victory was now his, her opponent sauntered back to his corner without bothering to press Mildred's shoulders to the mat and complete the pin. He started to put on his robe. That was a mistake. Mildred started coming around. "Rolling over and getting to my feet—somehow comprehending the need to get back into action at all costs—I shot over to my opponent's corner and pulled his robe off his back. As he turned in surprise, the bell rang. The ten-minute time limit was up, and he had not pinned me! My opponent had flubbed his challenge."

The ring doctor checked her neck and sent her on her way. Billy Wolfe drove her home to the apartment they shared in Kansas City. Then he left her with Joe and headed out to wrestle his own matches in St. Joseph. The next morning Millie awoke to find herself unable to move. She was alone with a crying toddler. Her own cries brought neighbors, who called a doctor. The paralysis lasted nearly four days. Toes, feet, fingers, hands, wrists, and arms only slowly regained their feeling. When Wolfe returned he had little sympathy for her. He had crab lice and wanted her help removing them. She refused. He got peeved. She asked him to feed Joe, and Billy responded by jabbing the spoon roughly into the toddler's mouth, cutting his lip. That was it. She told Wolfe she was leaving. Yet she still did not quite comprehend the man she had married. He punched her in the face. "I saw stars, then quickly lost sight of everything through that eye," she later wrote.

She left the house with Joe and went to the home of a girlfriend. Her mother and brother sent her a plane ticket and she flew to join them in California.

As Millie recovered in Los Angeles, Billy waged a charm offensive to win her back, she later recalled. He phoned every night from Kansas City to say he was sorry. He dangled as bait the dream of finally getting matches against other women in arenas. "I was the only woman he'd ever really loved. If I could just come back to him, we could get going on the arena matches," she wrote.

They had gone as far as they could with the carnivals and the mixed matches, which were banned in Missouri after the splash caused by Burke. Returning to the carnivals meant wearing out her body wrestling for peanuts. Women weren't allowed to wrestle at all in Kansas City, Chicago, or St. Louis. Wolfe and Burke were stymied in the Midwest. They needed to find someplace else. What she knew was in the ring. Outside of the ring she was lost without Wolfe. Gradually, she succumbed to his overtures. "What I told myself in the dark nights when I lay awake pondering my next move was that I would have to suffer Billy Wolfe—put up with the bastard—in order to get what I wanted in life." She wanted the bastard working for her. She considered him a small-timer, not much above a carny, ruled by the basest of passions. But she could use him exactly as he had used her. "My feeling was that if Bill turned his domineering, driving personality on the promoters, we would break in, all the way and for good."

She was right about that.

5

Becoming Champion

They turned their eyes to the South. In late 1936 Mildred Burke joined Billy Wolfe on a smaller carnival working the winter southern circuit out of Birmingham, Alabama. The show was shabbier than Landes and the audiences were segregated; the blacks watched silently, as if afraid to make noise. Burke couldn't stand it. It reminded her yet again of why she wanted to escape the carnivals. She had proven her talent as a wrestler. Now Wolfe needed to prove himself as her manager. Women had occasionally wrestled in arenas, but the act had never taken off as anything more than a one-off novelty, a freak show to relieve the tedium on a dull card of male wrestlers. Burke and Wolfe wanted far more than that. They wanted to establish women as permanent and popular arena performers, right up there with Strangler Lewis and Jim Londos.

Getting Burke into a match against another woman in a large arena required that Billy Wolfe convince a major promoter that women could wrestle well enough to win over a large crowd. It was a classic catch-22. Women could not wrestle unless they proved they could draw, but they could not prove they could draw unless they got the opportunity to wrestle. They had to start somewhere. Wolfe needed a willing promoter, but first he needed an opponent for Burke who would generate more excitement than any had so far.

He found that opponent in another female wrestler who was working in carnivals named Clara Mortensen, the twenty-year-old blonde who at sixteen had been the feature attraction of an at show out of California. If Wolfe was looking for the perfect woman to help him and Burke break through, it would appear that he could do little better than Mortensen. She was an accomplished wrestler who had already received national attention. Mortensen described herself as the reigning female lightweight champion, although the claim was confusing and unreliable. (Mortensen and Barbara Ware, for example, both said they had won the championship against the other in Topeka in 1932.) Four years earlier *Ring* magazine had touted her as among the top female wrestlers in the country along with Ware, Cora Livingston, and Virginia Mercereau. Better still, her good looks drew fans. A classic Nordic beauty with finely chiseled features and a long blonde bob, Mortensen would soon earn the nickname the "Eternal Woman."

Mortensen was about five pounds heavier than Burke, but she stretched it over a frame that was four inches longer. One newspaper account said that she possessed the "lithe, supple, shapely body of classic sculpture." Unlike Burke, Mortensen was born into wrestling. She had been trained since childhood by her father, the Danish light heavyweight champion Fred "Mart" Mortensen. When she was seven years old, Clara had taken on her brother in a professional ring before a paying crowd at an Elks Club picnic in Portland. The two kids allegedly split a purse of silver coins worth $81. As an adult, Clara had already wrestled in arenas, in some of the infrequent matches featuring women. In 1933 she appeared before 31,000 fans at Honolulu stadium. She sometimes wrestled in a yellow jersey, brown shorts, and yellow socks, looking for all the world like a high school girl who had wandered in after playing basketball in gym class. But she was skilled on the mat and like Burke she had a strong support system. Mortensen went on the road with her brother, who had also become a professional wrestler, and she was managed by a former pro mat man, Bluebeard Bill Lewis, who liked to appear at ringside sporting a beard and a three-piece suit. One of her signature holds was the airplane spin, also one of Jim Londos's favorites, where she would balance her opponent atop her shoulders and spin her around like an airplane propeller before flinging her from the ring.

With Mortensen in tow, Wolfe went looking for someone who would book women into an auditorium. He approached Birmingham wrestling promoter Chris Jordan, a former wrestler who now mainly booked male light heavyweights into arenas throughout Alabama. Wolfe showed up at Jordan's office with Burke, Mortensen, and Mortensen's managers. Burke later recounted the scene in her unpublished autobiography. It is a rare example of Burke giving Wolfe full credit for the break that made her career.

Jordan: "Whaddaya want?"

Wolfe: "Wanna talk to you about putting girl wrestlers on one of your cards. These two are the best."

Jordan: "You're kidding. All they'll do is pull hair. They'll kill the town for me. Can't think of anything that'd be worse for me than gal wrestlers. Business is bad enough, fella."

Jordan tried to shut the door in Wolfe's face, Burke wrote, but Billy jammed his foot into the doorway and assailed the promoter with his quick, insistent patter.

Wolfe: "If you'll put them on, and they don't bring you the biggest gate you've had in a year, they'll work for nothing. You don't have to pay them."

Their first match was in Dothan, Alabama, where Jordan thought the damage to his business would be minimal if they bombed. But the first match was a sellout, and Jordan got them more bouts around the state, including one in Mobile and another before 4,000 people in Birmingham. Mortensen quickly became one of the few people Burke would detest throughout her life. Because Mortensen was the bigger name, Burke had to agree to lose in their matches, which Burke derisively referred to in her autobiography as "worked exhibitions." Burke said she went along with it "for the good of the business." She later said this marked her initiation into the secret that pro wrestling was fixed, not just in the carnivals and at the lower levels of the game—she already knew that from her nearly two years on the road with Wolfe—but at the championship level as well. Burke maintained that the knowledge was devastating for her. "Being champion meant everything to me, in every way, and it wasn't something to be bought and sold," she wrote. She resolved that she would one day put herself in a position where she would never have to lay down for another match. "The only way to avoid these managed matches and managed decisions —as far as I was concerned personally—was to be unbeatable legitimately," she wrote.

What did it mean to be legitimately unbeatable in a world of managed matches? This was not as strange and contradictory as it sounds; indeed, it was already a tradition in pro wrestling. It meant that champions such as Strangler Lewis were "real" champions because they had shown they could beat all of their opponents in unstaged matches. Lewis did this by triumphing in private "shooting matches" held in closed gyms before other wrestlers and managers. It was an important way for the champion to achieve respect and standing. It also protected him from funny business in the ring. Lewis's skill made him a "hooker," a member of the ultimate fraternity of professional wrestlers, the small group of men whose knowledge of the most devastating wrestling holds allowed them to cripple their opponents at will. The vast majority of wrestlers, fearful of risking a broken arm or torn ligaments, avoided taking cheap shots or getting too rough when facing a hooker. Still, the possibility of a double cross in the ring was a constant threat. The men's title, with a lot of money at stake, had changed hands in 1925 and again in 1936 on double crosses, when a skilled challenger had turned a worked bout into a shooting match against a less skilled champion. Last and most important, even in staged matches shooting ability translated into the kind of authenticity needed to win over public audiences. As Liebling wrote, "Wrestlers with an honest background can lend a fake verisimilitude to their work that non-wrestlers find it hard to duplicate." When the ring action went public after the private shooting match, the champion and his opponent worked together to make their moves exciting in the slam-bang style of the era.

Lewis's dominance of the sport in the 1920s did not rest on his wrestling skill alone. He also had his managers and handlers, Billy Sandow and Toots Mondt, paving the way for him with other managers and promoters, as well as with the press. Lewis, Sandow, and Mondt were so successful they became known as the Gold Dust Trio. Finally, and most important, Lewis had the assent of those other promoters that he was the one true champion. Burke had the requisite skill, and she also had Billy Wolfe in her corner. But she had no promoters behind her who were willing to bill her as the champion. Mortensen, who was the bigger draw, had no reason to consent to a private shooting match with Burke. After all, Burke needed her more than she needed Burke. To become champion Burke had to find a way to get past Mortensen.

Burke said that Mortenson's triumphs in all those early worked matches made her arrogant and high-hatted. One night, to show the crowd who was the better woman, Burke said, she bounced Mortensen around the ring, repeatedly pinning her only to bring her shoulders off the mat at the count of two, before the fall was final. Only then did Burke allow Mortensen to pin her.

Wolfe parlayed the news of their success in Alabama to secure bigger matches in Tennessee. On January 28, 1937, a cold and rainy night, before 6,157 in the Memorial Auditorium in Chattanooga, Millie Burke, age twenty-one, realized her dream. She beat Mortensen and won a claim to the women's championship title. It was Burke's first victory against Mortensen after at least a dozen defeats. It was said to be Mortensen's first loss in five years. Why did Burke suddenly emerge as the winner? The answer, like many of the inner details of Burke's wrestling career, is ultimately unknowable. The very nature of professional wrestling is to deceive, with its carny origins, its public worked matches, and its private shooting matches. There is the possibility that the match was worked, like the other ones between Burke and Mortensen. Perhaps Mortensen finally agreed to let Burke win one, in order to pump the gate for upcoming matches. The local newspaper itself at the time openly speculated that the match was fixed, citing the fact that a third challenger was introduced before the match, and a better gate would result if that challenger had to beat both ex-champion Mortensen and new champion Burke.

There is also the possibility that the match was not worked, that Burke had broken the script and beaten Mortensen in a double cross. In her autobiography, Burke referred to Mortensen as Cora Jurgens and gave a very dramatic version of behind-the-scene events. Just before the match, Burke wrote, a beaten and disheveled Billy Wolfe came into her dressing room. Some pro wrestlers working in concert with Mortensen's people had thrown him against a wall and roughed him up. The message was clear: Burke had to continue losing to Mortensen. But now Wolfe was away from the goons and he was angry. He told Millie to wrestle her heart out. So she went out and won for the first time.

The *Chattanooga Times* noted the huge crowd but also predicted little future for women's wrestling. "There is no doubt but the girls put on a pleasing show and were a great attraction, but the continued practice of bringing them here each week will soon get old and the novelty will wear off, for it can be termed little more than a novelty."

To the fans, though, the match was a roaring success. "These two otherwise demure misses pulled hair, gouged eyes, tied each other in complicated knots, slugged and yanked arms and legs in the most approved wrestling manner," wrote one male fan, who said the crowd was one of the largest ever for the auditorium. "Grand opera and popular stage plays have never drawn near the crowd."

The match was a milestone for women's professional wrestling and the biggest boost yet for Burke, and to this day it is generally considered the starting point for the modern-day women's professional title. It put Burke's name in sports pages across the country. Never before had a women's match received such widespread publicity, and it was her great fortune that the attention came from a match that she had won rather than one of her many losses to Mortensen. The recently launched wire news photography services transmitted pictures of her triumph across the country, and over a period of weeks they appeared in papers from Olean, New York, to Ogden, Utah, from Port Arthur, Texas, to Bismarck, North Dakota. The pictures also made it into *Life* magazine, which after its launch the previous year had become the leading visual chronicle of mid-century American culture. The *Modesto Bee* in California featured a picture of a smiling Burke throttling Mortensen at the top of its sports page, near stories about Seabiscuit and James J. Braddock. Mildred also merited a sneering reference in the United Press national sports column of Henry McLemore: "I am sure that you would like to know that Miss Mildred Burke of Kansas City claims the women's heavyweight wrestling championship of the world, and she attributes her eminent position to what she terms the 'girdle grip.'"

Burke won again in Birmingham before Mortensen took the title back in Chattanooga on February 11, 1937. Again, the circumstances were murky. Burke later said that she had beaten Mortensen convincingly in the ring, only to have a bribed referee raise Clara's hand in victory after a quick count. The local paper supported Burke's version. "As a general rule, controversies arising from decisions in wrestling matches are just so much fuss," the *Chattanooga Times* reported. "But in the case of Mildred Burke, Thursday night, fans agree that she was 'robbed' to the extent that the referee awarded the final fall to Clara Mortensen on a very, very short count." Burke issued an immediate challenge to Mortensen. "Anxious to get another shot at Clara, Mildred called by the sports department today to announce that she would post a side bet of $100 and can beat Clara any time, anywhere," the paper concluded, giving a nod to the notion that the matches were fixed by pointing out that Mildred and Clara were supposed to wrestle again that very night in Knoxville.

They did not wrestle that night in Knoxville, however, for reasons unknown. Burke claimed she was so angry after the quick count that she stormed into Clara's dressing room and beat the blonde woman bloody. "Soon she was blubbering pitifully and begging me to stop, a sorry picture of a would-be champion. As the door was being broken in by the promoter's goons, I shook my finger at the sniveling girl. 'That'll teach you to pull a double cross on me.'"

In April 1937 they met again in Charleston, West Virginia, in the first women's match held in the city. It is the last documented match between the two women and provided ample evidence that female wrestlers were more than a novelty. "Those who are of the opinion that ladies are the weaker sex will see two distinct exceptions when Miss Burk [*sic*] and Miss Mortensen meet," local matchmaker Jack Dawson said in announcing the card. "They are stronger than many men wrestlers." They drew 2,500, a record for wrestling in Charleston. Five hundred more were turned away at the door. The wrestling drew a rave review in the local paper. "Some masterful science was applied," the Charleston *Gazette* reported.

The skullduggery that Burke described in her earlier matches with Mortensen seemed to continue. For one thing, a few weeks before the Charleston match, Mortensen apparently wrestled and beat a

"Molly Burke" in Norfolk. Mildred Burke at the time was wrestling in Texas, so the match could have been a ploy by Mortensen to cloud the title picture with a victory over a wrestler named Burke. To top things off, the Charleston paper reported the wrong result for the match in that town. It said that Mortensen had won two out of three falls in forty-five minutes. Two days later the paper issued a correction: "Miss Burke should have been credited with the victory, having beaten Miss Mortensen in two of three falls." Perhaps it was an innocent mistake. But in an age when wrestling promoters paid for good publicity, nothing can be taken at face value.

They were now the two most prominent and accomplished female wrestlers in the nation, and they could have made a lot of money in worked matches all over the country. But clearly they lacked the trust needed to continue in business together. They soon took separate paths to defend a title that both would continue to claim to the end of their days. Mortensen said that even though she lost the title to Burke in Chattanooga she won it back in a subsequent match. Burke just as determinedly maintained that she had won their last match. With records of the time so spotty the claims cannot be conclusively settled.

The enmity was lasting. More than forty years after their final match, the Cauliflower Alley Club, the leading organization of retired pro wrestlers, tried to honor both women at the group's annual function. But neither wanted to appear if the other did.

For a while Mortensen did well as a wrestler. She drew capacity crowds in Washington, D.C., and elsewhere, from California to Montana to Florida. *Time* magazine did a piece on her at the end of 1937 under the headline "Strong Sister." But she never became Mildred Burke. While Burke went on to increasing crowds, wealth, and fame, Mortensen's career slowly petered out. She suffered a major setback when the state of California, her home base, banned women's wrestling in 1939. She was also outmaneuvered by Wolfe and Burke.

At the time there were no formal bodies to determine and police titles for women wrestlers. Thus anyone could claim a title. The
Chattanooga match won by Burke had been advertised as the women's
lightweight championship, even though no organized body was making that claim, nobody in fact other than the promoters, Wolfe and
Burke, and the Mortensen camp. The title that mattered was the one
that received the most widespread recognition from the press and the
public. What Burke and Wolfe ultimately achieved was no less than a
national consensus on one person's claim above all others. They ef-
fected it by perceiving an opportunity and working incredibly hard
to seize it.

The two combined Burke's wrestling skill and her singular ring
style with Wolfe's drive and business acumen to build a moneymaking,
publicity-generating machine that no one could match. Key to their
success was the willingness to travel constantly so that Burke could be
seen defending her title by as many people as possible. A large part of
Burke's triumph was the creation of a stirring and powerful image that
was, to use one of her favorite words, eye-popping. The image was
grounded in sex appeal, the same quality that had elevated Jim Londos
above Strangler Lewis. Mortensen, for all of her physical beauty and
wrestling skill, came across as a bit drab, mechanical, and boyish in the
ring. Her loose-fitting costume hid her curves, her pretty face was hard
to see from the seats in the arenas, and she wrestled quickly and compe-
tently without undue drama. Burke compensated for her lack of standard beauty by the adroit use of makeup and by adopting tight-fitting
suits that accentuated her curves. She also set to building muscle defini-
tion that would be years ahead of its time and make the lanky Mortensen
look ordinary. A taunting, come-hither look was noticeable in Burke's
publicity photos, and soon Billy Wolfe would have her posed baring
her belly button in a zebra-striped two-piece, her sinewy muscles oiled
to a sophisticated sheen, her defined "six-pack" adominal muscles clearly

visible, a look that would not come into wide currency for women until the female bodybuilding craze of the 1980s. On her way to the ring Burke perfected a strut that drew all eyes and allowed her to bask in the crowd's adulation. In the ring, she crafted an act that mixed the mask of a thespian with the mastery of a thousand holds. Outside of the ring Burke and Wolfe would make sure the newspapers photographed her in the most feminine garb possible, always in long frilly dresses and, later, when she could afford them, diamonds and furs. Sex, muscles, and diamonds, that would be her formula.

Their joint triumph was so complete that when California opened up again to women wrestlers a few years later, even the local papers reported that Burke had "lifted the crown" from California native Mortensen and provided a much better show for the fans. "In contrast to the women wrestlers that worked here the past two or three years, Miss Burke and her opponents were big leaguers," the *Fresno Bee* noted. There was talk in 1943 of again matching Burke and Mortensen against each other. A promoter in Los Angeles offered a $500 purse to the winner. Burke said she was eager for the bout and would donate the money to the war effort. But the match never came off.

Mortensen provided the final proof of Burke's superiority with that ultimate loser's lament, a plea for just one more match with the champion. "I'd like another match with Mildred Burke," Mortensen told a newspaper reporter in 1945. "We have met on two occasions. Back in 1937, I lost to Mildred Burke but some weeks later pinned her in straight falls. We haven't met since that time." Mortensen continued to wrestle here and there, and she even appeared in a dreadful, low-budget wrestling film, titled *Racket Girls,* in 1951. She retired the next year and lived quietly as a housewife in Eureka, California, still maintaining that she had avenged her only loss, against Burke.

Mildred Burke's victory over Clara Mortensen started the avalanche. "The thing just started to take off on the basis of Chattanooga," Burke later wrote. "We had packed a big arena in a large city. In hard times, with money scarce and promoters living hand to mouth, that was a major achievement, and word spread." Behind it all was the hand of Billy Wolfe, pushing, prodding, and sending out newspaper clippings. All their lives Burke and Wolfe clipped stories out of newspapers. Burke saved them in scrapbooks. Wolfe mailed them around the country, turning the clippings into advertising and making them part of his pitch to various promoters and sports editors. To Burke and Wolfe, publicity was paramount, and not merely to drum up interest in their matches. Newspaper attention was validation, the only means for them to claim legitimacy in a business they were creating out of whole cloth. When Mortensen claimed she had beaten Burke in their last match, Burke produced newspaper clippings of her victories over Clara in Chattanooga and Birmingham. Their press coverage was a good barometer of how they were doing, and tracking it provides the best means available for gauging their rise. "Miss Burke is now on her second tour of the country and she has been attracting record crowds," the Mansfield, Ohio, *News-Journal* reported in the spring of 1937. The newspaper noted that Burke had recently attracted a record crowd of 7,000 in Chattanooga, "outdrawing Jim Londos by over 3,000 people." Who but Wolfe was making such comparisons and providing such details?

Wolfe had just added Ohio as the troupe's newest territory; it was his most important move so far to ensure their continued success. They came into the territory with enormous fanfare. A photograph of Burke signing for her first match in Columbus in April 1937 was splashed on the front page of the sports section in the biggest newspaper in town. "Mildred Burke, who could almost be called petite if her neck didn't measure nearly 14 inches and her arms didn't bulge with firm muscles, sat in Promoter Al Haft's office, Monday afternoon, and predicted that within five years there will be a women's match on every card," the *Columbus Dispatch* reported. The article featured Burke's earliest extant newspaper interview. "Afraid?" she said. "I don't think anyone my own weight can beat me and I've defeated lots of others out of my class!"

The story also gave the earliest description of Burke's style and persona in the ring. "Clean, scientific wrestling—that's Mildred Burke's formula," the newspaper said, noting the thrill she got from "a well-executed bodyslam or wristlock." Wrestling "scientific" meant that Burke did not often resort to gratuitous brutality or fouling moves such as punches, kicks, or bites. Scientific wrestling involved the mastery of hundreds of holds that had been handed down since antiquity. Throughout her career, Burke would perform as a "babyface," the noble wrestler who tolerates and finally overcomes the "heel," the dirty-fighting villain. "Miss Burke always plays the same role in her gripping dramas," a magazine pointed out a decade later. "She is the clean-fighting heroine mastering a less skilled, conniving vixen. . . . The script is the same—and not too full of suspense. The villain uses all sorts of foul tactics, even standing on Mildred's raven locks while bumping her head on the floor. But Miss Burke always triumphs." Playing the villain was easier, because it is always easier to be hated than loved, and villains could always be sure to get a rise out of the crowd with a dirty blow or kick. Burke had to win over the crowd without cheap violence. Her speed and skill made her wrestling a thing of beauty in the ring, full of careful shifts of balance and swift and surprising combinations that turned the straining of muscle and limb into a ballet of grace and power.

Al Haft, the promoter of Burke's first match in Columbus, would turn out to be the most important ally of Billy Wolfe's career. A former middleweight wrestler and coach at Ohio State University, Haft operated a training gym and controlled wrestling promotions in Columbus and surrounding environs through an organization called the Midwest Wrestling Association. Within two weeks of her signing with Haft, Burke won a tournament put on by Haft and Wolfe to give legitimacy to a new women's champion. With her victory, Burke finally received a recognized championship from a bona fide wrestling organization. Wolfe had a fancy MWA women's title belt fashioned for Burke, one made, they both claimed, of gold and precious stones. Wolfe said it cost $525, nearly the price of a new car in 1937. Burke would wear the belt for seventeen more years and use it to help spark the Golden Age of Wrestling.

All this did not happen a moment too soon. As Mildred Burke was coming onto the scene, the wrestling business was enduring its worst crisis ever.

Wrestling had always been plagued by the stain of fakery. In the nineteenth century, barnstorming wrestlers often mixed "exhibitions" with real matches without ever informing the audience. A fix had ruined the biggest wrestling match in America, the epic 1911 battle that pitted George "the Russian Lion" Hackenschmidt against Iowa farm boy Frank Gotch. Hackenschmidt was one of the strongest and most muscular men of the age, but three years earlier in Chicago he had suffered his first defeat at the hands of the lean-limbed Gotch, quitting in the ring after two hours of wrestling and claiming that Gotch was a dirty fighter who repeatedly fouled him. The first Gotch-Hackenschmidt bout had drawn wrestling's biggest crowd to date, more than 6,000, and a record gate of $38,828. The excitement surrounding the return bout could not have been higher. But days before the scheduled rematch Hackenschmidt was injured in training. Too much had been spent on promotion, however; the match would draw an unprecedented crowd of 33,000 to Chicago's Comiskey Park and a record gate of $87,000. Hack agreed to limp through the match with his leg in a plaster splint, provided that Gotch made him look good before beating him. Instead, Gotch, one of the meanest and toughest wrestlers born, dispatched the obviously hurt Hack in a quick nineteen minutes. Sportswriters vilified the match. "If ever there was a fraud perpetrated upon the American public in a big sporting event it was at Comiskey's park, Monday, when

Hackenschmidt 'laid down' to Frank Gotch and permitted the champion to gain two easy falls," wrote John C. Meyers. Another noted wrestling writer, Marcus Griffin, called it "the greatest fiasco ever perpetrated upon the American public."

Pro wrestling had to work hard to win back the public. The passage of time and the more exciting wrestling style that Strangler Lewis and Jim Londos brought forward after the war helped return the sport to prominence. For most of that period wrestling was controlled by a monopoly of promoters headquartered in New York City called the Trust. Members of the Trust often fought among themselves, promoted rival champions, and split off in combinations that formed and reformed with dizzying speed. In 1933 a new Trust came together that seemed to put everybody on the same side: the two biggest names in the business, Lewis and Londos, as well as all of the top promoters who ran wrestling's biggest territories, St. Louis, Chicago, Philadelphia, Boston, and New York. Each of the promoters ran his respective city like a mob boss, which is to say they brooked no competition. Most prominent were the New York promoters, matchmaker Toots Mondt, who had helped develop the slam-bang style with Lewis, and Mondt's boss, Jack Curley, who had promoted the second Gotch-Hackenschmidt bout. Liebling called Curley "a walking embodiment of the popular conception of a promoter." With his three-piece suits and ample girth Curley looked like a Tammany Hall political boss, but his gray hair, moon face, and inscrutable aspect hid one of the keenest promotional minds of the century. A former newspaper reporter, he went on to promote the boxer Jack Johnson, the tennis champion Bill Tilden, the actor Rudolph Valentino, and the opera star Enrico Caruso. Curley had ruled the wrestling game in New York City for nearly two decades and was widely thought of as the sport's elder statesman.

Londos, who had lost to Lewis on fourteen previous occasions, was made the Trust's new champion. On September 20, 1934, in a bout that seemed to bring everything together and serve as a passing of the torch, Londos beat Lewis, his old nemesis and new business partner, at Wrigley Field in Chicago. The match drew a record 35,265 and the gate of $96,000 broke the mark set twenty-three years earlier by Hack and Gotch across town.

Just two months after this milestone disaster struck as Londos was preparing to defend his title against Everett Marshall. On November 19, 1934, the New York *Daily News,* then the largest-circulation newspaper in America, blared a devastating headline that exposed the match as a fake: "Won 0, Lost 22, Marshall Tries Londos Again!"

It was a nearly mortal blow. "The fans read, and Curley, Mondt and the rest of the partners wept," Griffin wrote. "That evening the principals wrestled before a virtual gallery of ghosts."

The Trust had forgotten the old adage about honor among thieves. When they made their peace among themselves the previous year, they had kicked one member out of the club, a colorful character named Jack Pfefer. Born in Poland, Pfefer had been a porter for a touring Russian ballet company before becoming a U.S.-based talent scout for foreign wrestlers. By the late 1920s he was working for Curley and Mondt, who were promoting Londos as their champion. When Londos split from Curley and Mondt, Pfefer went with him; when Londos later made peace with Curley and Mondt, Pfefer was left out in the cold. He was legendary for his outrageous personal manner and his voluminous files and newspaper clippings on the wrestling game. After he found himself betrayed by his wrestling friends, Pfefer marched over to his newspaper friends in the New York City press armed with his facts, figures, and memories of the rotten insides of the business. He went to the *Daily News* and he also went to the New York *Daily Mirror,* where he spilled the beans about all the fixes to sports editor Dan Parker, the dean of wrestling writers. In a series of articles, Parker demolished wrestling's reputation. He portrayed the wrestling fraternity as a den of shady characters, and he made an extra effort to play up Pfefer's eastern European accent. "Them thiefs is stealin' and onless dey make me ha partner, den I won't play. I vant to steal vatches too if dem guys are goin' to rob the jewelry shop."

Many in wrestling would never forgive Pfefer for the destruction he had wrought. "It was through his own teeth that the story was given that was so damaging to us all," Mondt wrote to another promoter. Pfefer's revelations were devastating to the Trust, especially on the East Coast, but he saved his true revenge for two years later.

By then the Trust had arranged for the title to pass from Londos to Danno O'Mahoney, an Irishman shot-putter of limited wrestling skills but great ethnic appeal. Londos had allegedly received $70,000 to let "Danno Me Bye" win. For nearly a year, O'Mahoney made good on the Trust's investment by drawing all those Irish fans in New York City, and then a German wrestler named Dick Shikat doubled-crossed the Irishman and the Trust by beating O'Mahoney at Madison Square Garden. Shikat took O'Mahoney's title and threw in his lot with Jack Pfefer and Al Haft. In a match that came to be referred to as simply "the Great Double Cross," Shikat put O'Mahoney in a painful hammerlock, twisting his arm behind his back. "Stop him, he's killing me!" O'Mahoney begged the referee. He was not acting.

In April 1936 the Trust went into federal court in Columbus in a desperate bid to block Shikat from wrestling as champion for Pfefer and Haft. In doing so, the Trust allowed its secret deals to be laid bare. One of those was contained in a photostatic copy of an agreement showing that the Trust members had divided up the country among themselves. "Charges that a wrestling 'trust' exists in the eastern half of America, and that grapplers are forced to 'win or lose or draw,' according to order, or lose huge forfeits, whirled through federal court yesterday," the Ohio *State Journal* stated. Curley took the stand to swear that wrestling was "on the level." The papers had a field day. "Never did John Barrymore quiver a more disdainful nostril than did Mr. Curley in voicing his emphatic denial," wrote the sports editor of the

Columbus *Citizen*. "Never did John's sister, Ethel, give a more vivid portrayal of righteous indignation."

The irony was that even in this age of fakery wrestling skill mattered. As Shikat's double cross had shown, one wrestler could always turn a match from fake to real in an instant and take another's title. Time and again, experience had shown that the toughest men from other sports, professional boxers and football stars, no matter how big and strong, stood no chance in the ring against an experienced wrestler. And there was no doubt that the pro wrestlers of the era were highly skilled. One hooker, John Pesek, the 195-pound Nebraska Tigerman, had defeated Olympic silver medalist Nate Pendleton in a shooting match in 1923 by "hooking" Pendleton's foot in a toehold and tearing a ligament with an audible snap.

Skill mattered but the damage had been done. Undone by greed and mistrust the Trust split apart. No one could agree on a unified champion, so champions began to proliferate. The public, willing to forgive wrestling's foibles, did not take kindly to being played for chumps in exposé after exposé in the press. To make matters worse, a fragile recovery from the Depression was sidetracked by the so-called Roosevelt recession, which saw unemployment shoot back up to nearly 20 percent, reminding people of the worst days of the decade. Wrestling gate receipts went into a prolonged tailspin. Madison Square Garden stopping hosting wrestling altogether in 1938.

J. E. Wray, who covered wrestling for the *St. Louis Post-Dispatch,* summed it up in a letter to Pfefer. "As you observe, I have not been writing anything about wrestling. I can not stand the smell, and beside the customers out here are tired of the subject."

It was around this time that Mildred Burke emerged to help save the sport.

6

Building the Business

By August 1937 Billy Wolfe was looking to expand to more lucrative markets. He wrote to Jack Pfefer, who since his ouster from the Trust had carved a niche for himself in the New York territory promoting light heavyweights and what he called "freaks"— ugly wrestlers with misshapen heads, handle-bar mustaches, and tattoos who drew fans jaded by the business Pfefer had done so much to discredit. If Pfefer welcomed freaks, maybe he'd go for women.

Wolfe wrote to Pfefer that he had "the management of three splendid lady wrestlers. Which includes Miss Mildred Burke who is a Title claimant." The other two in Wolfe's troupe were the Nebraska sisters Mae Weston and Wilma Gordon. Wolfe told Pfefer they had drawn packed houses in Columbus, El Paso, Amarillo, Birmingham, Memphis, and Nashville. They were planning on making a tour of "Old Mexico." They did not come cheap. His wrestlers got 15 percent of the net proceeds; top male wrestlers usually got about 10 percent. But Wolfe argued that his wrestlers needed more money because of their special circumstances. Male wrestlers could set up in a single territory, such as St. Louis or New York City, and wrestle for months in the city and surrounding area, because they had dozens of male opponents. Female wrestlers had far fewer opponents and they had to wrestle less frequently in any territory they entered, lest the public tire of watching the same two or three women wrestle over and over. Shorter bookings meant more travel and greater expense. As a way of showing his commitment and investment in his women, Wolfe mentioned the $525 he had spent for "a very beautiful Championship belt" for Mildred.

Female wrestlers were banned in New York and New Jersey, though, and there was little Pfefer could do for Wolfe. In 1937 Wolfe and Burke were still largely confined to the South, the West, and the Midwest, hemmed in by attitudes and laws created by the various morals movements that had cracked down on drinking, gambling, and dancing as well as female boxing and wrestling. Women's groups and clergy led the opposition. The Very Reverend W. E. R. Morrow, provost of Chelmsford Cathedral in England, spoke for many. "To my mind, nothing is more calculated to degrade human nature to its most bestial depths than the sight of an apparently healthy pair of young women, wearing nothing more than a bathing suit, indulging in the repugnant postures of 'all-in' wrestling to the accompaniment of the jeers and promptings of a mixed crowd of onlookers." California banned women's wrestling as being "improper and vulgar," after the state athletic commissioner led a "purist movement against female encroachment on a man's sport." Nazi propagandists got into the act, running Burke's picture to show "how brutal Americans are."

Many male wrestlers also scoffed at the women. "It's terrible," Strangler Lewis, the most famous name in wrestling, told the *Los Angeles Times*. "Wrestling has been bumped around long enough without turning it into a burlesque." Lou Thesz, a superb technical wrestler who emerged in 1937 and would soon replace Lewis and Londos as the next great champion, also belittled the women. "I had nothing against the idea of girl wrestlers, but it's a fact I never actually met one—a wrestler, that is—during my career; every single one of them were performers, and their whole act was designed to titillate the males."

Even in the Midwest, which was fast becoming the bastion of the new business of women's wrestling, Burke was still barred in the two largest cities, St. Louis and Chicago, where athletic commissions simply refused to license females to enter the ring. Wolfe and Burke took bookings where they could, scattered across a large geographic area. Billy, Millie, her son, Joe, and his son, G. Bill, and the other wrestlers lived on the road, traveling from match to match in a car that towed a small trailer containing their wrestling gear and sleeping space. "Living in her trailer, Mildred possesses all the characteristics of the modern housewife," the *Ohio State Journal* reported. "She's tops at frying chicken—and there's always plenty of it."

They had no fixed address. "I am on the road with the girls in a different city every day so please do not try to answer this by wire as I may not get it," Wolfe told Pfefer in his letter. Wolfe was doing everything he could to promote his title claimant. His correspondence to Pfefer was on special stationery that bore at the top in big letters: "Miss Mildred Burke" and "THE GREATEST SENSATION IN WRESTLING ENTERTAINMENT."

Her career hurtled forward with accelerating speed. In September 1937 they drove down to Jacksonville, where she beat a local female champ who had recently triumphed in her own mixed match against a male pro. The match featured the by now familiar shtick where the female wrestlers got entangled with the referee and proceeded to tear off his shirt. The women's bout topped a card that included the Florida men's champion. The matches drew the biggest crowd that Jacksonville had ever seen for a bout not involving Jack Dempsey.

The next week they went to Cuba to take on Mayita Salmon at the Arena Cervaza Cristal. Millie floated into Havana harbor on a luxury liner, her stateroom filled with the scent of flowers sent by admirers. At the pier she was confronted with a throng bearing banners reading "Welcome Mildred Burke" and "Welcome Women's Champion." A military band played "Hail to the Chief." Reporters and newsreel crews boarded the ship for a press conference in English and Spanish on the promenade deck. Then she went by limousine with a motorcycle escort to meet President Ramón Grau San Martín at his mansion, a rock fortress inlaid with marble overlooking the Caribbean Sea. The president kissed her hand and presented her with a tiny white puppy. "This was a long way from Mom's Café in Kansas City," Burke recalled.

In three years she had become a star. "From a job banging typewriter keys in an office to fame as the world champion banger of females against mats is the story of the life of Mildred Burke for the last five years," the Tampa, Florida, *Daily Times* reported. "People usually laugh when they hear about women wrestlers," she told the newspaper. "But that's before they see us in action. At Atlanta and Columbus, Ohio, there wasn't even standing room for a second appearance when I defended my title. And the men hadn't been drawing nearly as well."

The moment that showed Burke had truly arrived came in December 1937, when she made her debut in the East in Cumberland, Maryland. Topping the card was the great Jim Londos. Burke had risen far enough to warrant mention in the prefight publicity along with Londos, who was on the other side of forty and beginning the downward slope of his career. In the wrestling ring that night, the women outshined the men. "Despite the fact that the much ballyhooed champion, Jim Londos, was appearing in the main bout, two women wrestlers 'stole' the show last night at the state armory, where a gathering of over one thousand persons turned out to witness Cumberland's first 'grunt and groan carnival' in two years," read the story in the Cumberland *Daily News*. The description in the local paper reflected how the faster women's matches electrified crowds that had grown bored with the slower strainings of muscle-bound men. "Putting their act on with plenty of vim, vigor and vitality, Miss Mildred 'Muscles' Burke, 132-pounder, of Kansas City, Mo., and Miss Betty Lee, 133, of Chicago really scored a hit," the paper said. "Even those who booed and jeered the male wrestlers in the three other bouts on the program gave the female tumblers a 'big' hand throughout their lively contest, which lasted thirteen minutes. There was not a dull moment in this match, and it was so fast and good that it made the other performers on the program look like a quintet of second raters. . . . Of all the matches ever staged in this city, the Burke-Lee grappling affair was 'tops.'"

For one night, Burke had trumped Londos, the biggest star in the game.

Millie Burke was making real money now, and at the end of 1937 she was able to come off the road to spend the holidays with Joe, her mother, and her brother in Los Angeles. After her last booking of the year in Tulsa she headed to California in a Buick purchased with her wrestling proceeds. Along the way, she passed the sad columns of Depression-battered Okies fleeing the Dust Bowl in hopes of a better life out West. She was making the same trip, at least geographically, and the irony of her privileged position did not escape her. She saw the unshaven hollow-eyed men and the gaunt women suckling babies. The possessions of a lifetime were scattered along the road or piled atop rusting buses and decrepit cars. Dust coated everything. In California, she stopped outside of a restaurant, where the proprietor refused to sell bread to an emaciated man. They were told that if they wanted bread they needed to buy a hamburger. So Burke bought sixteen hamburgers, two dozen bottles of milk, and all the pie and cupcakes in sight. She gave it all to the Okies along with a $20 bill. "This'll get you to LA," she told them. "Cross the desert at night, or you won't make it in that truck." They wept.

★ ★ ★

Billy Wolfe's genius at garnering publicity continued to propel Burke's rise. In January 1938 she appeared in *Life* magazine again, this time in a seven-photo spread with Wilma Gordon, about the first female mud wrestling match in the country, held before 2,500 people in Akron, Ohio. Mud matches, known as "Hindu style," had started on the West coast featuring male wrestlers. Millie hated the mud but she gave in to Wolfe's promotional instincts. She got her revenge. After she pinned Gordon she saw Wolfe walking toward her wearing his three-piece suit and his "Halloween pumpkin smile." Her hair was matted with mud, slime filled her nostrils, and grit lodged in her eyes and teeth. She took a couple of steps and jumped into the air, shooting her legs forward and landing on her backside. "Whizzing through the sticky night air, the muck smothered Bill from head to foot—cigar, smile and all," she recalled. "He was now wearing a brown suit. The crowd went wild."

Newsreel cameras were ringside and the match brought Millie even more publicity than she got when she'd beaten Mortensen. "That touching bit of sentiment about a woman's place being in the kitchen might be okay in its place, but there's no place for it in the life of Mildred (Cyclone) Burke," wrote Jerry Brondfield in a syndicated article that ran in papers from Lowell, Massachusetts, to Kingsport, Tennessee. Burke talked about "rassling" and the growing number of women doing it. "A lot of wrestlers' wives—maybe through association —I don't know— now have the idea they can wrestle. So I ought to have a lot of competition before very long. Bring 'em on. Any of 'em. All of 'em. I'll rassle 'em any time. Any place. And in mud if they care to!"

Newspapers profiled her all the time now, and she cultivated a brash, tough-talking persona that was more Billy Wolfe than Millie Bliss. A few days after the mud match she bristled when a sports columnist for the *Mobile* (Alabama) *Times* questioned her commitment to the wrestling ring. "If those so-called he-men can do it, so can we girls," she said. She won over reporters with her disarming frankness. In the newsroom at the Norfolk, Virginia, *Ledger-Dispatch* she took off her coat and told the sports columnist, "Here, feel my arm . . . Now, feel my back." As he did so, the man noticed that the customary newsroom din had subsided. All the typewriters had fallen silent. When he looked around he saw the "smug smirks and sly smiles" of his colleagues. "To be perfectly frank, I was in a bit of a dither." Melville Carico, a *Roanoke Times* cub reporter who interviewed her that same day, was "surprised to find a trim 22-year-old girl with sandy hair who weighs 128 pounds. Well, when I first saw her I was so astonished that I could not think of anything to ask her. Finally, I managed to stammer out enough words to ask what are her favorite holds. 'A flying leg scissors and a body slam,' she said, giving a big Missouri smile." Then the reporter said, "I don't just exactly understand what a flying leg scissors is." Billy Wolfe knew his cue. "Why don't you let her demonstrate?" he helpfully offered. The embarrassed young reporter soldiered on. "Her biceps are larger than the average man's and are as hard as rocks, her back muscles have the rhythmic flow of a professional boxer or any well-trained man athlete. And as for her punch, well, I didn't question that."

In an interview a week later with a female reporter at the *Charlotte Observer,* Millie dropped the hardboiled act and came across much less cartoonish. Expecting a "lady rassler," LeGette Blythe found a thoughtful, self-possessed woman. In a long piece that ran on the front page of the newspaper, the reporter etched a serious portrait of a young woman trying to make her way in the world, "a neat looking girl, who might have been a secretary. She was neatly dressed, wore a tiny gold wrist watch on her left arm and a small bracelet on her right, two inconspicuous rings and her dress was one of those new bolero outfits in dark blue with some red about the neck—which was pretty tight, I noticed—not the dress, I mean, but the neck of it. I noticed that she had just had her hair curled . . . She talked quietly in a nicely restrained voice that occasionally dropped into the jargon of the wrestlers and boxers, and she was very modest in discussing her exploits." She had taken up wrestling because she thought it was a good way for an athletically inclined woman to earn a living, and now she made more than many professional men. She wasn't boastful or coarse. Instead, she allowed a rare glimpse of the woman behind the wrestler's mask. She wasn't eager to wrestle men or in the mud. "No, I don't often wrestle men," Burke said. "In the first place, I don't think a woman wrestler is as good as a man wrestler of her weight. And there are many reasons against it. If I should beat a man wrestler the fans would claim it was a frame-up, and if he beat me, they would say that I was no good—just a woman."

Burke said she trained carefully, did not smoke, and was temperate in her eating habits. She did not eat for several hours before a match. Afterward, "I'm usually pretty hungry then, and I eat a big steak, maybe." Billy Wolfe was present and he piped up at an opportunity to trot out one of his pet theories on health and nutrition. "Yeh," he said, "she eats too much steak. I'm always trying to get her to eat more green stuff. Spinach and that sort of stuff. She doesn't get enough of it." Mildred responded, "Well, I eat vegetables but my manager won't let me put vinegar on my spinach and I don't like it without vinegar." Wolfe said, "Yeh. Vinegar's not healthy. It's the wrong kind of acid. She oughtn't to eat spinach with vinegar." Lemon juice would be okay but not vinegar, he said. "It ain't healthy."

The reporter noticed Wolfe's cauliflowered left ear. She asked Mildred if she worried about her ears. "I once thought maybe I'd get a little bit of a cauliflower on my ear, but then I decided I didn't want one. So I'm mighty careful. I rub Vaseline on my ears and I take good care of them. I had a little lump on my right ear lately, but now it's gone and I'm mighty glad of it."

The reporter asked if Burke was married. "Not yet," she lied. "One rich old oil man in Texas asked me to marry him, but I didn't.

And I've been too busy moving about over the country. I want to stay in the game a good while yet. A married woman wouldn't draw so well, do you think?"

Billy and Millie still had no fixed address, but business was good. In July 1938 Wolfe contacted Jack Pfefer again, still hoping to get some matches on the East Coast. "Mildred and I are very thankful that we have been making splendid money," Wolfe wrote from Wheatland, Missouri, where his older brother, George, ran the telephone exchange and maintained a mail drop for Billy. Now he had stationery with a full-body shot of Mildred in the ring wearing her championship belt. Wolfe was full of ideas for promoting his champion: "I am planning on having a beautiful sound car, equipped with large loud speakers, so that I can advertise your show on the streets all day the day of Mildred's match. As a matter of fact I have already bought all of the sound equipment, which cost me $224.00 and I will install it on a new 1939 car as soon as the new cars come out."

Millie continued to win every match. It was a testament to her skill and charisma, as well as to Wolfe's strategy of keeping her perpetually on the road, that her constant winning did not affect her ability to draw. The pattern of unbroken victories ended with a stunning series of matches Wolfe put on for Al Haft in Columbus in the fall of 1938. On November 17, she faced off with Betty Nichols of Boston at Memorial Hall. The first five hundred women were admitted free. Nichols was fast and at 126 pounds a little smaller even than Burke. The headline after the match was a stunner, one never to be repeated: "Mildred Burke Is Loser," the Ohio *State Journal* proclaimed. The paper reported that Nichols had polished Burke off in nine and a half minutes to take her title. The women's bout "was even more thrilling than the feature bout and just about all the rough stuff known to wrestling was attempted by these capable performers. . . . It was by far the best women's match ever staged here." Eight years later, Burke published a piece in the *National Police Gazette* explaining her surprising loss. Under the headline "My Bloodiest Bout," Burke wrote that she had never taken such punishment in the ring. When she first saw Nichols, she recounted, she was lulled by her size. "Most of my opponents have outweighed me a good deal," Burke wrote. "I figured this would be easy. Far from it."

In Burke's account, after a bruising and even ring battle ("We were both fighting with everything we had"), Nichols simply sucker punched her. "I received the hardest, swiftest punch on the chin I ever felt in my life. I was out like a light. The next thing I knew I was in the dressing room with smelling salts waving under my nose." Burke said the referee declared the bout a "no contest" because she had been "knocked out by an unfair lick." This was important to the Burke legend, for throughout her life Burke would maintain that she never lost a match, other than those exhibitions with Mortensen. But the newspapers of the time make clear that Burke had indeed lost the match in Columbus to Nichols along with her title.

After "two hours of arguing between the promoters," Burke wrote, a rematch was planned for the following week. The two women dispensed with wrestling and fought like street fighters, punching, kicking, and pulling hair, the newspapers reported. The match was approaching its thirty-minute time limit when Burke said Nichols grabbed her in a headlock and smashed a knee into Burke's face. "Blood ran all the way down my suit, my legs and on to the mat," she wrote. "My eye puffed up completely and was shut in a minute. The audience was amazed at how quickly it swelled. It stood out like a baseball." Somehow Burke made it through the rest of the match and a draw was declared. "When the bell rang we were both covered with blood from my eye, and the mat was splattered with crimson," she wrote.

A week later there was yet another rematch. Nichols now had her picture in the paper under the headline "Champion." She was described as a great favorite of the Columbus fans and, in a line that could have been stolen straight from Burke's publicity, "the surprise package of the wrestling world . . . 126 pounds of dynamite."

Burke took the third match, winning with a body slam in twelve minutes, twenty-two seconds. At one point, Millie tossed Betty over the ropes and Nichols seemed to injure her hip as she landed. "Betty did not appear to have the power and fight last night that she displayed in two previous bouts with Mildred," the Ohio *State Journal* reported. Burke wrote in the *Police Gazette* that "Betty had used her best licks in the first two matches and had nothing left to surprise me with . . . She had put everything she had into those matches against me and when I defeated her, I did so both physically and mentally." Burke later told the Associated Press, "Betty was so broken hearted she gave up wrestling."

Burke and Nichols wrestled again, four days later, in Charleston, West Virginia. Mildred won in two straight falls. Nichols quickly faded from wrestling. It is interesting to speculate on the Burke-Nichols matches, but in the end nothing can be known for certain. Did Betty Nichols really knock out Mildred Burke with a sudden punch or was this just a brilliant stratagem dreamed up by Billy Wolfe to boost the gate? The Columbus *Dispatch* pointed out that Burke had to be carried from the ring after that first match, which certainly matches Burke's description in the *Police Gazette*. Was she out or was she acting? Whatever the case, Burke's knockout did wonders for the gate; she wrote that thousands were turned away from the sold-out second match.

Millie Burke's upward trajectory continued. "Wrestling is one of the last remaining frontiers of male achievement and Miss Burke is definite proof that even this rugged diversion will fall before the invading fair sex," the Mansfield, Ohio, *News-Journal* reported. Her powerful image served as a beacon to other Millie Blisses trapped in hard and hopeless lives. "Every booking brought me new fans, and produced new converts to my dream," she later wrote. "Streams of tough and hungry girls wanted to break into the sport." One of them was nineteen-year-old Gladys Gillem, who was helping her invalid mother run a boardinghouse in Birmingham when Wolfe's troupe came to a nearby town. After seeing Burke wrestle, Gillem made a decision. "I didn't want to work in a 10-cent store. I didn't want to be a waitress. I didn't want to clean houses," she recalled in an interview sixty-eight years later. She told Wolfe she wanted to join up. "Just tie me on the car roof, because I'm leaving this place," she said. He gave her a tryout. "He had Wilma Gordon beat the hell out of me," Gillem remembered. But she was a tough tomboy; she could take a "bump," in the parlance of wrestlers. They added her to their group. "This is when Billy and Mildred wasn't rich," Gillem recalled. "They were just poor people then. My daddy told them, 'If you don't treat my daughter right, I'll travel across the United States to take care of you.'"

In the early days Wolfe appears to have had a hard time settling on a name for Gladys. For a while, he tried Gladys Ryan. Then Gladys Gilliam. Finally, he stuck with the name she was born with. That proved to be particularly apt, for Gladys "Kill 'em" Gillem would turn out to be one of the most colorful and best-fitting ring monikers in the entire wrestling game. She was not beautiful and she was never allowed to win. But she was a terrific performer and she played a key role in Mildred Burke's rise. With the addition of Gillem, Wolfe took a major step in the direction of building a stable of women wrestlers who could make Burke look good and at the same time draw fans of their own. This would be the linchpin of their success.

Gillem's style in the ring brought out the best in Burke. The blonde Gillem was a wildcat, a crowd-pleasing bundle of energy whose roughhouse tactics could be counted on to whip up a big response. The auburn-haired Burke represented fortitude, fair play, hard work, and honor. Gillem brought mayhem, chaos, rule breaking, and sheer entertainment. She was the black-hearted villain every white-hatted hero needs, lest they become vanilla and boring. Their contrasting styles always ensured magic in the ring. "Miss Burke is a wonderful straight wrestler and Miss Gilliam is downright mean and contemptible," Galveston promoter Jerry Schultz told his local paper in October 1939.

The sports columnist in Galveston captured a candid locker room scene with Burke and Gillem. Wolfe was also there, chomping on his ever-present cigar. He convinced the journalist to feel Mildred's back and shoulder muscles. Mildred smiled an even row of white teeth and flashed her blue eyes. Then Wolfe left the columnist alone with the two women. The man was struck by what he now saw in Gillem, who moments earlier had been dragging Burke around the ring by her hair. Backstage, Gillem was "just a demure and sober-faced lassie whose eyes criticized or admired Miss Burke's clothes as the champ stowed them away in an alligator bag which—she burbled like a school girl—she had bought on a recent trip to Mexico." The columnist wanted to know why they had deserted "home, hearth and the pursuit of man" for the wrestling ring. "Well, I don't know for sure," Gillem answered. "Maybe it runs in the family. I have a brother who was a boxer in the Navy. Or maybe I do it because of the excitement. I guess that's it." Burke, by contrast, was as definite as an arrow in a bull's-eye. "I promised myself a long time ago that whatever I did with my life it would be different," she said, smiling. "I guess being a lady wrestler is being different, isn't it?" Wolfe returned, the interview ended, and Burke "in a flutter of excitement" gathered hat and purse to get on with their life on the road. "It was time to move on to another town, to another barren dressing room, another strange crowd, another session of hair-yanking," the columnist wrote. "Women are peculiar people."

The next month, a reporter in Ohio tried the get-to-know-the-lady-wrestlers angle and caught Burke giving one of her hard-boiled performances.

"Tell us, Miss Burke," the reporter asked, "do you like your Amazonian occupation?"

"Don't get flip wit' me, buddy," Burke answered. "This job is as respectable as any."

At this point Wolfe entered and joined the interview. Listening, the reporter nonchalantly leaned against what felt like a "hard cast-iron stove." It was Burke. As always, Wolfe was quick with a quip. "Better not lean on Miss Burke too hard, Al, you might muss up her tights."

Her tights, or rather the color of them, would soon become a big part of her act. Over the next few years, Burke and Wolfe built her into the champion who would capture the national imagination and dominate her sport for fifteen years. It was a project that took considerable thought and effort. Nothing was left to chance. Wolfe's voluminous address book lists all the details that demanded attention: Major Papers for Publicity, Man Who Does Silhouettes, Cartoon Artist and Statuette Molders, Best Place to Have Pictures Made, People that Make Robes, Man that Can Have Wrestling Shoes Made to Order in Boston, Mildred's Colored Enlargements Delivered to, Men that Make Cuts and Mats, Studio that Makes Negatives and Colored Enlargements, Men Who Get Splashes in Magazines and Newspapers, People that Has and Trains Girl Wrestlers, Jewelry Dealers, the Man that Makes My Mountings, Girls Who Applied for Stenographic Work, Girl Wrestling Students, Available Girls to Train, Girls Wanting to Learn Wrestling, Colored Girls.

Millie designed her own suits. The first reference to her "white togs" occurred in a newspaper article in December 1939. From then on it became her standard look. "Ninety percent of my wrestling was in white tights and white shoes," she later said. "I always kept a real good tan. The white satin made it show up real good." The white was a large part of the image she was trying to build. The color was both functional and symbolic. The bright white suit caught the light in the ring and stood out starkly against the darker costumes of the other wrestlers. Covering one Burke-Gillem match, the paper in Charleston noted that Burke was "wearing white wrestling attire in sharp contrast to the coal black shade" of Gillem's suit. The white also conveyed purity and underscored Burke's good-girl role as the troupe's virtuous champion.

Always there was great sensitivity about what the women wrestlers wore. "Her working garments vary with the town she plays," one journalist wrote. "Sometimes she wears a one-piece white bathing suit. Other towns demand that she don a pair of Lastex trunks over her suit, so that if one layer gets torn off, the other will remain, leaving her decent. A great many towns demand that Mildred wear tights under her suit."

To get to wear the white she had to overcome the fears that she would reveal too much. "Most state commission rulings said you couldn't wear white tights 'cause that looked too much like your own skin," she later recalled. "So I said, 'I've got white on and I'm goin' to wear it.' That first night I got in the ring with white tights and a beautiful suntan and the commissioner himself came back to tell me how absolutely gorgeous it was. He'd never seen anything look that pretty in the ring before."

She matched the white suits with white leather boots and rhinestone-covered robes that she had designed, hand-made by her mother, who had seen her wrestle in a newsreel and had become her biggest fan. "I'd have some beautiful colored robe, maybe fuchsia or something, with white-satin lining," Burke recalled. "I had one robe that cost me $1,100. It was solid cut rhinestones. It weighed, I think, twenty-six pounds. There was nothing else in it, it was solid. . . . It was clear to the floor from the shoulders. I got tired of carrying it because, you know, twenty-six pounds in the suitcase besides the tights and shoes and everything else. Then I had it cut in two and had two short jackets made out of it. Oh, it just glistened like diamonds! It was just fabulous."

Outside the ring, she favored mink coats and custom-made full-length floral dresses tailored to her unique physique. "Out of her wrestling garb, she's all woman," a reporter noted. "She owns five fur coats and a bunch of girlish frilly dresses, instead of the tailored attire one would expect of a female athlete." This was another conscious choice. "Women's wrestling wasn't going to be any freak show while I was champion," she later wrote. "Dressing like a top movie star was the order of the day, in high fashion, stunning design and the best of taste." The idea was always to sell women wrestlers to the public by playing up their womanliness. "My resolve was to be a woman and a lady first, and a champion wrestler second," she wrote. "Every woman was a potential wrestling fan, and it was good business, on top of my own personal motivation, to project a shining new image. This meant the right kind of clothes, in and out of the ring, so there would be no doubt as to my femininity."

One of Burke's favorite coats was a gift from Billy, a heavy woolen article that was bright pink and trimmed in black and white skunk fur. "Worn with a tasteful turquoise dress that I also adored, this coat really went over with the public," she wrote. "The combination always landed me in the women's section of the local newspapers when I wore it to the arenas." Image was everything. No detail was too small. She even started signing autographs in green ink, just to make a distinctive impression.

On her way to the ring she chose a special piece of music, "her favorite song," the fast and madcap instrumental "Sabre Dance," from Armenian composer Aram Khachaturian's ballet *Gayane*. The whirling war dance was a favorite of circuses and acrobats. To Burke, it conjured the energy she felt in the ring. "This exciting melody always filled me with fighting spirit," she said.

She entered the ring perfectly coiffed and made up, with lipstick, rouge, and eyeliner. The prebout preparations were full of frenzied primping in front of a mirror. "The girls dress backstage like actresses," a magazine noted. "The makeup kit is brought out and the face is adjusted perfectly before it gets the subsequent terrific beating. No self-respecting lady wrestler would think of climbing into the ring unless her hair were properly set and her nails newly manicured."

The body that went into the suits and dresses got equal attention. On the road Burke kept to a vigorous schedule of self-improvement that, like everything else about her, ended up published in the papers: Breakfast—Steak and Potatoes; Training—One hour during the morning; Exercise—One hour in the afternoon, including roadwork; Wrestling—Twice a week; Cocktails, candy and nightclubs—none. She threw herself into sculpting her body. Using dumbbells, she built up and refined the cut and defined musculature that so many found so striking when she entered the ring. She took care to be muscular without being muscle-bound. She used weights, but kept them light, to avoid "any grotesque buildup of my muscles," she wrote. "Top condition was my goal, but I also wanted to appear feminine and attractive in an evening gown." Still, she ended up looking somewhat like a female body builder in the days before female body builders existed, but many fans found that attractive. "I wouldn't say she was built like a man, but she was chunky, kind of muscled up," said Tommy Fooshee, a wrestling referee who never forgot his first sight of Burke when he was a fourteen-year-old fan in Houston. "She looked more like a weight lifter than a wrestler, but she wasn't stiff like some of the weight lifters. She could move very well in the ring. She had a body that was very flexible. It was just kind of a pleasure to look at something like that."

On the road, she exercised constantly in her hotel room. Pushups, situps, deep-knee bends and dynamic tension exercises followed each other in a set routine, and she finished with body bridges, which became a standard part of her act. She would lie on her back in the ring and bridge her body upward, using the muscles in her legs and her neck, and the crowd would count along as she reached eighty, a good number for a male athlete. "Once I started doing these body bridges at the arenas, they added to my fame," she said.

The overall effect was mesmerizing. Lillian Ellison, a young girl from Tookiedoo, South Carolina, saw the champion when her father took her to the Tuesday night wrestling matches at the Township Auditorium in Columbia. "Every eye in the place was on her," recalled Ellison, who had grown up with twelve brothers and no mother since the age of ten. "She carried herself the way a champion should. She strutted. I could just tell that here was someone—a lady—who kicked ass and took names. After all this time I had spent surrounded by and competing with boys, here was a woman like Amelia Earhart who I could model myself after." When Ellison came of age, she made it her mission to join up with Burke and Wolfe and become a wrestler. After Burke's era ended Ellison would adopt the moniker the "Fabulous Moolah" and become the most famous female wrestler in the world. She never forgot the first sight in the ring that had inspired her. "Wow! Women can do that?" she recalled decades later. "Right then, I knew what I wanted to be."

7

"Pulchritude on Parade"

In the spring of 1940, after the New Jersey athletic commissioner decided to allow women's wrestling in the state, Billy Wolfe finally got a prominent promoter and former wrestler named Rudy Dusek to book Mildred Burke for some matches around Newark. Then Jack Pfefer wrote Wolfe saying that he could now book Burke in New Jersey. Suddenly Wolfe had a problem, caught between two powerful promoters, neither of whom he could afford to offend. He asked for Pfefer's forbearance while he worked things out with Dusek, who had connections to the old wrestling Trust and, with his three wrestling brothers, had formed a popular act in the 1930s known as the Riot Squad.

Wolfe's attempt to smooth things over ran into trouble. Pfefer tried to book Burke into Atlantic City, but Dusek was already claiming that date. Now Pfefer was complaining to Wolfe about his expensive phone calls and telegrams trying to arrange a booking. The promoter said he couldn't wait four weeks and was threatening to book other women wrestlers. Wolfe turned on his particular brand of charm, a combination of genuflection, subservience, and pained but muted indignation. "I am very well aware of the fact, that I am a very small person in this big wrestling world," Wolfe wrote from Baltimore on June 30, 1940. "I want to explain to you the spot I have been in since this affair came up. . . . Mr. Pfefer please understand what an unpleasant situation that was for me. I have sent you publicity for several years with out you booking my girls. I can't understand why you say to me that I must work for you with-in three weeks time or you will get other girls . . . I regret this situation very much, and will pay you for your calls and wires." In an early sign of his business acumen, Wolfe managed to avert the crisis and have his dates with both Dusek and Pfefer.

The forty-five-year-old Pfefer was just the man to take Wolfe's wrestlers into the stratosphere. Thin and just a few inches over five feet tall, Pfefer was one of the most memorable characters in a sport with far more than its share. He was the kind of shrewd, fast-patter operator who could make even Billy Wolfe look sluggish. Pfefer also had an encyclopedic knowledge of wrestling backed up by the voluminous files he kept filled with clippings on every wrestler and promoter. A. J. Liebling accurately described him as "a frail, corvine man," but then pointed out that Pfefer had changed wrestling by pushing its entertainment value far beyond where even Jack Curley was willing to go. "The difference between Pfefer's productions and Curley's was like that between avowed fiction and a Hearst news story," Liebling wrote. "Pfefer's productions were weak in acrobatics but rich in humorous characterization." Throughout his war with the Trust, Pfefer had managed to stay in business. Now, women wrestlers would join the freaks, midgets, and ethnic wrestlers he employed to pull in business in the worst market anybody had seen for pro wrestling in some time. "Jack, as he is affectionately known to his intimates, is reported to have told his boys, who he refers to as palookas, to 'Hit the road, you bums; ve got glamour gurls now,'" the *Newark Star-Ledger* reported.

Pfefer was as notable for his personal aura as he was for his wrestling promotions. He had a different standard of personal hygiene, and the wrestlers who knew him insisted that he didn't bother to bathe, picked his nose, and had breath bad enough to get him nicknamed the Halitosis Kid. Although he always sported a three-piece suit, people noted that it wasn't clean. He let his hair and fingernails grow far longer than any fashion would allow, wore his hat at a raffish angle, and put a carnation in his lapel. People may have derided him but they also flocked to see what he was up to. He got more and better publicity than any of his rivals. Even though Dusek brought Burke into New Jersey first, it was Pfefer who grabbed the headlines. The *Star-Ledger* broke the news that he was launching "a new phase of his multi-colored career when he makes his first attempt to become the 'Ziegfield of Wrestling' by presenting matdom's glamour girl, Mildred Burke."

Pfefer relished the spotlight Burke's matches gave him. "I didn't tink that gurl vesslers vould be a good idea," Pfefer told the paper, "but after vatching palookas for so long even Carrie Nation vould be a relief. Dees Mildred Burke ach but she is vonderful. I hear she vessles men when she runs out of vomen opponents but I vouldn't vant her to vessle some of mine bums, she vould ruin their rep, their reptu . . . you know what I means."

When Jack Pfefer entered the ring and addressed the crowd before Burke's first bout for him on July 10, 1940, the paper let its scorn show, but it also gave him plenty of ink. "Jack Pfefer made a short speech of a few thousand poorly chosen words and wound up declaring, 'Geev a look at dees leetle gurls' muskles,'" the *Star-Ledger* reported. "Even the speech couldn't spoil Mildred's hour of triumph and she climbed above the introduction to win the fans."

Droves of women eager to see women wrestle had packed the Meadowbrook Bowl, a two-year-old outdoor boxing arena on Orange Avenue in Newark. At first the crowd was for Gillem, with many yelling, "C'mon, Blondie geev it to her." But as Gillem excellently performed her role as the heel—slugging, biting, kicking, hair pulling—the fans quickly shifted. "The bout was only a minute old when Blondie showed that she was a dyed-in-the-wool villainess and the majority of the fans switched to the heroine," the Star-Ledger reported. Gillem rushed out of her corner, grabbed Burke's hair, and kneed her to the ground. Burke was on the defensive but then regained control with a dropkick. Her wrestling ability won many fans. One writer, in an article headlined, "They Know Their Stuff," was so impressed that he listed the holds: back-drops, flying mares, dropkicks, flying tackles, hammer-locks, and the Japanese wristlock. "The fans gasped when Milly landed her dropkick for they never expected to see a lady wrestler land such a blow," the Star-Ledger reported, adding that "one leather-lung" fan in the bleachers yelled, "Lookit, a female Dr. Dropkick Murphy," referring to the top male wrestler on the card. The fans had no way of knowing that Burke outearned Murphy for the evening, $94.70 to $20, but the price ratio reflected their sentiments. In addition to the legitimate holds, the two women also slapped each other, manhandled the referee, and pulled hair. After Gillem retaliated with some more dirty tactics, Burke sent her flying across the ring with an uppercut. The fans jumped up in their seats and roared: "Keep the dames here and send the bums back to the minors." Burke ended the match with her famous new hold, the "alligator clutch," which "left Gladys tied up like a pretzel made by a punch-drunk pretzel bender." The fans gave the two women a rousing ovation.

The Irish Angel, one of Pfefer's massive and freakish male wres-tlers, who was waiting to enter the ring next, put Burke in a headlock after her match as flashbulbs exploded around them. He was roundly booed. "Hit the road, you bum," the fans yelled. "Don't get her mad or she'll throw you into the next county." A newspaper photogra-pher captured a winded Millie, her hair still mussed from her match, smiling gamely in the grasp of the Irish Angel, a muscle-bound bruiser with a shaved head and huge sideburns that crept along his jaw like giant caterpillars. The photo ran the next day in a long story that featured Burke. The Angel, who was paid $5 for his match, got one line at the bottom. The *Star-Ledger* called it "a humdinger of a show."

For Wolfe and Burke all the pieces had come together, all the careful thought and arduous preparation, and allowed them to make their finest showing yet. They created a sensation, drawing the media from New York City, where women's wrestling was still banned. There was a blizzard of stories in the New Jersey newspapers. "Beauty Via Milly Burke Shoos Beast from Local Mat," ran the headline in the *Star-Ledger*. The "trim, compact" Burke was described as "wrestling's gift of pulchritude to the world." Much leering attention was given to her ring outfit. "Miss Burke was clad in extremely tight shorts of white satin," Willie Ratner wrote in the *Newark Evening News*. "She certainly put a lot of faith in those narrow strips that hold up her costume. She would have made a great hit on the beach."

The women were hailed as the answer to pro wrestling's ailments. "While the male villains haven't churned up any box office interest to speak of, the women have," the *Star-Ledger* noted. "They have done an amazing business wherever they have shown. Maybe that's the trouble with wrestling. Maybe we haven't had enough of the women's touch as well as body slams." Burke was back the next week, this time for a match with Mexico's Lupe Acosta before another big crowd at the Meadowbrook Bowl. "With Pulchritude on Parade again featuring the show another large crowd turned out to welcome the girls and once more went home talking about the fast and furious action provided," the paper reported.

A month later, the return match between Burke and Gillem attracted the largest crowd in the history of the Meadowbrook Bowl. They wrestled to a draw in fourteen minutes, thirty-one seconds. Gillem, termed "the blonde bombshell of biff," slugged Burke at the opening bell, and the two women traded punches throughout the match. At one point, Gillem picked up the smaller Burke and choked her in the middle of the ring. Burke broke the hold, gasping for breath. "This has gone far enough," she shouted. "It's time to call a halt." Then she knocked Gillem out of the ring "with a couple of dropkicks that would have made Dr. Dropkick Murphy, the master of the hold, green with envy," the paper reported. Gillem came tearing back as the crowd roiled in amazement. She ripped the shirt off the referee's back when he tried to interfere "and soon all three were tumbling around the ring in a mad maelstrom of flying fists." The two women ended up slugging each other outside the ring, fans all around them. The referee tried to stop them, counting to twenty—they had ten seconds to get back in the ring or be disqualified—to no avail. Burke had Gillem bent over backward on one of the seats when three police officers and a couple of bowl attendants pulled them apart. "I didn't beat her as I promised," Gillem said in the dressing room, "but I didn't lose and I sure messed her up a lot."

It was nothing but a good show. As Gillem would say in a letter twenty-five years later and repeat in an interview forty-two years after that, all of her matches with Burke were worked. "I never wrestled Mildred the real thing," Gillem said.

A part of Gillem's act was going crazy and biting in the ring. Occasionally, she went too far. "Crazy Gladys actually bit me on the thigh and she wouldn't let go," Burke said years later in a magazine interview about an incident that happened in Cleveland in 1940. "Her teeth cut through the tights and drew blood. I finally got loose with a forearm smash which broke her nose. You heard of cauliflowered ears, well that Gillem had a cauliflowered head."

To stoke the box office, Pfefer arranged for his male wrestlers to form a union, Wrestlers Association No. 1234, and picket outside the Laurel Garden in Newark against the "unfair invasion" by women. "Male Pachyderms Stage Protest Parade," the *Star-Ledger* dutifully headlined. The men carried signs proclaiming, "Women Wrestlers Go Home and

Wash Your Dishes." The men told a reporter that brawn could not compete with beauty in the ring. "Cauliflower ears, bashed-in noses, looks to frighten children, all these have been our assets, but now the dames come in with pulchritude, powdered noses and looks about which men rave, and ring antics which have the women flocking to see them in the thousands." The next article pointed out that the whole thing was one of Pfefer's put-up jobs. "We were just kidding," one of the strikers said. "But we figured we had to do something to get our pictures in the paper again."

Burke's matches for Pfefer had the desired effect. In New Jersey and New York City in the summer of 1940 Millie Burke was the toast of the town. She may have been banned from wrestling in the Empire State, but soon she and Wolfe were sampling the Manhattan nightclubs with Pfefer. "I ran into Jake on Broadway with a nifty, one Mildred (Call me Millie) Burke, of Kansas City, a feminine Hackenschmidt who learned her art watching the lads around the local slaughterhouses put headlocks on steers," wrote Louis Royal in the New York *Daily Advocate*. Mildred told the reporter she was angry that women's wrestling was banned in New York City. The columnist was sympathetic. "The novelty of lady rassling has saved the mat racket across the river," he wrote, adding, "Miss Burke doesn't look like a muscle moll but when you shake hands with her it is like getting your fingers caught in a taxi door. The best way to meet her is to keep your hands in your pocket and give her a polite nod." Millie was everywhere. The next day, she appeared in the *Washington Post* in a photograph with Jack Dempsey feeling her biceps under the headline, "Whaddayamean, the Weaker Sex?" Two days later, a syndicated cartoon featuring Millie in Ripley's *Believe It or Not* appeared in newspapers around the country. She was depicted as the champion woman wrestler who had "never lost a bout" and could do "80 body bridges in succession!"

Burke and Wolfe were now signing their letters to Pfefer together, "Sincerely Your Friends, Mildred and Billy." They were riding high, and their letters reflected their high spirits. "Dear Jack," they wrote. "We received your splendid letter this morning and many thanks to you. The write-up was wonderful." Millie added a separate, personal note: "Dear Jack: Bill is not playing any more Poker. I think we have him worried. Ha. Ha. Regards from Your Champ, Mildred." For the first time, Wolfe had added his own picture to the stationery, a small mug shot in a cameo at the lower left-hand corner, "Billy Wolfe, Manager." His cauliflower ear was clearly visible.

Behind the scenes, the marriage continued as a loveless match. Wolfe had moved on from Mae Weston and was now sleeping with Gillem; sex with him appeared to be the initiation fee for any woman who wanted to wrestle for him. Gillem, a fun-loving, adventurous young woman, didn't care and even developed some affection for Wolfe. "He wanted to play musical beds with all the girls," Gillem later recalled. "He tried all the girls. He'd go from one room to the other. If you went to bed with him, you got a good booking." Burke turned a blind eye to Wolfe's open philandering and kept to herself when they went on the road.

Professionally, they could do no wrong. Mildred wrestled in the roof garden of the Gibson Hotel in Cincinnati. Triumph followed triumph. "We wrestled in Lima, Ohio, last night and more then [sic] doubled their business there and made a big hit in the town," Wolfe wrote Pfefer. "Mildred wrestle's [sic] here in Toledo tonight and a big house is expected in spite of the fact the news-papers [sic] here are against lady wrestling and won't even mention the girls," Wolfe wrote on another occasion. Time and again, the newspapers pointed out that the faster women's matches were more entertaining than the men. "It was the usual blistering match with both female grapplers making the males on the card look as if they were nailed to the mat," the *San Antonio Light* observed of a Burke match in October 1940.

They wrestled in open-air arenas in the summer and unair-conditioned auditoriums in the winter. Occasionally, a promoter would set up blocks of ice and fans to blow cool air over the spectators. By now, Wolfe and Burke and the other women were driving around the country in a 1939 DeSoto pulling the trailer filled with their gear. But the days of sleeping in the trailer were long past. They could now afford cheap motels. Still, there was no time for lying around a swimming pool. As the car racked up the miles on dusty roads throughout the Midwest, Burke and the women would sprawl on the fenders in their bathing suits to get that deep tan that looked good in the ring. "They couldn't afford to stop before they got to the next match," Burke's son, Joe, recalled. The road was long and arduous in the days before the national Interstate Highway System and air-conditioning. Increasingly, Joe, who had just turned six and needed to be in school, was left with relatives, in either Missouri or Los Angeles. "When Mom was on the road working she'd send me a dollar every month, so I'd have a little pocket money," he said. "That was a pretty big thing in those days." He had grown up watching her train and wrestle and understood that her absences were part of their life together; he didn't think there was anything unusual about any of it. "I was on top of the world, all the time," he recalled. "I never felt abandoned. I never felt like I didn't have a mom. Maybe because I was raised from birth that way."

Wolfe's stationery now featured a seven-inch photograph of Mildred Burke in her white suit under the words, "A Great Athlete and One of the Finest Attractions in the Wrestling World." He now had a stable of seven women wrestlers who could be deployed to support his champion. By the end of 1940 Burke was hands down the most prominent female wrestler in the country. The *National Police Gazette* printed the most detailed word portrait of her yet, a profile of a champion in her prime. "Her attractive face with its up-turned nose and strong, white teeth is heavily made up for the lights which shine down upon her. Her light brown hair is carefully marcelled, and her nails are manicured. Her double-layered bathing suit clings to her muscular torso. All in all, Mildred looks as glamorous as any showgirl, if a lot more massive."

Her transformation under Billy Wolfe was now complete. The interview in the *Police Gazette* was taken over by the hard-boiled Mildred. She didn't even sound like the same person from only two years earlier. "Looka hyar," she was quoted. "It's all the bunk about gal and boy wrestlin' bein' funny business; this here is jest as serious as any other angle of the game. There ain't no room for messin' around in our racket. If I wrestle a boy or a girl, it's all the same, we mix it up, for real." On getting made up for the ring: "I gotta git all prettied-up, so I can look good while I'm gittin' messed up." And on her diet: "To be on the level, I don't really have to exercise hard and I don' have to diet, either. I eat steak for breakfast, steak for lunch, steak for supper, and then a nice juicy porterhouse or T-bone steak after the match." The next year she would tell another reporter, "You can leave that perfume and powder stuff for those guys who have been crawling in and out of the ring with Joe Louis on a monthly basis. I'll take a good chaw of seaweed every time."

Despite all the attention and money women were bringing into a business that desperately needed both, the obstacles to full acceptance remained. Many male promoters only grudgingly accepted females, even as they profited from them. "Regarding the girls—I had booked Mildred Burke in the territory for a couple weeks," Al Haft, who had been so instrumental in opening up Ohio for Burke, wrote to Jack Pfefer in December 1940. "They start today. I bring them in about twice a year. Once in the summer and once in the holiday season. I dont [sic] like to feature too much lady wrestling. After all, it is a mans [sic] sport."

Billy Wolfe's attitude toward the women he managed came out in his writings to Pfefer when he found out that his friend was trying to develop and manage his own women wrestlers without Wolfe.

"Jack, I really do think that you are to [*sic*] big a man in the wrestling business to spend much time developing your own lady wrestlers, when you have got a stooge like me, that wants to do it for you," Wolfe wrote. "Handling lady wrestlers and trying to make a dollar out of it is really a headacke [*sic*]. About the time you get a girl that will make you a little money, she may get sick and go to the Hospital with female troubles, or run off with some wrestler and some times want to go back to some husband they have left." Pfefer's own attitude toward women wrestlers and the general disgust that many male promoters retained was touched on in a letter that a former wrestler named Herbie Freeman sent to Pfefer seventeen years later. "You're 100% right about the girl wrestlers, they are low, very low," Freeman wrote. "Dogs are insulted when you call them that."

Pfefer ignored Wolfe and plunged forward with his own female matches. He also ignored Wolfe's sage advice to use women sparingly in the same territory lest they wear out their appeal. Pfefer's wrestlers drew crowds for a while but faded out when New Jersey, responding to a clamor about the indecency of it all, banned women's wrestling once again. Pfefer was an ingenious and energetic promoter, but if he really wanted to compete with Wolfe he would have to take his women on the road and carefully build his own stable to support his stars. Pfefer would continue to promote the odd woman wrestler here and there, but in the end he lacked what Billy Wolfe had in abundance: a single-minded willingness to do whatever it took to put his women over.

8

Mat Mamas Maul for Millions

As the country made a slow progression toward war, women were increasingly coming out to watch women wrestle. Millie Burke told a reporter she planned on opening a gym when she retired in another fifteen years to serve this new onslaught of female interest. "I get letters all the time from girls who want to know how they can become professional wrestlers—even some from mothers and fathers who want their daughters to wrestle," she said. When she wrestled in Charleston the crowd was 51 percent female.

When they went to Tulsa a big, tough tomboy named Johnnie Mae Young was among the women in the audience. She had grown up one of nine children under the care of a single mother in a "boxcar house" outside of town. At five feet, seven inches and 140 pounds, Johnnie Mae was one of the most natural athletes the coaches ever saw at Sand Springs High School, a girl who could throw and kick with the boys. She played on a national championship softball team as well as a local women's football team. As a reward, a coach took her to see Mildred Burke wrestle at the Tulsa Coliseum. Young was smitten. She was also amazingly confident. She thought she could beat either Burke or Gillem. A challenge was issued and a tryout arranged. By her own account Young, the inexperienced amateur, quickly dispatched Gillem; Gillem disputes that to this day.

Whatever happened, Young made enough of an impression that Billy Wolfe immediately added the seventeen-year-old to his stable. She would go on to a stellar career in wrestling, though never as a champion. A striking blonde beauty when she started out, she was also an electrifying, rough-and-tumble performer in the ring, one whose dirty tactics and obvious athletic ability made her a great villain and never failed to stir the crowd. Within the sisterhood of female wrestlers, she would become legendary for her toughness and bravado. "She had men's shoes on, men's pants on with a zipper down the front, a cigar hanging out of her mouth," recalled Penny Banner, a nineteen-year-old prospect from St. Louis who joined Wolfe's troupe years later. "And she looked at me and said, 'Hi, fuck face.'" Young was a devil-may-care free spirit, willing to fight at the drop of a hat in a bar or hotel room. "She'd play poker with the boys, and lift up her leg and let out a big fart," recalled Freddie Blassie, a noted male heel of the era. "If a guy did something to piss her off, she'd try to provoke him into a fight. She knew how to take a punch from a man, then kick his ass." She would later make the papers when she was arrested for robbery in Reno for allegedly slugging a 210-pound man and taking $100 from him after a tour of the bars; she told police he made "certain improper advances."

Soon Young would take over from Gillem as the troupe's leading heel. Within months of graduating from high school the Tulsa tomboy was going up against Mildred Burke before thousands. The new prospect soon left her mark on the champion. "Mae's rough and she knows how to wrestle," Burke later said of Young, displaying the scar above her eye left where Young had slugged her while Burke was tied up in the ring ropes during a match in Texas. "The first lick she hit me, it just swelled up, it didn't cut," Burke said. "Then she hit again and it just laid it open. That was a twenty-foot ring there and the blood was shooting clear to the center. And I wore white satin, so you can imagine how all that red blood looked."

The national publicity continued. In September 1941, the Associated Press ran a feature on Burke that appeared in newspapers throughout the country portraying the polite, demure Millie. "The average American woman spends too much time smoking and drinking," she said. "Every woman would be much better off with a little wrestling—just for exercise. They'd learn to take care of themselves." The nation's capital became a regular stop for her. Al Jolson visited her before a match at Turner's Arena there, and the flashbulbs caught them examining her gold belt. "You're a wrestler, and you're beautiful," he told her. "I don't understand it." Senator Elmer Thomas, the Democratic New Dealer from Oklahoma, became a big fan and invited her to dinner parties when she came to town. "At these dinners I met virtually every Washington figure of the period at one time or another," she wrote. "Not all were wrestling fans, of course, but they all seemed to get a big boot out of finding me in gorgeous clothes and only five feet, two inches tall."

Then the country was at war. Millions of men joined the armed forces. In a demographic shift of seismic proportions, two million women entered the workforce in 1942 alone, stepping into defense industry jobs and a host of other occupations that once had been almost solely the province of men. The age of Rosie the Riveter also saw the rise of the female wrestler. "Many wrestlers have been drafted and some have taken defense jobs and good men are getting scarce," Al Haft wrote Jack Pfefer. "I could use a couple good men right now." Max Clayton, the promoter in Omaha, predicted that there were "enough men to last about a year" and resorted to bears and women to make up for the shortage. "Max has a lot of respect for the woman champ,

Mildred Burke," the International News Service reported in May 1942. "At a weight of 135 pounds, Clayton says, she can toss about half the pro wrestlers he uses."

Two weeks later, Burke herself was saying that women were about to take over wrestling. "If the predictions of Mildred 'Muscles' Burke come true, the nation's wrestling rings will soon be filled with cute young things in flowered tights and painted fingernails, and the customary grunting giant will become extinct," United Press reporter Berneice Schlemmer wrote. Burke offered wrestling as a sensible career opportunity for women during wartime. "The war will take away the top-flight men wrestlers, leaving the field to the girls," she said, adding that they "needn't be powerful Katrinkas, either." As promoters braced for a shortage of male wrestlers, big names from the past who were too old for military service came out of retirement. Among them was Strangler Lewis, now fifty-one and long past his prime but still a legend whose name alone could draw. Soon Mildred Burke's matches were headlining with Lewis's as the co–main attraction. Lewis had been one of the most adamantly opposed to the women when Wolfe's wrestlers began appearing in force in the late 1930s; the Strangler's presence on cards with Burke spoke volumes about the position female wrestlers had attained.

In 1941 three million spectators paid an average of seventy-five cents apiece to see pro wrestling; 40 percent of the national audience was now made up of women, with an additional 10 percent children of grammar-school age. Billy Wolfe got his share of that money. His troupe now included most of the best female wrestlers in the country: the champion Mildred Burke, the Alabama villainess Gladys "Kill 'em" Gillem, the Tulsa toughie Johnnie Mae Young, the Nebraska sisters Mae Weston and Wilma Gordon, an athletic young woman from Columbus named Ann Laverne, and Elviry Snodgrass, a hillbilly wrestler from Tennessee who fought in bare feet and overalls.

"Mildred and I are still poor people trying to get by, but for poor people we have been doing very good," Wolfe wrote to Pfefer in July 1942, announcing sellout business in Columbus and Dallas. Millie wrote Pfefer that same month with the same sentiment, but she worried that the war was about to end it all. "For poor people we have been doing very nicely but it is beginning to look more all the time like every body may have to stop unnecessary accupations [*sic*] and start doing something to help Uncle Sam win the war," she wrote. Instead, Wolfe's wrestlers remained in demand as entertainment for the troops and the civilian workforce in warmaking industries. With gas rationed nationwide, Millie rode troop trains and found her fans among the soldiers, including one who had seen her wrestle that first arena match in Bethany, Missouri. Wolfe's wrestlers did a series of shows in Nebraska, where servicemen were admitted free. "Manpower shortage doesn't hurt rassling; women battle," the local paper noted.

The end of the year brought Burke her highest honors and recognition yet. She made it into the annual Associated Press poll of sports editors for the outstanding figure in women's sports. Gloria Callen, a record-breaking backstroke swimmer, topped the poll and Burke received only one vote, but that was enough to get her named in the *New York Times* on a list with Alice Marble, Babe Didrikson Zaharias, and Sonja Henie. No female wrestler had ever made the list; the state of wrestling had fallen so low in the eyes of sportswriters that only one male wrestler had ever made the list. Apparently Burke had somehow—through her sex appeal or athleticism or perhaps someone's idea of a joke—found her way into the flinty heart of a sports hack. Though it was only one vote it did serve as a gauge of her emergence into the national consciousness.

Her coronation was completed in a long story on the state of female wrestlers in one of the nation's most notable literary journals, the *American Mercury*. The august publication elevated the "girl wrestlers" to "lady wrestlers" and managed to be both celebratory and condescending. Burke was described as "the only recognized female champion in the business, having won the belt offered by the Midwestern Wrestling Association for proficiency in that region." The article tried to parse the rise of women's wrestling, expressing complete puzzlement that families would cram smoky arenas to watch "a pair of females, complete with lipstick, rouge, false eyelashes and skimpy bathing suits, grappling on the floor in a five-minute act billed as 'Girl Wrestlers.'" The attraction for the wrestlers was nothing less than a chance at the kind of glamour that was inaccessible outside of Hollywood. Once again, Jack Pfefer, in his thick Yiddish accent, put it best. "A girl what has a svell shape, a good-lookin' face and wants to be in pictures, should foist be a rastler," he said.

The article in the *American Mercury* had pointed out that for all its popularity women's wrestling was still a sports stepchild. It was permitted in Washington, D.C., but banned in most of the other biggest cities on the East Coast. Its strongholds remained in the smaller towns of the South and Midwest. Then, in January 1943, women wrestlers got news of the opening of the biggest territory yet. The California State Athletic Commission made a slight crack in the state's ban, allowing females to make two appearances every six months in cities that had wrestling promotions. Mildred Burke had been one of those petitioning the state, and her cause found support even in the male-dominated wrestling press. "Time was when we might have agreed with the commissioners that rassling was no business for a woman," wrote Prescott Sullivan, the respected *San Francisco Examiner* sports columnist. "But at that time we might have argued, too, that driving a truck also was out of a lady's line. Times have changed. The State Athletic Commission must keep in stride. The ladies are not to be denied."

Billy Wolfe quickly took advantage of the opportunity, and soon he had Burke squaring off against old standby Gladys Gillem at the venerable Hollywood Legion Stadium. He touted his champion as a movie star in the making. "She has an offer from a big studio to make a full-length picture and may accept, although she has no aspirations as a glamour girl," the *Los Angeles Times* reported. "Her heart is in wrestling." On her California tours, the papers took note of her unique combination of sex appeal and skill. "Mildred came to town bally-hooed heavily as the real McCoy and she lived up to advance notices in her good looks and ability to wrestle," the *Fresno Bee* noted.

It was in Fresno that she wrestled for the first time before her father, in a bout with Johnnie Mae Young at Ryan's Auditorium. The local paper said it was just a coincidence that Bruce Bliss was in the capacity crowd. He was now a farmer living a few miles south of town. "Strange as it seems it was the first time he ever saw his daughter in a match, although she has had some 500," the *Bee* reported. "Naturally the champion's papa was tremendously pleased with the performance of his daughter." But there were no pictures of father and daughter together, no heartwarming quotes of acceptance. Burke makes no mention of it in her autobiography. And there is no record of Bruce Bliss ever seeing his daughter again.

After the California tour, Millie and Billy bought their first home together, a little stucco bungalow at 1151 West 52nd Street in the South Vermont Avenue district of Los Angeles. The home sat in a leafy neighborhood full of birds and children. A *Times* reporter visited Burke in July 1943 and found "a very feminine homebody" wearing "a little old" house dress with an apron making a lemon meringue pie with her mother. Among the sofa pillows and knickknacks were two large stuffed animals, an elephant and a bear. Millie grabbed the dolls and beamed for the flashbulbs as her brother, Louis, looked on. "It was a comfy family group," the reporter noted. Her son, Joe, of course, was kept out of sight. In the heart of wartime austerity the reporter was struck immediately by Billy Wolfe's jewelry, "a lot of diamond rings and a jeweled watch charm." Around the same time, Burke had told another reporter that she had paid taxes on $22,000, more income than any baseball player was earning at the time except for Joe DiMaggio or Ted Williams. Millie brought out her gold-plated championship belt, which now featured a six-carat diamond and a miniature picture of herself. As Wolfe boasted about Burke's appeal, the writer sized up the champion Wolfe and Burke had both created, noting that she was gracefully built even though she carried 135 pounds on a five-foot, two-inch frame. Her arms were powerful but not masculine. The reporter spotted the five-inch scar above one of her ankles, courtesy of a loose nail that had ripped her leg to the bone when she was tossed from the ring. She managed to blush when the reporter asked her why she had not married. She didn't talk much about wrestling, but she did let slip a revealing glimpse of her life in the ring. "The women fans kid lady wrestlers for their looks mostly," she said. " 'Pee-roxide,' they yell at blondes. Or, 'Go get your face lifted.' You know, catty. The thing that burns me up is when they call me 'Shorty.'"

The family scene was a carefully constructed facade. Mildred and Billy were not presiding over a comfy household; while Burke was on the road her mother shared the two-bedroom bungalow with Louis and Joe, who found his first permanent home in the Los Angeles house. In the summer, when Burke came to town to rest up from the road, she stayed in a smaller one-bedroom bungalow in back. The man who stayed with her was not her husband. It was her husband's son.

For Millie, her husband's affairs had been simply a price paid to achieve a dream. The marriage was merely a contract that bound their business interests, not their feelings. "We had a promotional and professional partnership within the legal bounds of our marriage, but there was no emotional or sexual tie," she wrote years later. In the early days, he had sheperded her on the road and sat beside her for the newspaper interviews. But with the business expanding and the demand for women wrestlers growing astronomically, Wolfe soon had several groups of wrestlers driving to matches in different cities. Increasingly, he drove on the road with the new girls. Millie was left more and more to drive herself or go with other girls to her matches. A woman alone was too easy prey. Burke kept a snub-nose .38 in the glove compartment, but she also needed an escort to help her deal with the rigors of the road. It was too easy to fall asleep while driving the hundreds of miles in the dead of night. When they weren't driving, women wrestlers had to deal with constant unwanted forays from male wolves. Worse was the threat of bandits on the road. Promoters paid the women in cash, and that and the diamonds Burke had started wearing drew highwaymen looking for an easy score; she once had to resort to a high-speed car chase to get away from some men who had been eyeing her jewelry suspiciously in a diner in Texas.

Billy Wolfe assigned the job of guarding and driving Burke to his son, George William, known to everyone as "G. Bill." He had been barely a teenager when Burke started barnstorming with the carnivals in the mid-1930s. Occasionally, Billy, Millie, G. Bill, and Joe went on the road together, looking like a family that was minus the mother. Now G. Bill was in his early twenties, and at six feet tall he looked like a leaner, prettier version of his father. Like Billy, he was always in a suit with a fedora on his head. He had the same dark-rimmed glasses and slicked-back hair. But G. Bill had no cauliflower ears and was handsome in the style of a movie star who cultivated a pencil-thin mustache to make himself look older. Like his father and stepmother, he was passionate about fancy clothes and diamond jewelry, but where his father was domineering, hard-charging, and larger than life, G. Bill was quieter, friendlier, softer. He was good company, a nice guy with a sense of humor.

When precisely Mildred and G. Bill began their affair and the exact nature of it are lost to history. Her son, Joe, recalls that they were together before she acquired the Los Angeles house in mid-1943, which would make him twenty-one and her twenty-seven at the time the affair started. Joe said he and Mildred and G. Bill first lived together in the Greystone Apartments near the Angel's Flight funicular railway in the Bunker Hill district of downtown Los Angeles. Gladys Gillem remembers that Mildred and G. Bill were a couple while she was seeing Billy in the early 1940s. "He had a big old sloppy boy, his son, G. Bill," Gillem said. "He was about twenty-something. And he was fucking Mildred. And Billy was fucking me and half those girls. Bill approved of it. Maybe he couldn't take care of her himself. I don't know." Johnnie Mae Young also thought the affair between Burke and G. Bill had been sanctioned by the boss. "I think that Billy Wolfe was the instigator of G. Bill and Mildred living together," an eighty-four-year-old Young recalled decades later. "He and his son got along fine. Apparently, he sent his son over there to pacify Mildred while he was screwing around with other girls."

In her unpublished autobiography, Burke is vague about the details of her arrangement with Billy and her affair with G. Bill. The pain of how things turned out obviously influenced what she wrote decades later. She went out of her way to minimize her time with G. Bill, and she left out entirely Billy Wolfe's reaction to the affair as it unfolded, save for the final blowup. The available evidence suggests that Billy tacitly tolerated or approved of the affair, just as Millie tolerated Billy's infidelities.

Burke wrote that she and G. Bill grew close during the long hours and miles on the road. "When he was first assigned to me to act as driver, bodyguard, chaperone, business manager and spy for his father, he was a likeable kid," Burke wrote. "Six years younger than me, he was much closer in both age and outlook to me than his dad had ever been." Above all, she appreciated his help and sensitivity on the road. "G. Bill made it possible for me to snatch some sleep on the road each day, something I had been previously unable to do," she wrote. "Sharing all the chores and working in a successful, winning venture brought us close. G. Bill was attentive, considerate of my needs, and took over all the physical tasks such as lugging baggage. He drank somewhat, but nothing objectionable. Our attachment grew and deepened through what we shared."

G. Bill drove Mildred as much as four hundred miles in a single day or night between bouts. He also collected her earnings from promoters. She wrote that G. Bill was embarrassed that the money was handed to him rather than to the woman who had earned it in the ring. She maintained that she felt affection toward G. Bill but did not believe it was more than that. "He would occasionally lay up with other girl wrestlers on the road, but I thought nothing of this because a permanent, emotional relationship with G. Bill just had not occurred to me," she later wrote. Besides, the marriage to Billy Wolfe was still in force and was the deal that sealed everything else. "I was constantly running into problems when girl wrestlers he had laid turned up as opponents in the ring. I felt I needed the legal shield of the marriage. No one had come along with whom I could fall in love in the classical style that would mesh with my moral upbringing, and this certainly included G. Bill." But G. Bill fell in love with her, she wrote. "I was fond of him, grateful for all he did for me daily, and I had a love for him without being *in love* with him. There's a mighty gulf between those two states of love. For G. Bill, the whole affair was a giddying, a continuous whirl of excitement as he lived on the road with a woman who was a star."

Burke's son, Joe, the only living witness, believes "there was love" between his mother and G. Bill. To Joe, G. Bill was "always a brother and more." It was G. Bill who taught him how to ride a bicycle and then a motorcycle and some of the other things boys need to know growing up. They were together constantly when Millie and G. Bill came off the road. For their vacations, the three of them would go to the Florida Keys or Acapulco. Once, when a hospital in Miami refused to admit a very sick Joe, it was G. Bill who argued angrily until the boy was treated. Joe knew that G. Bill was acting as some kind of surrogate. "Your mom and your dad don't live together and he's surrounded by a bunch of pretty attractive women," Joe recalled. "I don't think it takes too much of a leap of the imagination to see something is going wrong." With Millie and Billy, Joe didn't dwell on what he couldn't see. "I never saw any overt affection," Joe recalled. "I've never seen them kiss. I never saw them holding hands. I can't remember anything like that."

Joe hardly ever saw Billy Wolfe, but when they were together his stepfather never mistreated him. The older man did like to flick his index finger against the boy's skull. One time Billy went into a store and came out with a tin wind-up toy, an animal riding a motorcycle; Joe was thrilled. "It's not yours, it's mine," Billy said. He eventually gave it to the boy, but only after making him suffer. Billy Wolfe was not the least bit sentimental. "He always made the comment he didn't believe in Christmas," Joe recalled. "He believed that if you wanted to buy somebody a gift you do it then, you didn't wait for Christmas." To Joe, he was strength, toughness, and smarts personified. "He should have been a politician," Joe said. "Looking at one of his photographs will give you an idea of the strength of his character. He held that business together, along with my mother, of course. And I might add my mother was the kingpin. Without her the business would have fallen apart. But he held an organization together that was up against all kinds of adversity, people trying to take the business over. He could have been a governor or a senator."

At the end of 1943 Mildred Burke once again got a vote in the Associated Press poll for sportswoman of the year. Everywhere she went, she was now getting prominent play on the sports pages alongside the likes of Joe DiMaggio and Bob Feller. In article after article she got the headline while the male wrestlers were relegated to the bottom of the story. Billy Wolfe kept up the promotional activities behind her. He sent out calendars to sports editors and wrestling promoters featuring Millie in various poses in her wrestling suits as well as in cheese-cake photos of her in her zebra-striped two-piece outfit, which showed off her muscular stomach and anticipated the arrival of the bikini by more than two years. He included a proud note with the calendar he sent to Jack Pfefer. "The Picture on my Calendar this year is a splendid painting, in beautiful colors, of my little Champion," Wolfe wrote. "The painting is finished in Oil which will preserve the picture for many years and can be cleaned at any time with a damp cloth." The calendars created a stir at newspapers all over the country. "Yes, Billy we have made her our pinup girl," wrote a sportswriter at the *Fresno Bee*.

Time magazine called her the "Queen of the Mat" in March 1944. She was described as twenty-eight, unmarried, and the winner of 750 matches without a defeat. She had recently drawn 12,000 into Mexico City's vast Arena Coliseo, entering the ring with "her sinuous tights girdled with her sparkling championship belt" and drawing cries of "Esa es mi vieja!" Women's wrestling had finally earned its place as a legitimate, dependable arena attraction. "While the novelty was wearing off the feminine tuggers were developing science, color and toughness and today they can stand fore as wrestlers and not just pulchritude putting on a different kind of revue," Associate Press writer Harold V. Ratliff noted. Some promoters even thought that the women were better wrestlers than the men. "Women are cooler and more relaxed in a wrestling ring," said Karl Sarpolis, the Dallas promoter. "That's why they can take more spills. You don't get hurt so much if you fall like a bag of salt."

The rise of the women was not without its setbacks. Clergymen appeared before Congress to argue that women's wrestling was nothing but a burlesque show that contributed to juvenile delinquency. "All wrestling bouts should be placed under the boxing commission," argued the Reverend Oscar Fisher Blackwelder, an important Lutheran pastor from Washington, D.C. "Then only professionals would wrestle—and there are no professional women wrestlers." The splash Burke created in California also brought a backlash among, of all people, other women. The Los Angeles Women's Council, representing women's groups affiliated with churches, began protesting women's wrestling and asking the state athletic commission to ban it. The commission resisted the pressure and voted at the end of 1943 to allow women to continue under the current restrictions. But a few months later the movement to ban women came back stronger than ever.

Alan Ward, a sports columnist with the *Oakland Tribune* who said he was no fan of female wrestlers, nonetheless came to their defense. They were "clever, capable performers," he said, and they drew the fans that kept the game going. "Certainly, the gals can't, or shouldn't, be any more objectionable than such performers as your Man Mountain Deans, your Daniel Boon Savages and a couple of importations from the East weighing in the neighborhood of 400 pounds." It didn't matter. The Women's Council appealed directly to Governor Earl Warren, who would later go on to set the tone as chief justice for the most liberal Supreme Court in the nation's history. In a letter to the governor in April 1944, the Women's Council complained that women's wrestling was "characterized by biting, hair-pulling, choking and loud cries of 'break her neck, break her neck.'" Later that month, the commission set a vote on the matter in Los Angeles. A large contingent of protesters camped outside the meeting room in the state building. A United Press reporter described them as "matronly representatives of 30 girls' organizations, welfare groups, social services, churches and women's clubs." The reporter quoted one of them as saying, "Women's wrestling is degrading. Men who come to see the female matches don't come because of the interest in the bouts as a sport but to see women in often peculiar positions."

The commission members, clearly cowed, waited for the women to leave before appearing in the meeting room two hours late. The UP reporter noted that the commission chairman Jules Covey glanced "out of the corner of his eye" to make sure the protesters were gone. "The commission has carefully considered the problem of women's wrestling," Covey said. A commission member made a motion to rescind the action allowing women to wrestle. There was no discussion. The motion carried without dissent. That was it. Mildred Burke was banned from wrestling in her home state.

Six months later she was in the Houston coliseum wrestling before 11,000 as part of a campaign to raise $20 million for war bonds. "Mat Mamas Maul for Millions," Ed Herlihy intoned on the newsreel coverage of the match. Wartime was her time. "Mildred Burke, champion lady wrestler, went for Mae Weston like Montgomery went for El Alamein," the columnist in the Ogden, Utah, *Standard-Examiner* wrote in January 1945 of a match that took place before 2,000 fans jammed into the local high school gym. "Fans agreed the femme bout was the fastest and wildest match they'd ever seen on a local mat card. The tactics of these two gals definitely marked wrestling as a woman's sport." The women in the audience in conservative Utah ate it up. "She is sensational," said one. "My goodness, I'd like to use some of those holds and tricks on my husband when he gets rough," said another.

Wolfe and Burke made sure to balance the roughness with a feminine side in her publicity, providing newspapers with many shots of Millie cooking in the kitchen. "Catch her in a housewifely pose brewing up one of her special Swiss steaks or all decked out in silver fox and five-carat diamonds, and you'd call her downright winsome," the Nashville *Banner* reported in a profile. Another profile written by the women's page editor in the Waterloo, Iowa, *Sunday Courier* described Mildred's carefully penciled eyebrows and modest amount of mascara. Mildred mentioned that the nylon wrestling suits were much easier to wash than the prewar Lastex. She confided an unusual aspiration. "I know my English isn't very good and I guess there are too many writers as it is, but I want to write murder mysteries. They're my

favorite reading. I don't know why I like to read about killings. I hope
it doesn't have anything to do with my work."

The United Press seized on the glamorous, feminine image in a
detailed profile of Burke datelined from the nation's capital. She sat
for the interview in a low-cut black satin dress and high heels, and
with a gardenia in her wavy black hair. She proudly showed off a
certificate from Admiral Ernest J. King, the commander in chief of
the U.S. Navy, given to her for entertaining the troops, and she mentioned that she was the pinup girl of the USS *Romulus,* a landing-craft
repair ship that served in the Pacific theater. She had recently been
featured in the Marine Corps magazine *Leatherneck,* "so the boys over
there will know what is going on at home." She predicted that military training for women would swell the ranks of female wrestlers.
"There are about 150 women wrestlers in this country and there will
be a lot more—the WACS and WAVES are learning how." With the
war coming to an end, Burke made it clear that she and her fellow
females were not about to surrender their place in the ring to the men.
"Miss Burke, a slight but solid five-foot two-inch girl, who likes diamond rings and fur coats and makes enough money to buy them, said
that she and her colleagues would show the men wrestlers a thing or
two after the war," the UP writer noted.

Two weeks after Germany surrendered, a match occurred that
aptly demonstrated the wartime ascension of women. Mildred Burke
was back in Ogden, appearing on the card with Wild Bill Longson, a
Utah native and then the heavyweight champion of the National
Wrestling Association, the sport's ruling body. Longson, whose age
and marital status kept him out of the war, was the biggest man in
wrestling, having drawn a series of huge crowds in St. Louis, which
had become the wrestling capital of the nation. But it was Burke who
dominated the headline in Utah: "Girl Mat Champion Wins 1,000
Consecutive Bouts." The paper printed an unrestrained rave. "Miss

Burke is just reaching her peak in the wrestling profession. She's only 28 and getting better every season. Last year, she was paid $30,000 for her work, more than any other wrestler in the game, man or woman, excepting Salt Lake's own Bill Longson."

She was on top of the wrestling world.

9

Billy Wolfe's Harem

With the end of the war, Mildred Burke and Billy Wolfe prospered at an even greater rate. Her $25,000-a-year income—more than ten times the average annual salary and five times the price of an average home—became a standard part of the pre-match publicity. Burke and Wolfe used their burgeoning wealth in the gaudiest way possible, draping themselves with gems. They bought what Mildred called "desperation diamonds," stones that had been sold at cut-rate prices by people in dire straits. Along with wrestling, diamonds were one of their few shared passions. They had started buying the stones during the war but now that wartime austerity was a thing of the past they could really go to town. "I collect diamonds as a hobby, I guess," she told a reporter. "I put them in the bank the minute I get back to Los Angeles and wear them while I am on tour. If I see one that's just a little bit larger than one I have, why, I just trade mine in!"

Soon they were hanging diamonds on just about every place on their persons. Millie wore four rings totaling ten carats and a "well-iced" wrist watch. "I wore diamond necklaces, bracelets, earrings and brooches," she wrote in her autobiography. "Diamond rings grace fingers on both hands. Never was I without at least two diamond watches . . . Diamond tiaras and diamond hairpins took care of the top story. . . . My favorite piece was a breathtaking diamond ring set in the form of a crown."

In the unpublished autobiography, she took a stab at explaining her obsession with diamonds. The gems meant something deeper than wealth and status for the poor little girl who grew up with nothing and gave her life to wrestling. The key to understanding it was that ring in the shape of a crown. "Most of my other pieces I changed fairly often, to give the impression that I owned a much larger collection than I did," she wrote. "Whatever else went in trade, the royal ring stayed. Already I was known far and wide as 'The Queen of the Lady Wrestlers,' so I let that ring symbolize my sports royalty. I wore my crown on my third finger. I was married to wrestling."

Her diamonds were outshined by Billy Wolfe's. He told a male wrestler that his ambition was to outdo Diamond Jim Brady, the notorious Gilded Age gourmand and financier. One magazine writer pointed out that Wolfe "carries around enough ice for a Sonja Henie movie"—three stones of eleven, six, and five carats. A few years later, when Wolfe was at his height, another reporter did a complete accounting. The total was fifty-five carats. Two rings on his left hand, one with five carats. On his right hand, just one ring, but an astounding ten carats. Dangling from his watch chain was a double horseshoe fob with sixty stones totaling fourteen carats. The belt buckle had a five-carat canary stone nestled among eight two-carat stones. The stickpin totaled eight carats. The tie clasp had four blue sapphires arranged between five half-carat diamonds. "They're pretty," Wolfe said, "but you should see us when Mildred and my son and I are all together. We wear $75,000 worth of diamonds all told."

The effect when he was out in public was an almost comical rococo excess. One writer outstripped his metaphors trying to capture Wolfe in all his sparkly glory: "He sported a diamond belt buckle featuring a stone with the brilliance of a locomotive headlight; cuff links that sparkled like the sun on a wind-rippled lake; a stickpin with the moonless-night glare of a blue-white neon sign; a horseshoe-shaped watch fob that made me wish I had worn sun glasses; rings on his fingers—four of them, but a solitaire given exclusive right to one hand, is the daddy of them all. Although two carats were lost in cutting to a modern setting, the stone weighed in at 10 carats." Bobby Bruns, a heavyweight wrestler who was even tougher than Wolfe, bumped into him on the street in Kansas City and told him the only thing he was lacking was a pair of diamond earrings.

With midwestern practicality, Wolfe tried to explain that the stones were not sheer vanity. "It's show business and an investment both," he said. "It makes people notice you."

Billy Wolfe's other grand passion was women. His stable of wrestlers soon coalesced into what wrestling wags referred to as "Billy Wolfe's Harem." For years Gladys Gillem was his steady girl on the road, but there were many others. Somewhere along the line he had an assignation that resulted in a pregnancy with Ann Laverne, the wrestler from Columbus. Decades later Gillem said his affairs were more about control than love. "He couldn't get a good hard-on," recalled Gillem, still a salty character with a lot of spunk at age eighty-seven. "If you weren't very nice to him, you couldn't get the good bookings . . . There was never any love between us." In one form or another, all of the women felt the heat of his sexual need. "He would never force himself on anybody, but he let you know he was willing," said Barbara Jean Baker, one of the many young girls who approached Wolfe wanting to wrestle. Bette Carter, another of the young ones trying to get Wolfe to take her on, said he was blunt about the sex. "The first time I talked to Billy," Carter told sportswriter Frank Deford four decades later, "he said to me, 'I got two questions for you: Are you a lesbian, and if you're not, will you sleep with me?'" To the first question Carter, then a teenager, answered no, but none of your business. To the second question, she simply answered with a firm no. Wolfe shrugged, "OK, then you'll never get to be champion." Carter went to work for him any way.

Johnnie Mae Young thought Wolfe was a sexual opportunist. "Any girl that would screw around with Billy, he would screw around with her," Young recalled decades later. "I don't really think Billy was in love with anybody. I don't think Billy had the capability of being in love with any person. He was for Billy Wolfe." Of the women who slept with Wolfe, Young said, "The thing they were interested in was getting bookings and they didn't have brains enough to know they could have got them without screwing that old fart."

He had a penchant for May–December pairings. As he grew older, the women grew younger. Still, several of them retained fond memories of him. "Billy, of course, had all the women," recalled Ethel Brown, a young wrestler from Columbus who joined up with Wolfe when she was eighteen. "They used to say he had a harem. It's not really so, he was more like a father. He did do a little womanizing."

There was one woman who stood out among all the others. Johnnie Mae Young spotted a portly young waitress in a diner on Fifth Avenue in Birmingham, Alabama, and introduced her to Wolfe in 1942. Her name was Verdie Nell Stewart and she was all of fifteen years old. At first, she didn't seem like she would amount to much. She was a raw country girl, as backward as could be, a butterball with a big pile of brunette hair. But she also had a sunny disposition and an endearing Georgia drawl. And she had an athleticism and beauty that was obvious even under the extra poundage. "I kidded her all the time, 'Nell, why don't you become a wrestler?'" Young remembered. "Nell was a beautiful girl."

Stewart had lost her father at fourteen and had to help her mother support her two younger brothers. A job that would pay more than waitressing was a welcome opportunity. "The first time I attended a wrestling match, I saw the gals get to grips and I knew I fitted right into the picture," Stewart later recalled. "Mildred Burke at the time was reputed to be making about $30,000 a year, and I must admit that helped me make up my mind." Wolfe put her in the professional ring before her sixteenth birthday. She made her debut in Mexico City against a small Mexican woman. "I was so scared she whipped me in five minutes," Stewart recalled. Young and Gillem showed her the ropes. "I always thought a lot of Nell," Young recalled. "She was a sweet girl. She was never a tough broad. She was a good little worker." Gillem, responsible for Nell's training, didn't think so much of her. "I lent her a black dress to wear," Gillem said. "The poor girl didn't have nothin'. She wasn't used to modern things. Where she came from, they still used outhouses." On a trip to Houston, Gillem said, Stewart "called the bellboy up to show her how to flush the toilet."

Gillem disliked Nell for another reason; Billy Wolfe had started sleeping with her. Soon Wolfe was telling Gillem that, in addition to having to lose all of her matches to Millie and Young, she would have to start losing to a fifteen-year-old as well. Wolfe was so enamored of Stewart that he got into the act with her, allowing the girl to chase him around the ring and rip the shirt off his back when he appeared as a guest referee. He even put her in against his champion; Millie triumphed in a twelve-minute bout that featured "choking and general roughing." For Gillem it was the final straw. "Bill says put Mae over, put Nell over," Gillem recalled. "That really hurt." She didn't mind being behind Millie as the top mistress but she wasn't about to stand for being in second place to second place. "I was number one; when number two came along, I took off," Gillem recalled. "I said, 'Bill, you can have this. I'm going home to Birmingham.'"

Gillem left wrestling to become a lion tamer, then an alligator wrestler. She remained bitter decades later. "I spent ten years traveling with Mildred Burke and Billy Wolfe, put diamonds on his fingers after giving him fifty percent off what I made, had my nose broken twice by Mildred, didn't dare hit her back or would lose my job," Gillem, who by then was running a flower shop in Birmingham, wrote to the editor of *Ring* magazine in 1965. "It hurts to know I put Mildred over for ten years and wrestled her more matches than any living girl."

Over the years, Nell Stewart would become Billy Wolfe's personal project, in many ways his proudest creation. At five feet, four inches tall and 140 pounds, she was a lot of raw material for him to work with. As he had with Burke he put Stewart on an exercise regimen and special diet: steak, salads, fresh fruit, whole-wheat bread, honey in place of sugar. He molded her in the image of the actress Betty Grable, the box office queen of 1943. Grable's blonde beauty had been poured like a milk shake into a white bathing suit for a classic cheese-cake photo that emphasized her derriere and won her immortality as the top pinup of World War II soldiers. Under Wolfe's tutelage Nell Stewart became "the Betty Grable of the mat." The Alabama girl lost fat, gained muscle, dyed her hair blonde, and eventually won her place as the most glamorous woman in wrestling. Billy Wolfe delighted in sending the newspapers before-and-after pictures of the fat brunette side by side with the blonde bombshell that had emerged from his oversight and dreams. "Nell Stewart wasn't glamorized in Hollywood but by wrestling," he proudly wrote.

In an era when a woman's measurements carried a lot of weight with male spectators, Stewart's were a stunning 38-26-38—Burke by contrast had the same waist size but her chest was a boyish 31 inches. Stewart's blonde mane and her large bust became her trademarks, but she could also wrestle. She followed in the footsteps of Gillem and Young and wrestled as a roughhousing, blonde-headed heel. She liked to tell reporters that women were more rugged than men when it came to wrestling. "We're meaner in the ring, wrestle faster and stand holds longer," she said. She herself employed every possible dirty move. "Miss Stewart's tactics at times are not too becoming a lady and usually after her opponent has taken considerable hair-pulling, finger-biting and the like from the quick-tempered blonde they proceed to return in kind, much to Nell's dismay," one reporter wrote. Her looks and ring style would soon make her the top box office draw in women's wrestling and a credible challenger to Burke. She was not as fast or as technically proficient in the ring as Burke, but she was the next iteration as a sex symbol. The thought of all that fleshy pneumatic softness battering around in the wrestling ring was both incongruous and undeniably erotic, a key part of her immense attraction among male fans. How could someone so beautiful and feminine be so violent and rough? However she looked on the outside, she was not soft and fragile; her curves were complemented by bulging biceps.

A couple of years after he discovered Stewart, Wolfe made another important find on a swing through Texas. One night while watching Morris Sigel's "Friday Night Wrestling" program in Houston, Wolfe looked into the ring and saw strapping twenty-one-year-old June Byers trading holds with 300-pound Krippler Karl Davis, much to the crowd's delight. Byers was a big, tough, thick-lipped Texas gal well acquainted with heartache. She was also fast, muscular, and strong, the most physically gifted female wrestler of her age. At five feet, seven inches and

150 pounds, she was bigger than almost all the wrestlers in Wolfe's stable, which reflected his preference for feminine-looking types over the Amazons who had dominated women's wrestling at the turn of the century. But in Byers Wolfe was staring at the future of women's wrestling.

She had been christened DeAlva Eyvonnie Sibley. Her parents called her June because it had taken that long to find a name for her after she was born on May 25, 1922, in Houston. She grew up in a huge family. "When I was a youngster I boxed and wrestled," she said. "We had a family of fourteen, six sisters and seven brothers, and you learn in that kind of family. You learn to defend yourself, but you also learn lots of other things to help your family. I was a nut on wrestling." Her uncle Ottawa "Shorty" Roberts was a light heavyweight who started showing her the moves when she was seven. He put her on a conditioning and body-building program and, by thirteen, she could beat any kid in the neighborhood. After winning the girls' wrestling title at Kline High School, she challenged the boys on the wrestling team. But life after high school had not turned out well for her. Her lot was crushing poverty. By twenty she had been married twice and had two young children. The boy, from her second marriage, lived with her; the girl, from her first, had been adopted out to a family member. To support herself and her son, Byers worked as a seamstress making $37.50 a week. As Millie Bliss had done a decade earlier, June Byers sought relief at the wrestling matches.

The sight of Mildred Burke and the others transformed her life. She was attracted to their money as much as anything else. "I used to see the lady wrestlers when they came to town and nearly died when I saw the diamonds they were wearing," Byers later recalled. "So I said to myself if they can get all that just by wrestling, I'm all for it." Encouraged by her uncle, she took to entering the ring between matches to fool around with the male wrestlers, friends of hers and her uncle's. After being spotted by Wolfe, Byers made her debut in 1944 in Wilmington, Delaware, where Mae Weston tossed her in seven minutes. Byers also became a Wolfe project. Johnnie Mae Young trained her, teaching her the roughed-edge ways of a heel in the ring. Wolfe taught her his vicious "cupped chest lick," which had brought him all of that notoriety and condemnation back in Chillicothe.

As the years passed, the powerful Byers became an increasingly important wrestler in Wolfe's stable. She started out as a mid-carder working her way through preliminary matches, where she beat wrestlers of small standing and regularly lost to stars such as Burke and Young. Some of the other women complained that Byers worked "stiff" in the ring; that is, she was so rough that her matches were more like real fights than choreographed dances. Nevertheless, Byers was a convincing villain, and she drew record crowds when she appeared with Burke in Boston and El Paso. "Byers had Champ Burke groggy and ready for the kill, but a bit of carelessness at the wrong time prevented June from winning the crown and wearing the belt that Mildred displayed so proudly," the *El Paso Post* noted in an account that captures the flavor of their matches. "After drop kicking her opponent, June was a little slow in getting up. That's all the Champ needed. She quickly pulled June's legs from under her and pinned her to the mat."

It took June Byers eight years to win her first title, and that was a lesser one given out to the two wrestlers billed as the best women's tag team, where two wrestlers would face off against two others, with only one from each team allowed in the ring at a time. Byers had the look and aura of someone who was biding her time, awaiting her moment. She exuded rude good health, wearing it like a silent accusation against the less physically fortunate. She drank orange juice by the gallon and she used to say that it made her sweat smell like orange blossoms. She seemed apart from the other women in other ways as well. In photographs, Mildred increasingly adopted a stern, determined look while Nell was full of come-hither provocation; June just smiled. It was an enigmatic smile, though, one that held people at a distance, as if June knew something no one else did, a secret that amused her. She had a hard practicality that Nell and the others lacked. They dreamed of becoming champions or movie stars; June dreamed of becoming a wrestling promoter.

She had something else that was very tangible; Billy Wolfe had bought her an ostentatious five-carat diamond ring. She, too, became one of his girlfriends. She had taken up with Wolfe even though he was married to Burke and heavily involved with Stewart. Byers, who had already given up a child to adoption, was not held back by pride or compunction. "He had Nell Stewart, June Byers on the string and whomever else," Young recalled. "He'd go from one territory and meet June one night and he'd go to another territory and meet Nell." Among the wrestlers, the whole arrangement was pretty well out in the open. "Nell Stewart, June Byers, those were his main girls," remembered Gloria Barattini, who joined the stable in 1950. "When June was in town, Billy was with June. When Nell was in town, Billy was with Nell. It was just one of those things. There wasn't too much said about that." Lillian Ellison, the South Carolina girl who became one of Wolfe's wrestlers several years after being inspired by the sight of Mildred Burke in the ring, also described the sleeping arrangements on the road. "We traveled in two separate groups. So when Billy would go with Mildred's group, he'd sleep with her. But sometimes he'd go with June's group, and that's when he'd get her or Nell in bed. June and Nell wanted the best bookings, so they slept with Billy whenever he liked. These were wild times—and there were a lot of wild girls on the road."

There was a large category of women in his troupe whom he did not sleep with. They were the lesbians; at least a dozen of his wrestlers were gay. He was remarkably tolerant for the time and so were the women in his stable. The clash of young female bodies and overt sexuality, gay and straight, made for interesting situations on the road. Gladys Gillem, curious as always, said she found herself in bed with one of the lesbian wrestlers but didn't know what to do, so she just got up and left. Another young wrestler said she was confronted in the shower by an older wrestler, who the younger one described as a "trisexual, because she would try anything." The younger girl ran screaming into the hall, where another of the lesbian wrestlers, one of the biggest and toughest in the troupe, came to her defense.

One time on the road, Wolfe suggested to Millie that they share their room with one of the lesbian wrestlers. He said it would save them money. "This idea didn't set well with me, but those Depression dollars were tough and short, and this was a way to save," she wrote in her autobiography. "I went along." But when the time came and the lights were turned out the woman jumped into bed with the couple. Still, Burke said nothing. Then the woman started groping Burke's breasts and running her hands over Millie's body. Burke said she caused a fuss, forcing the woman to sleep on the floor. "Billy Wolfe made a poor effort to appear bewildered," she said. The woman and Wolfe also cracked jokes about Burke's "prudery." From then on, Burke never shared a room with another woman wrestler. Whatever prejudices she may have had toward lesbianism, she remained practical about its existence in her sport. "Many lesbians are drawn to wrestling," she wrote. "They are not a majority by any means, despite the assertions sometimes made in anti-feminist propaganda. They make excellent wrestlers, there's no doubt about that."

By the mid-1940s the women who would form the core of Wolfe's business had been assembled. A newspaper photograph captured several of them dressed up for an interview with a reporter for the Dayton paper looking for all the world like a ladies' gardening club: Stewart, Gillem, Young, Weston, and the hillybilly wrestler Elviry Snodgrass. Another photograph showed Stewart, Gillem, Young, and Weston on the road posing together on the front bumper of their car. Revealingly, Burke is never in the group shots. While the other women traveled together she rode separately with G. Bill, and she stayed in a separate hotel. "Wolfe's practice for some time had been never to accommodate me in a hotel with any of the other girls," she wrote. "His con man's explanation for this was that the champion shouldn't be seen around with challengers or lesser wrestlers. The real explanation was that he knew how women talk. He also knew how many of his wrestlers hated his guts. He ruled their lives and careers with an iron hand. If they weren't pliant sexually they were usually shunted out of his life, reduced to chattels and chips in the games he played. No wonder they hated him."

Lillian Ellison was one of those who hated him. She said that when she first approached Billy Wolfe he told her she was, at 115 pounds, too skinny. He told her to "go back home and sit on some attorney's knee and be his southern doll," Ellison later recalled. Burke later said Wolfe rejected Ellison "because she had a real funny body. She was built all top and no bottom, you know what I mean? The legs were funny." But Ellison gained weight, came back, and convinced Wolfe to let her join in 1948. Like Burke and Byers, Ellison was a single mother with a young child when she came into Wolfe's orbit. "Billy never really cared about the girls," Ellison wrote in her autobiography. "You'd get fifty dollars a week, whether you wrestled once or twenty times. And it was usually twenty times. Now out of that whole fifty dollars, you'd have to pay for a motel room, your food and gas." Once, she said, she left her sick father's bedside for a match in Columbus, Ohio. After the match she learned her father had died. She asked Wolfe to loan her a hundred dollars so she could attend the funeral in South Carolina. She said he refused. "You just left home two days ago. What do you want to do, go home and hold his hand?" The heartbroken Ellison was dumbfounded and furious. "I hope you die in the damned gutter and the worms eat your body before they find you!" she told Wolfe.

10

"The Public Likes the Puss"

S omehow Billy Wolfe managed to keep everything in balance and the business booming. He did it with a blend of paternal-ism, discipline, and guile. For many of the women, he was the father figure they never had. Soon several of them were calling him "Papa." He was far older than any of them, wiser in the ways of the world, smarter in business. His judgment was not questioned and he seemed to know everything about the industry in which the women had decided to make their living. He liked to play poker with the ad-venturous ones and take away their ring earnings. He levied fines, ranging from $5 for biting in the ring to $10 or $15 for wearing slacks or getting drunk to $50 for sleeping with a male wrestler. He loaned them money when they needed it, keeping the amounts in his book along with the fines. He took 50 percent of their earnings and made them pay for their own hotel rooms, two cents per mile in gas, and their own wrestling suits and boots. And he did it all without signing a contract with any of them. That arrangement alone was enough to get Billy Wolfe a mention in Walter Winchell's influential column.

"The Easy Street discovered by Billy Wolfe of Wheatland, Missouri, a former wrestler and the husband of Mildred Burke, the world's top matgal. He has the monopoly on all femme wrasslers. No contracts. Just verbal agreements. Gets half their loot."

Wolfe played the women off against one another, stoked their jealousies, worked on their insecurities. "Billy Wolfe was the daddy of us all, but he was a terrible bully," Bette Carter recalled. "He loved to pit girls against each other outside the ring. He loved to see the girls fighting." They competed for his attention and approval. He also looked out for them, dispensed fatherly advice, and made it possible for them to be stars. He held all the cards. And now it was all coming together, both for him and for Mildred. In February 1946 a newspaper finally printed that they were married. Several months later Burke would tell another paper that the writer had been misinformed and a correction had been printed. "Why Billy has a son and a daughter both of whom are older than I," she said with contrived indignation and sheer inaccuracy—she was older than both G. Bill and Violet.

Mildred and G. Bill were very discreet. In all the publicity about her, there are only fleeting glimpses of her lover and ubiquitous traveling companion. In a long piece in *Sportfolio* magazine in April 1947, cleverly titled "Queen of the Seize," there was only this: "When she travels, Miss Burke usually is accompanied by her trainer-husband Billy Wolfe or her step-son, 24-year-old Billy Jr." Around this time, G. Bill put on wrestling togs and engaged Mildred in a mixed match for the benefit of the wire service's cameras; judging only from G. Bill's tortured grimace and the painful pretzel-like positions Burke put him in, none of the casual newspaper readers could have known that they were watching two lovers at play.

The *Sportfolio* writer pointed out that Burke was an unlikely star: a stocky torso fit only for the covers of physical culture magazines, a voice "as flat and mid-western as her native prairie," intelligence "no higher than the next gal's." But she was also "probably the only actress who makes $25,000 a year with her muscles." The magazine provided the definitive description of Burke's ring style. "To acknowledge a mat introduction Mildred prances from her corner and waves at ringsiders. Then she hands her flimsy white robe to her husband or step-son. She stands in the glare, clad in a lavender satin bathing suit and her championship belt. Mildred licks the tips of her fingers, like an old time spitballer, as she goes into action. After a tug on her trunks she begins to pull at her adversary's limbs like a hungry man eating Sunday chicken. . . . For the first 20 minutes or so, Mildred's antagonists, Amazons like Nell Stewart, Mae Young or Elvira Snodgrass, run the gamut of dastardly mat tricks. Through it all, Mildred suffers silently, her deep blue eyes mirroring a pained appeal for justice from the referee. The official repeatedly warns the challenger. Challenger disregards injunctions. Crowds boo challenger. Mildred, a look of deep determination on her face, tugs at her tights, licks the tips of her fingers and marches right into her unsporting tormenter. Follows a crack to her opponent's jaw. Crowd cheers champion. Challenger runs like a cry baby to the referee, howling and rubbing her jaw. Mildred, the picture of innocence, rubs her elbow significantly and points to it. Referee nods his head and overrules the objection. Crowd applauds. Mildred gets down to work, using all the accepted scientific holds— headlock, armlock, scissors, the Nelsons (full and half-measure). She administers the coup de grace with a patented Burke standby, the Alligator Clutch. This special arm stretcher generally does it. Millie is the winner and still champion. The crowd cheers."

Millie was now at her zenith. In early 1948 she made her highest showing yet in the annual Associated Press poll for woman athlete of the year. She finished sixth out of sixteen receiving votes, trailing only golfer Babe Didrikson Zaharias, tennis players Pauline Betz and Louise Brough, swimmer Ann Curtis, and golfer Louise Suggs. Even with the war long over, Burke was still outdrawing male wrestlers. In July

1948, her bout with June Byers in Boston drew fourteen thousand fans, the largest wrestling crowd in the United States that year.

Female wrestlers were making Haft a lot of money but he wasn't entirely happy about it. He was one of the many male promoters who had retained their disgust with women's wrestling even though it had helped save their business. Describing an upcoming Burke match in September 1948 Haft wrote to Jack Pfefer, "It has a big advance and with weather we will turn them away tonite. Not for the wrestling, mind you, but for the puss." The next day he wrote Pfefer again. "The girls had a big night here last night. Looks like the public likes the puss. Others [*sic*] folks too, I guess. Enclosed is a clipping which will show you what the girls did here. They are drawing nearly as well as Gorgous [*sic*] George."

The reference to "Gorgeous George" Wagner was more than a little ironic. After years as a journeyman wrestler, Wagner had in the late 1940s become the biggest star in the business by feminizing it. He was small for a pro wrestler—190 pounds, five feet, nine inches tall—but he quickly became wrestling's first superstar as it entered the television era. His appeal was in his outrageousness. He let his wavy hair grow out and dyed it platinum blonde, handed out roses, and wore silk sequined robes into the ring. He entered to strains of "Pomp and Circumstance." He was usually accompanied by a female or male valet, who "disinfected" the canvas with an atomizer filled with a perfume Wagner called Chanel No. 10. In action he was fey and treacherous, the leading heel of the age. His antics in the ring were matched by his boasting outside of it, and his trash talk with ring announcers became a staple of his appeal. The fans ate it up, bellowing for George's destruction. Instead, he got bigger. His style was so distinctive and his cultural impact so great that among those who later admitted to being influenced by him were Elvis Presley, Bob Dylan, and Muhammad Ali.

Wagner was the same age as Mildred Burke and had been wrestling since the late 1930s. Born in Nebraska, he was raised in Houston
and worked during the war at a shipyard in Oregon. It was not until
he created his flamboyant ring persona—at first he called himself the
"Human Orchid"—that he took off as an attraction. He first came to
wide public notice through wrestling's first big incursion into television, the weekly wrestling program put on by KTLA in Los Angeles.
George made his debut on the show in November 1947 at the Olympic Auditorium, and national syndication soon made him a household
name. By 1949 George's appeal was so great that he was acclaimed
"Mr. Television" and appeared in a Hollywood B-movie, *Alias, the
Champ*. When men's pro wrestling was reintroduced that year to
Madison Square Garden after a twelve-year absence, Gorgeous George
was the headliner. The next year his earnings were said to be $160,000,
at least three times what Burke was earning.

Mildred Burke later maintained that she had had a hand in that.
"Gorgeous George never forgot or failed to acknowledge that the
source of his whole Gorgeous George format was Mildred Burke,"
she later wrote. "When my lavish robes and ring regalia injected class
and style into a sport that was visually drab, George Wagner read the
signals correctly. On a tour of Mexico he saw the impact of all this on
the crowd. We discussed it in the dressing room afterwards, as he
wondrously examined the magnificent rhinestone robe made by my
mother."

In May 1949 Frank Eck, the sports editor for the Associated Press,
wrote a long feature about her that ran in papers all over the country.
Unlike the female feature writers who interviewed Burke, Eck did
not describe her makeup, clothing, or diamonds. He wrote that she
now grossed $50,000 a year by wrestling anywhere from three to six
nights a week for eight months of the year, driving a hundred thousand miles. She spent $4,500 each year buying a new car and $200 a

week for phone bills. "Some people might say it's almost impossible for Mildred Burke to lose a wrestling match because her husband, Billy Wolfe, makes the matches. Of course, those people would be the ones who don't know the inside story," Eck concluded.

Wolfe remained master of all publicity, writing a detailed promotional sheet for each of his women, stories he half-invented to hype them as gate attractions. Burke became the former high school track star with sisters preaching for Aimee Semple McPherson, the never-defeated female champion and conqueror of two hundred male wrestlers. Stewart became the "Betty Grable of Wrestling" and the "Alabama Assassin," who was wrestling to help put her brothers through nice schools. Much of what he wrote wound up word for word in the newspaper articles. There was at the time a culture of petty payola in some corners of the press that covered wrestling, where slipping a few bucks into the right pocket ensured mention in the newspaper. There is no evidence that Wolfe did this; but if he did not he was an exception. Wolfe, with his tight control of the publicity engine, pitched both Stewart and Byers as the coming champion.

In June 1947 the *Washington Post* stated that Byers was "recognized as the number one contender for Mildred Burke's title." The next month, the Portland, Maine, *Sunday Telegram and Press Herald* reported that Stewart "has long been the number one contender for Miss Burke's crown." To keep Stewart and Byers happy while the years passed and Burke stayed champion, Billy Wolfe made them champions in their own right, albeit in lesser realms. Stewart became Texas champion, Ohio champion, and TV champion. Byers became the women's tag team champion. They rarely wrestled each other. Wolfe also rarely booked Stewart against Burke, but Byers became, along with Johnnie Mae Young, one of Mildred's most frequent opponents. With Burke ensconced as the virtuous babyface "world" champion, both Stewart and Byers spent most of their time wrestling as the villainous heels.

★ ★ ★

Nell Stewart acted as Billy Wolfe's lieutenant on the road. She helped him train girls and she kept them in line. She and Wolfe sometimes acted like an old married couple. When he sweated, she mopped his face with a handkerchief. When he complained about his ulcers, she tended to him with a glass of water and phenobarbital. Nell herself suffered from asthma, and Wolfe left instructions to all his wrestlers on what to do if Stewart got an attack in the ring. He also told her that she should stand on her head to drain the mucous out of her body.

But Billy Wolfe continued to split his time on the road between Nell Stewart and June Byers. In mid-1950, he was with Byers in New York City appearing in one of the most prominent entertainment columns of the day, *On Broadway with Earl Wilson*. For the columnist's benefit, Wolfe asked Byers to demonstrate the cupped chest lick he had taught her on Dot Dotson, one of his newest wrestlers. Dotson, a former Orlando cabdriver, was also one of his biggest, at five feet, nine inches and 155 pounds. Wilson wrote that Byers "removed about 30 carats of diamonds from her fingers, stood back and walloped Dot on the chest with a sock that crashed through the building."

Byers accompanied Wolfe at Churchill Downs two months later when he tried to buy a half interest in a colt minutes before the running of the Kentucky Derby. Wolfe had read about the horse, Hallieboy, and became enamored after watching it work out. On race day Wolfe approached Hallieboy's owner, Walter Fugate, while he was having breakfast at his hotel. The madcap scene was captured by a *Washington Post* columnist, Walter Haight, who was enlisted by Fugate as a witness. Everyone adjourned to the hotel's nightclub bar where, at 10:30 a.m. with bartenders wiping off glasses nearby, the two men tried to strike a deal. Haight noted that at that hour the bar was empty of customers save for Wolfe and "a girl wrestler lolling in a chair beside him."

That was June Byers, a "feminine Londos," Haight wrote. The columnist was struck immediately by Wolfe's diamonds, which made him look like "a combination of walking jewelry store and human 'milky way.'" A Latin orchestra started warming up in the bar, the musicians openly gaping at Wolfe, "each seeming to have picked out a Wolfe diamond." A girl vocalist started singing. Wolfe began to talk about his diamonds but Fugate steered him back to Hallieboy. Finally, Wolfe said, "We'll complete the deal for Hallieboy at the track. Where can I meet you at 2 o'clock?" Fugate replied, "In front of stall No. 15 in the paddock and if it's a deal we can sign the papers in the secretary's office nearby." Wolfe left and Fugate told Haight "to get every reporter, photographer, movie man and radio announcer to come to stall No. 15 at 2 o'clock. I believe this fellow will go for $20,000."

When two o'clock came, Wolfe came to stall No. 15 with both Byers and Millie Burke in tow. His female bodyguard was an amusing sight, and Wolfe couldn't resist injecting a quip into the tense circumstances. "Anyway, I'm well protected," he remarked. But he'd had a phone call with his lawyer, who had cooled him on the deal. It was off. Hallieboy, a hundred-to-one shot, ran tenth in the fourteen-horse field.

Two months after that, Wolfe accompanied Byers as she sat for a profile with a United Press reporter in New York City, the sort of national publicity that was usually reserved for Burke. Byers's practical side came out in the interview. "Dripping in diamonds but smoking a 12-cent brand of cigarette, Blonde June Byers frankly admitted today that she got into the female wrestling trade because she had a weakness for jewelry and big cars." The reporter wrote that Byers was careful to include a nod to Burke, whom she called "the greatest lady wrestler of all time," noting that the much smaller champion had once cracked her pelvis with a body slam. Wolfe quickly piped up and agreed that Mildred Burke was the best of them all. "Sure is," he said. "And that's being conservative."

★　★　★

For the first time, Wolfe started getting publicity of his own that rivaled what he generated for Burke. Always he had been in the background. Now he was becoming the star. Newspapers and magazines around the country hailed him as the genius who had invented the women's wrestling business in America. "As Mahout of the Pulchritudinous Pachyderms, Billy turns a pretty penny annually by booking Bevies of Beautiful Burping Babes for the entertainment of those who like to see how the girls act when they let their hair down," wrote Dan Parker, the New York *Daily Mirror* columnist whose exposés on fake matches rocked the wrestling world in the 1930s. The syndicated article was the first profile of Wolfe to appear since the Chillicothe paper had singled him out as a vicious wrestler fifteen years earlier.

Wolfe got his own national feature profile from United Press two months after June Byers did. The article called him "Diamond Billy Wolfe" and said he wore $30,000 worth of the stones. "Now some of the catch-as-catch-can customers may take issue with this, but I think Billy and his diamonds and his methods are much more interesting than Mildred's Muscles," reporter Oscar Fraley wrote. "Especially his diamonds." Wolfe made a point to break up all the talk about diamonds and give proper credit to Mildred Burke. As Fraley wrote, "But, Billy interrupts, Mildred not only makes the dough for all those diamonds—she convinced the public women could wrestle." The St. Louis *Globe-Democrat* did its own fawning profile of Wolfe. "Self made Mahout of Muscle, Billy was a famous wrestler in the Midwest before he parlayed an idea into a multi-million-dollar business," the paper reported. The *National Police Gazette* put Wolfe's wrestlers on its cover and described him as "the self-made Maharajah of Muscle," who had "lifted women's wrestling out of the murky confines of carnivals and burlesques to make it one of the top-drawing attractions in America."

Wrestling and TV Sports magazine captured "the Ziegfeld of Wrestling" at his height. "Perhaps the best proof that distaff wrestling is on the boom can be found in the person of Billy Wolfe himself. As retiring as a peacock, Billy, without question, is one of the most picturesque figures in the sports world, combining in his mannerism the showmanship qualities of a W. C. Fields and an old time circus owner. Not an especially flashy dresser, Wolfe sets himself apart from other impresarios by the number of diamonds he wears." The writer noted Wolfe's flat midwestern diction and said that without his jewelry Wolfe "could be mistaken for the average small-town businessman. Broadfaced, slightly better than average height, he bears a faint resemblance to President Truman. It is only when Wolfe talks that he takes on the aura of the showman. And never at a loss for words he is ready to convince anyone that femme wrestling is the biggest thing that ever hit the grunt-and-groan emporiums. His favorite claim is that gal rassling has revived interest in the mat game throughout the country."

The article ran with what stands as the quintessential picture of Billy Wolfe: a photo illustration showing five images of Wolfe sitting around a table playing cards with himself. The message was clear. He held all the cards in women's wrestling. Wolfe liked the picture so much that he used it as a publicity shot with the caption, "Billy Wolfe who plays the game all by himself of booking girl wrestlers in Western Canada, Puerto Rico, Cuba, Old Mexico and through-out the United States."

The *Wrestling and TV Sports* article told a different story about how the business began: it had started before Mildred Burke. Wolfe, the article said, had staged his first women's wrestling bout in 1932 in a burlesque theater in Kansas City. "Seeing the customers tearing down the box office to get in, Wolfe realized he had hit the jackpot," according to the article. Two years later he hooked up with Burke, and two years after that they went on to make the first breakthrough into arena wrestling in Missouri, Alabama, and Tennessee. This version did not sit well with Burke. In her view it was she, not Wolfe, who was the one who had seen the future of women's wrestling and pushed for it.

To her mind, she had to force him to accept her as a wrestler and then force him to put her into the arena matches. Without her, she believed, Wolfe would have never gotten out of the carnivals. "Billy had now conveniently forgotten how it all started," she wrote. "He began cultivating the lie about how he had discovered and trained me, and how he had first seen the financial and professional future of girl wrestling."

The publicity had another side effect. Wolfe, filled with pride at the business he had created, had started ballyhooing women wrestlers as better than men. "Women's wrestling definitely is more exciting than men's," he told the *Globe-Democrat*. "A girl has to be tough to stand it." That sort of thing was fine. But it got more problematic when he started emphasizing the violent aspects of his women's ring exploits. The *National Police Gazette* gave Wolfe the lurid cover headline "Women Wrestlers—More Brutal Than Men!" And Wolfe did his best in the magazine's pages to give the readers their money's worth. "There's no doubt that women's wrestling is more brutal than men's," he said. "The girls don't stop to think or reason. They just get mad. And they carry grudges to the grave—or it would be the grave, if the referee didn't stop the girls from killing each other."

Wolfe's hype may have been good for the gate but it also played into the hands of those who hated the sight of women wrestlers and wanted them banned. Forty-odd states allowed female wrestlers by 1950—but California, New York, Illinois, Connecticut, Michigan, Oregon, Pennsylvania, and Kansas still refused to license women wrestlers; New Jersey had just opened up again but a third of Missouri was still off-limits. In Mildred and Billy's home state, where she had started out in mixed matches against men, the chairman of the State Athletic Commission still prevented women from wrestling in St. Louis. "I think it is undignified to womanhood," Colonel Charles P. Orchard told the *Globe-Democrat*.

The same month the *Police Gazette* story appeared, a city council-man in Cleveland tried to ban women wrestlers as "loathsome and degrading to womanhood and public good taste." The city attorney quickly found a law banning exhibitions that were "offensive to womanly modesty or common decency" but backed off using it against female wrestlers for fear that could open up the city to lawsuits. Soon the whole city was talking about the controversy. The secretary of the Cleveland Boxing Commission threw his support behind the women. "It should be borne in mind that we are not living in an era when legs must be referred to as limbs and women's garters and hose be called unmentionables." The papers couldn't resist entering the fray. "A threat against the right of one lady to kick another lady in the stomach is a blow to the very foundation of our liberties," wrote the Cleveland *Plain Dealer* sports editor Gordon Cobbledick, tongue firmly in cheek. The local promoter promptly booked two women for the Cleveland Arena. But times had changed since the showdown in Los Angeles in 1944. Interestingly, there was no full-scale women's movement to ban female wrestlers in Cleveland, as there had been in California. With only men to drive it the effort to ban women in Cleveland fizzled.

Before the hubbub died down, the Cleveland *News* did a man-in-the-street poll. It came out five to one in favor of women wrestlers. "Women are better wrestlers than men and more fun to watch," said a male cabdriver named P. H. Collins.

Billy Wolfe's business continued to improve. By the middle of 1950 he had two dozen women in his stable earning more than $10,000 a year and drawing single gates as high as $25,000. Mildred Burke had drawn huge crowds in Mexico City and Boston, but most of the time the women were constantly on the road blanketing the small towns of America. In July 1950 Burke and Nell Stewart drew a record crowd of over 1,300 in Kingsport, Tennessee, for a match that featured "plenty of slugging, hair-pulling and good wrestling." Three weeks later Burke and June Byers drew another record crowd in Panama City, Florida. "The women displayed a far rougher brand of grappling than their male counterparts, presenting a slam-bang display of fistic arts, kicking and jumping to the delight of the largest crowd ever believed to attend a fight card in Bay county," the Panama City *News-Herald* reported in a story that also featured a large photograph of Byers stomping on a prostrate Burke.

A few days earlier Burke had made headlines around the country when she reacted angrily to a Radio Moscow propaganda broadcast that condemned women's wrestling in America as a "barbarous" capitalist exploitation of women. Burke told reporters that she would like to go to Moscow and "clean out Uncle Joe and the rest of his whole rotten gang personally . . . I'm sure I could beat any woman athlete Stalin has to offer." Burke said the women who wrestled had good morals, led clean lives, and were mostly married with children. "The only bad habit I have is coffee," Burke said. The writer added, "Mildred, herself, is happily married to her manager, Billy Wolf [*sic*]. She says that he is the boss and that there are no arguments in the family." The stream of publicity was endless. At the beginning of 1951 the sports editor of the Miami *Daily News* named her as one of the five reliable drawing cards in the wrestling business, along with Gorgeous George, the former boxers Primo Carnera and "Two Ton" Tony Galento, and Ginger the wrestling bear.

11

The Golden Age

All of Billy Wolfe's hard work was paying off now. For years he had had no fixed address. While Millie and G. Bill lived their separate life on the road and in Los Angeles, Billy lived in hotels such as the Holland in Manhattan and the Park in Columbus, Ohio. He always used as a mailing address his brother's telephone exchange in tiny Wheatland, Missouri. Wheatland was not as remote as it seemed, centrally located as it was among the territories that Wolfe's women worked as they crisscrossed the South, West, and Midwest. But he was now managing thirty-two women wrestlers with another dozen in training in a business that put on nine shows a day nationwide and had a reported gross of more than $250,000 a year. The women needed somewhere to train other than in hotel rooms with Nell Stewart and in the arenas before matches with Johnnie Mae Young. Wolfe needed a more permanent base for his operations. He found it in Columbus, the territory run by his friend and ally Al Haft. In early 1951 Wolfe established his booking business there, moving into an office suite next to Haft's in the building that housed Haft's Gym at 261 South High Street in downtown Columbus.

Haft had ruled wrestling in the Ohio River basin and beyond for more than two decades. Like Billy Wolfe, Haft had been among that generation of American boys who were inspired to go into wrestling after Frank Gotch dethroned George Hackenschmidt. Haft was a sixty-four-year-old former wrestler and college wrestling coach who had seen every aspect and worked every angle of the business, from coaching Olympic competitors to backing male professional heavyweight champions to paving the way for "Billy's Girls." Called by some the Big Dutchman, Haft was a tough, bullet-headed man who by the early 1950s had a business that reportedly was grossing $1 million a year, four times what Wolfe was pulling in. In addition to his gym, Haft also operated Haft's Acre, the 6,000-seat open-air arena that was one of the most important wrestling venues in the region. The gym on High Street was the center of his wrestling empire. Top male wrestlers could be found there working out with weights and training in the regulation-sized ring. "To say that the gym is the most pretentious and fully equipped layout in the United States, used exclusively by and for wrestlers, is putting it mildly," a wrestling magazine noted. Wolfe quickly established a training school there for all the women who had been besieging him, and soon Billy's Girls were working out side by side with some of the best male wrestlers in the business, who occasionally doubled as the women's instructors. The men also used the gym to engage in private shooting matches to decide their place in the wrestling hierarchy. Wolfe, too, would match his women against each other in shoots to see who was toughest. "Some of the best wrestling matches occurred there, hidden away from the public, and Haft's Gym was a place where reputations were made and destroyed," Tim Hornbaker wrote in a history of wrestling in the 1950s.

Billy Wolfe moved his few personal belongings into a suite with a large window on the ground floor of the Park Hotel at 465 South High Street, two blocks from Haft's Gym. For the next several years the hotel would be his permanent home. The hotel itself was an aging four-story brick structure just north of the brewery district that had been built during the gaslight era a dozen years after the Civil War. Once it had been grand, featuring the city's first hotel elevator, a 185-foot observatory overlooking a park festooned with fountains, and hot and cold running water in every room. By the middle of the twentieth century the old hotel was still imposing but also seedy and badly in need of renovation. Its shady, worn-out glamour suited Wolfe well. While he occupied one of the hotel's twenty suites, his wrestlers would move into some of the 150 small and shabby rooms. "Like little cells," one of the women remembered. Each room had a beat-up dresser, a single chair, a bed with a bedspread and thin sheets that were falling apart. There was a small, desultory lobby and crooked hallways that were sometimes prowled by bats. The girls joked that there had been a dungeon in the basement; actually, in better days it had been a billiard parlor. In both the gym and his private office at the Park, Wolfe put up posters of Mildred Burke flexing her muscles in her zebra-striped two-piece and high heels.

Haft's Gym and the Park Hotel became a mecca for women wrestlers from all over the country. Each applicant had to fill out a questionnaire establishing that "she is single, intelligent, physically agile, and of sound character," a wrestling magazine noted without irony, given the goings-on in Wolfe's harem. He also had strict physical parameters for his recruits: aged eighteen to twenty-four, weight 130 to 150 pounds, and height five feet, two inches to five feet, seven inches, in other words no one smaller than Mildred Burke or bigger than June Byers. Appearance was a plus. "We used to choose trainees according to brawn," Wolfe said. "Now they have to be photogenic."

Applicants who were accepted for tryouts had to pay their own round-trip fare to Columbus, where they were put up at the Park Hotel. They were required to deposit $100 at the hotel to cover expenses while they underwent two weeks of training bouts. The ring training amounted to about an hour a day at Haft's Gym, four days a week, in practice sessions with some of Wolfe's top women and a top male pro. The women were taught how to take hard bumps and falls and also spent hours working out with light dumbbells, the medicine ball, and free-style calisthenics. They practiced putting headlocks on a spring-loaded wooden dummy called Oscar. If the applicant passed this point, she was taken on at a salary of $50 a week, until she was ready to make her debut and start earning at the box office. That could take anywhere from one to eight months.

Wolfe estimated that one in four women made it through the training and thus far he had produced "about 60 high-caliber femme wrestlers." He claimed that he turned down a hundred women a month and had to screen forty applicants to find one worthy prospect. "Turn-over in personnel is high, but no higher than it is in business and industry," he said. "Some trainees quit when they get their first bump on the mat. Another, after the first couple of matches and the accompanying publicity makes her more glamorous to the boyfriend and he proposes. I won't take married girls or keep them after they're married. A wife that's traveling continually doesn't make for any kind of homelife. I've lost plenty of money. Like the $1,700 invested in a Seattle school teacher. She was making good, then suddenly decided to get married."

The women spent most of their time on the road. When they were in Columbus, they lived a simple life along High Street, walking back and forth over the three blocks between their rooms at the Park and Haft's Gym. In between, they stopped for lunch or dinner at the Hi-Fulton Grill at 427 South High Street. The place was a plain little restaurant but it was clean and the food was good. A waitress named Ruth took care of them. With comfortable red leather booths, comfort food like chili dogs, and mirrors along the walls, the Hi-Fulton became their home away from home. Framed glossies of Billy's Girls, posed like Hollywood stars, adorned the restaurant walls. Billy Wolfe like to admire the photos and himself, in those mirrors. "He would be sitting in the booth and the mirror would be to his right," recalled Ruth Boatcallie, one of the new women who joined up around this time. "He would talk to you, but he would be looking at himself in the mirror. Once, he was talking to this girl. He would talk to her and then look at himself in the mirror. And one of the girls talked to him and then looked at herself in the mirror. We all got the giggles."

New prospects quickly became new stars. The scattered geography of their origins stood as a testament to the vast reach of Wolfe's business. Unlike his earliest recruits, who were drawn largely from the Midwest and South, the new women were from all over. Gloria Barattini, a stunning twenty-year-old with an opera-trained voice, came from a family that ran a hotel and filing station in Fort Meade, Maryland. Wolfe had her sing for reporters and called her a Baltimore heiress. Cora Combs, a perky twenty-six-year-old redhead, came from a family of coal miners in Hazard, Kentucky; she was so energetic that Billy called her his "Hadacol Kid" after the patent medicine that was 12 percent alcohol. Twenty-one-year-old Ella Waldek, a powerfully built, 150-pound softball and roller derby star, had grown up in a German family in Custer, Washington. There was a twenty-year-old Jewish girl who had been abused and abandoned in Connecticut who Wolfe turned into Ida May Martinez, the Mexican Champ. Martinez joined the group at the same time as Boatcallie, a physically imposing twenty-year-old from Houston who had also left roller derby for wrestling. The two women came to tryouts Wolfe was holding at a Houston hotel. The shooting matches Wolfe put on to weed out the weaker women served only to stoke the rivalries and jealousies. "He was a manipulator, and he pitted the girls one against the other," Martinez recalled. "When you handle twenty-some female wrestlers who are always bitching and arguing and fighting, what do you do? You have to be tough with them. He was stern and gruff sometimes. And sometimes he would tell a joke and somebody would laugh."

His joking left a lasting memory with some of the women. "He always seemed to have this great sense of humor," recalled Ethel Brown, the young wrestler from Columbus. "He wouldn't admonish you for doing something if you gave him an off-kilter answer. He would laugh about it. Kind of like a father. One of the girls told him I was man-crazy. I said, 'Gee, Billy, I was worried you were going to say I was girl-crazy.' And he laughed and laughed about it."

Martinez said she and Boatcallie came up to Columbus on the train together two weeks after their tryout; Martinez sold her guitar for the fare. They checked into the Park Hotel, which Martinez recalled as "third or fourth rate." They immediately ran into Johnnie Mae Young and went to have a drink at a biker bar across the street. Young, as always, made an immediate impression on the young prospects, leaving them wide-eyed that any woman could be that tough. "All of a sudden I hear this arguing, and Mae Young was arguing with this woman," Martinez recalled. "And when the woman turned around, Mae threw a sucker punch at her and it started a riot. I got out of there because I didn't want to get arrested on my first day as a wrestler." The stories about Young were legion. Joe Wolfe heard that she got into a bar fight with a man in Columbus. "Somebody was flirting with her girlfriend, she got pissed and beat the shit out of him," Joe recalled. "I understand she actually bit his genitals." On another occasion, Young fought with a woman in the back of the Hi-Fulton. Another time Young supposedly decked a male wrestler who pulled down his trunks and exposed himself to her in the locker room.

Sometimes Billy Wolfe instigated the fights. Martinez remembered decades later the shock she got from watching Young slugging it out in a room at the Park Hotel with Mars Bennett, a muscular former trapeze artist and another of Wolfe's girls. "All of a sudden they're in a fistfight on the floor, and Billy has a big smile on his face," Martinez said. "He accomplished what he set out to do."

The girls were strong, athletic, and in the full flower of their youth. Their heads were dazzled with images of diamonds and ring stardom. "We were all just young kids and we were having fun," Boatcallie recalled. "We were all just immature, we were thrown into it, in these huge big cars, driving out in the night." Their reality was bruises and long hours on the road.

Mildred kept away from the Park, the Hi-Fulton, and Haft's Gym. When she came into town she stayed at the much nicer Southern Hotel farther up High Street. Her relationship with G. Bill and Wolfe's strategy of housing her in separate hotels had succeeded in isolating her from the other women, leaving Mae Weston and Cora Combs as two of the few close friends she had among the other wrestlers. "She was low-key," Ida May Martinez recalled. "I think she made herself scarce from the whole scene. She was the champion. Maybe she figured she ought to be off by herself." Burke missed out on the fun and camaraderie. "Mildred was more of a serious person," Barattini recalled. "She wasn't a crack-joke person. But she was nice." Others were offended by her aloofness. "Mildred was a snob," recalled Barbara Jean Baker, another new wrestler who had been accepted after graduating from high school in Charleston, West Virginia. "I only met her twice and she thought she was better than anybody else." Burke's remoteness played into an image that some of the women had that she was a coddled, "fake" champion who owed her long reign entirely to Billy Wolfe. Ella Waldek said Burke had been "cloistered" by Wolfe and "kept away from everyone. She worked six months a year and worked out for the other six months." Gladys Gillem pointed out that she had never wrestled Burke in a real match. Johnnie Mae Young insisted that she could have beaten Burke if given the chance. "I could have beat her any time I wanted to," Young said in an interview decades later. "Mildred was not a great wrestler, but she made a good presentation."

Martinez recalled that Burke lacked the flair of Nell Stewart, who always made a big entrance by flashing her blonde mane and swiveling her curves on her way into the ring. Martinez quickly became fond of Stewart and they became lifelong friends. "She was beautiful and I thought she was a helluva good wrestler," Martinez recalled. She called Stewart "Skipper" or "Skippy" and found her to be good company, even though underneath that sweet Georgia drawl Stewart flashed a temper that often broke out in arguments. Once she and Wolfe got into an argument in the lobby of the Park Hotel and he hit her with his open hand; Nell was so mad she rushed to get the pearl-handled .38 she kept in the glove compartment of her car. Ida May talked her out of it. "Skipper, you just kind of forget about it," Martinez told Stewart. "If you kill Billy, your life will be over and you'll have to spend it in jail."

In the end, Nell's star quality always won people over. One of Wolfe's young recruits, Penny Banner, recalled the awe she felt upon meeting the legendary Nell Stewart, "the beautiful girl I'd seen only in a huge picture hanging in the Hi Fulton Restaurant. . . . I was amazed watching Nell wrestle. She was a real artist in the ring. It was like watching June Byers, everything was precise and she never missed a move." Gloria Barattini, who had trained with Nell in Boston, also liked Stewart. "Nell was a beautiful girl," Barattini recalled. "She was a very good wrestler. I worked with Nell many, many times. She was always kind."

Byers was not so popular. "June was one of the hardest workers I ever worked with," Barattini recalled. "When you got hit, you got hit with June. You would land across the ring." Byers was always flashing the big diamond ring that Wolfe had purchased for her. All the girls knew about it, and what it meant about her place in their universe. And none of them liked the other thing that Wolfe had given her, the "cupped chest lick" that he had taught her from his own wrestling past. "She had a June Byers slap," Ella Waldek recalled years later. "She would take an open hand like this and right between the throat and the breastbone right here she would lay that thing in and not only would it sting, it would damn near knock your head off. There was no reason to be that vicious with that kind of a slap. There wasn't anything. It didn't make any sense. It wasn't a hold, it didn't get a rise out of anybody. It wasn't fun. And there was no reason to do it." Ethel Brown said Byers liked to test the other girls. "June had a habit of seeing if the girls could take it," Brown recalled. "When I was still new she took her fist and went straight into my face. It broke my nose and blacked both of my eyes." But Brown got her revenge by accidentally head-butting Byers and knocking her out in the ring. "Later she acknowledged that she had hit me on purpose and she wanted to see if I could take it," Brown said. "Now we should put it all behind us and we should be friends. I never lost that feeling that I had, not liking her." Johnnie Mae Young said she never had any trouble with Byers. "She didn't do it to me. The only ones that she laid the boot on were the one's she didn't expect to retaliate. If you hit me, I'm going to hit you back."

Wolfe eventually tired of Young's independence and the implicit challenge it carried to his authority. During a tour in Mexico City with Young, Nell Stewart, Violet Viann, and Lillian Ellison, he chose his moment. "Billy Wolfe always hated my guts," Young recalled decades later. "He did not like me, period, because I didn't take his bullshit. He never went to bed with me, and that made it worse. Billy

Wolfe was always looking for somebody to beat my ass and he never could." She said she believed he picked Mexico City "because he wanted to kick my ass literally and he might go to jail in the United States. He made an excuse to take me to Mexico." Then he picked a fight with her. "I came in late and he didn't like it," she recalled. "Billy Wolfe wanted to have some trouble with the girls, period. So I told him, 'Kiss my ass.'" Instead, he came at her with his fists. "We got in a fight in the hotel room. He knocked the shit out of me. He knocked me down and got me on the floor and choked me." He did not flinch at hitting a woman. He worked her over thoroughly. The toughest of the female wrestlers was no match for him in a real fight. "Billy Wolfe could wrestle, and he was tough," Young recalled. She said she left Wolfe for a while after that and worked for him only sporadically from then on. For Lillian Ellison, who was close to Young, it was the final straw. "He got mad at Johnnie Mae about something and he just beat the heck out of her," Ellison recalled decades later. "And I said, well, that's the end of here. If I have to walk back to the United States, I'm not staying in this mess. That's when I quit Billy Wolfe."

The first black girls joined in 1951. Wolfe deserves credit for being one of the first bookers to integrate pro wrestling on a systematic basis. He said he got the idea after watching the great strides made by black baseball players. "Negro men have been competing in pro wrestling almost since the origin of catch-as-catch-can matches in the United States, 63 years ago," Wolfe was quoted as saying in a Kansas City wrestling program. "They have met with success wherever they have wrestled, even in such faraway places as Thailand (Siam), Burma, and Indonesia. Then, why wouldn't the Negro girl athletes stand an equal chance of making the grade? That's the way I figured it. And from the tremendous fan support given the Negro girls' matches I have not been wrong in my figuring." He asked his white women for approval before he started using black women. "Billy called a meeting and said we were going to have a vote on this," Martinez recalled. "Do you want to wrestle black people or not? And of course we voted yes." Ethel Johnson and Babs Wingo, two sisters, were the first, followed by Kathleen Wimbley. She had been a star at a local high school in Columbus, captain of the girls' basketball team, a debater, the only Negro member of the marching band, and winner of a modeling scholarship. She contacted Wolfe after seeing his women wrestling on television. Wolfe came to her parents' house for dinner. One of the smartest women to work for Wolfe, she went on to a career as a supervisor at a banking conglomerate based in Manhattan. "Billy should get one hundred percent credit for integrating women's wrestling," Wimbley said decades later. "He was the first one to have the chance to do it. I broke many color lines. He took a chance where nobody else would."

With more women on the road wrestling for him, the money poured in, allowing Wolfe to indulge his passions: women, diamonds, gambling, and, to a lesser extent, drinking. "Billy liked his booze, but he was never drunk," Barbara Jean Baker recalled. "Not around us. But he liked a shot of bourbon every now and then." He liked his good times, but he also liked to be in control. He was much more ardent about gambling. He used to frequent the underground bookie joints in the red-light district a few blocks away from the Park Hotel. There the Victorian mansions were filled with hookers and there were card rooms up and down the strip. Both catered to the conventioneers staying at the big hotels on High Street. When he wasn't working Wolfe could be found there looking for the big-money games.

On the road with his women, Wolfe was quick to get out the deck. Several of his wrestlers recall playing poker with him and losing their hard-earned money to him. "We used to play poker all the time," Johnnie Mae Young remembered. "He was good. He could beat you. He used to beat the girls all the time. A lot of the girls would get in debt to him, and he'd put them on the books. He kept them on the books to keep them obligated to him so they'd have to wrestle for him." The women were his universe and the force driving its expansion was sex, the thing he buffed and sold to the public, the thing he took in private when he wanted pleasure or to exert control. He worked hard and spent his hard-earned money training and promoting the women, and he felt their bodies were his due. The Park Hotel became a scene where sex could be traded for power. Occasionally, Wolfe's friends were invited to partake. Burke was aware of what was going on and was disgusted by it. "His orgies and trafficking in the sexual favors of some of his girls were infamous in the business," she later wrote. "Some promoters happily took part in this lavish whoring, envying Wolfe his access to so much female flesh."

He was in a rare position for a man in America in 1950, and he knew it. Only Hollywood moguls and their casting couches in sunny Los Angeles, and a few years later Hugh Hefner and his Playboy bunnies in Chicago, could compare to the operation Wolfe had established in, of all places, staunchly Republican southern Ohio. "He was just an ordinary guy, surrounded by a lot of pretty, young girls, trying to make a buck," Boatcallie recalled. At times he was like a kid in a candy store. One of his wrestlers recalled walking into his office at Al Haft's gym when she was eighteen and catching the fifty-six-year-old Wolfe and the sixty-six-year-old Haft literally with their pants down. "They both had erections and Al was knocking over chairs to show how strong it was," the woman recalled. "They didn't even apologize or act embarrassed." The male wrestlers may have envied Wolfe for his access to so many beautiful young girls, but the men were also disgusted by the way he treated the women who wrestled for him. "Even though Billy had been a wrestler, he kept away from us and we kept away from him," recalled "Classy" Freddie Blassie. "He wasn't one of the boys, as far as we were concerned. We thought of him as a pimp."

Burke said that it was during this period when Wolfe began to think that she was expendable. "Ensconced now in the Park Hotel, with diamonds sprouting all over him and surrounded by dozens of attractive women that he could force to sleep with him, he began to have bad thoughts about me," Burke wrote in her autobiography. "He began to think that my integrity as a champion was just another commodity. I was something that you could throw away when you were done with it—like an old shoe."

She was already upset that he was taking so much credit for their joint enterprise; soon she became convinced he was actively plotting to replace her. She came to believe that he was putting women up to double-cross her and take the title, just as Dick Shikat went rogue to betray the trust and snatch Danno O'Mahoney's title in 1936. "A double cross was a sudden, violent switch on my opponent's part into a full shooting match," she wrote. "This was a deliberate effort to knock me cold for a quick pin, or to injure or disable me." Women began swinging for her face or her stomach, she said, going for the quick knockout. "What got through to me in the late forties and early fifties was that everyone was beginning to have a go at the double cross, even green kids out of school. . . . The girl in a match could be induced to take the risk of a double cross by means of a tax free, under-the-table C-note. Girls could be bribed also with a promise that she would be champion for a long while if she were successful in knocking me off. Numerous such promises were made by Billy Wolfe. He paid out thousands in bribes as well." She said she was told this by other women wrestlers, promoters, and referees, but she offers no details, other than to say that Ann Laverne once hit her with a straight right on the jaw and then ran from the ring when she didn't go down.

As she became more wary of Wolfe, her suspicions grew into paranoia; she wrote in her autobiography that she believed he twice had her car tampered with to cause accidents and on a third occasion planned to have her murdered in Mexico. "Everything misfired or fell apart, even his last ditch plan to murder me on the bus coming back from Mexico," she wrote. She offers no confirming details, nothing but a reference to an unnamed female wrestler who told her the story.

After Billy Wolfe came down with jaundice in 1951, Joe Wolfe was taken out of school in Los Angeles at sixteen and sent to Columbus to work for his stepfather in the gym and the business. Up until then they had not seen much of each other. "The experiences I had had with Billy were very minimal," Joe said years later. "Even when Mom was on the road I didn't get to see him, and when she was home it was rare that I would see him. Eventually, I would see him maybe once every two years and for a relatively brief time." Once a year, Billy took him deep-sea fishing, for salmon in Seattle, tarpon in the Gulf of Mexico, dorado off Acapulco. Now that Wolfe was sick and needed him, Joe finally got to spend an extended period of time with his stepfather. The boy enjoyed it and felt that Wolfe was making room for him in the business. "He was grooming me," Joe recalled. "Like he did G. Bill."

Joe was assigned to drive some of the wrestlers to their matches. One time, he was stopped by cops in the Deep South with a couple of the black wrestlers and told to get out of town. Back in Columbus, at Haft's Gym and the Park Hotel, the boy did not notice any funny stuff going on. Burke and Wolfe had taken care to keep Joe in the dark. "All of the trouble that was going on between my mother and Billy Wolfe was more or less shielded from me," Joe said. "I really have nothing to hold against Billy Wolfe."

Joe enjoyed working out in the gym with the pretty young women and had his own summer affair with a young girl wrestler. He was never allowed to work with Nell Stewart or June Byers. That was no accident. Wolfe was careful to keep his affairs compartmentalized. "He was extremely discreet," Joe said. "That's how it was back then."

Even though Joe had worn Billy's last name since he was an infant, Wolfe had never formally adopted him, and it was G. Bill who had always acted as more of a father to him. Now, the older Wolfe took Joe under his wing for the first time. Billy allowed him to share in the wealth and also taught him how to spend it. He taught the boy how to play poker. Wolfe brought Joe into a game with the powerful promoter Salvador Lutteroth, a multimillionaire who ran wrestling in Mexico City, and was extremely proud when the boy walked away with a considerable amount of Lutteroth's money. Joe recalls Billy playing poker for two straight days, sleeping on couches, and sitting down in another game with the famed stripper Gypsy Rose Lee. His stepfather also introduced him to the famed promoter Jack Pfefer, but he told Joe in advance not to shake Pfefer's hand or get too close because the man had a venereal disease. Billy also bought Joe one of his proudest possessions, a 1.25-carat diamond-and-emerald ring in the shape of a serpent's head from the jeweler Wolfe frequented in Baltimore. "It could have been like any dad or any son," Joe recalled. Sometimes Billy took him to business meetings, and he saw the side of the man that had built the wrestling business. "If we were meeting with any promoters or anybody of significance, he would always turn around before we walked into the room and say, 'Just keep your mouth shut and don't say anything unless we talk about it first.' He was just afraid it was only going to take one sentence that could be taken wrong and it would screw everything up. This man had total control. And he didn't have to threaten you. All he had to do was tell you, and you'd listen. If he said, shhh, you kept your mouth shut, because you were afraid of him."

★   ★   ★

By 1951, Wolfe and Burke were surfing on cultural changes in American society and structural changes in the wrestling business that were about to peak as never before. The shifting currents could be summed up in one word: television. Unlike baseball, boxing, and horseracing, wrestling had been a poor fit for radio when it had arrived and transformed American life in the 1920s. Soon after NBC did its first experiments with commercial television in 1939, however, it quickly became apparent that wrestling and the new medium were made for each other. Wrestling required no sets, writers, or actors, and it was perfect for the early TV cameras that were heavy, hard to move, and needed very bright light to produce a usable picture. By 1948 NBC, ABC, and the DuMont network were broadcasting weekly wrestling shows to the nation, and small local stations were joining in. Bars used wrestling to draw customers. "Come in and see Mildred Burke and Elvira Snodgrass, two of the Best Women Wrestlers on Television," advertised the Embassy Bar in Elyria, Ohio. In May 1949, the same month that he profiled Mildred Burke, AP sports editor Frank Eck published a piece on the phenomenon. "Wrestling—grunts, groans and grimaces intact—has taken better hold thanks to television. An Associated Press survey of the nation's wrestling cities which have television shows that the sport is attracting its largest crowd in years." Between 1942 and 1950 attendance at wrestling matches increased 800 percent.

The television age helped to change the style of wrestling in the ring as well. Televised bouts encouraged flair, flamboyance, and speed, in other words, an even higher degree of fakery. Aerial maneuvers, including flying leaps by wrestlers such as Antonino Rocca, began to gain in prominence. "We have a new generation and the bobby soxers and feminine fans want the flying tackle and mayhem," St. Louis promoter Sam Muchnick told Eck. "I could try to be reformer, but I'd have an empty house." Female fans drawn in through television were fueling wrestling's rise, just as female fans attracted to Jim Londos had done two decades earlier. Women were now 60 percent of the audience at wrestling shows. One promoter estimated that 90 percent of the TV wrestling audience was female.

The surge in interest was deemed as vaguely unsettling. "Explanations for this are a dime a dozen," *Business Week* reported in October 1950. "The most common is that watching a wrestling match gives women a mental release for some kind of sexual frustration." In addition to the more sensational style of TV wrestling, women were also drawn to "the display of performers' muscled bodies on television," Chad Dell noted in *The Revenge of Hatpin Mary*. He added that attending wrestling matches allowed women to express freedom, sexuality, and assertiveness at a time when postwar societal pressures urged docility, domesticity, and conformity.

The number of TV sets grew from several thousand in 1946 to 10.5 million in 1950. Late that year, the Crosley Broadcasting corporation in Cincinnati enlisted Al Haft to put on the first women's wrestling championship tournament for television on WLW-TV's Saturday night wrestling feature. Billy Wolfe supplied the women to Haft, and Nell Stewart became the first WLW-TV champion. Wolfe's surviving records show twenty-four of his wrestlers under the heading Girls That Have Signed Television and Film Contracts. "There's no doubt that television has made a difference," Wolfe said. "We're now screening applicants for looks and glamour as well as ability . . . Amazons are on the way out . . . I've given orders no girl is to enter the ring without makeup and carefully made up coiffure."

Television turned female wrestlers into lodestars for the public's fascination. Wolfe's women were coming into the national consciousness at a peculiar period in the sexual history of America, a strange halftime of wants and desires lurking below a surface of normalcy.

World War II had liberated libidos and given women a new measure of social freedom, yet the time of true sexual freedom and blatantly sexualized imagery was still off in the distance. An erotic photography industry had arisen by mid-century but it was still underground. Bettie Page was posing for her first famous bondage photos by 1951, but Marilyn Monroe's nude centerfold in the first issue of *Playboy* was still a few years off. Mainstream men had to make do with the sight of legs and busts, and for many Wolfe's women were nothing but a nationally touring burlesque show that enticed some and appalled others. As such, they were harbingers of the sexual revolution that was coming, and the disturbance they created in the cultural realm had its ripple effect.

Historian William Manchester later described Wolfe's wrestlers as "great hulking earth bitches with breasts like half-loaded gunnysacks and pubic hair dangling down their thighs. They always seemed to have cut themselves shaving." Others liked what they saw. Randy Roberts and John S. Olson wrote in *Winning Is the Only Thing: Sports in America Since 1945* that women wrestlers may have been denigrated as "earth bitches" or celebrated as "muscular beauties," but either way they held the attention of television viewers. "Just as Gorgeous George owed part of his success to America's fascination with homosexuality, female wrestlers capitalized on male daydreams of lesbianism and erotic masochism."

One of the most malignant receptors of these currents coursing through mid-century America was an Egyptian academic named Sayyid Qutb. A mild-mannered and unassuming sort, Qutb studied at the Colorado State College of Education in Greeley on a State Department grant. He was in Greeley when Mildred Burke wrestled there, but he left no indication that he saw her. If he had, his outrage would have been beyond the apoplectic. As it was, he was most intensely offended by two aspects of American culture that were uniquely combined in Mildred Burke: overt female sexuality and spectator sports such as pro wrestling. Of women he later wrote, "The American girl is well acquainted with her body's seductive capacity. She knows it lies in the face, and in expressive eyes, and thirsty lips. She knows seductiveness lies in the round breasts, full buttocks, and in the shapely thighs, sleek legs—and she shows all this and does not hide it." Wrestling, he wrote, evoked all that was worst in American society. "Bloody monstrous wrestling matches" left "no room for doubt as to the primitiveness of the feelings of those who are enamored with muscular strength and desire it." When Qutb returned to Egypt he set to writing a monumental work arguing that the only hope for civilization was a retreat into the religious strictures of seventh-century Islam. These writings would later become the theoretical underpinnings for many radical Islamic groups, including al Qaeda.

The second great transformation that Billy Wolfe rode had to do with the wrestling business itself. Wrestling had never had a single, effective official sanctioning body. The National Wrestling Association, a collection of state athletic commissioners, had been the closest. But it was a weak group that existed mainly to license wrestlers for the collection of fees; policing of the title picture was beyond its authority. Powerful promoters working in concert still controlled the game. The association had sanctioned a male heavyweight champion since 1929, but after the scandals of the mid-1930s individual promoters went their separate ways and named their own champions. One of those promoters was Al Haft, who started the Midwest Wrestling Association, which developed its own male champions and had sanctioned Mildred Burke's title. In July 1949 a small group of midwestern promoters met in Waterloo, Iowa, and formed a new organization, the National Wrestling Alliance, with the goal of unifying the men's heavyweight title. The alliance, known as the NWA, would become the most powerful sanctioning body yet for pro wrestling.

Key to the alliance's power was the ability of each member to unilaterally suspend or "blacklist" wrestlers from working in NWA territories if they were deemed to have done anything "detrimental to the interests of a promoter." Haft was one of the six charter members of the NWA and his Midwest Wrestling Association was merged into the new organization.

Mildred Burke's MWA title was not recognized by the new NWA, which focused exclusively on men's wrestling. Still, Wolfe was allowed to join the NWA in December 1949. Some NWA members indicated that they wanted him in the club so they could keep an eye on him. "I suggest you accept Billy Wolfes [*sic*] membership," Pinkie George, the promoter in Iowa and the first NWA president, wrote to St. Louis promoter Sam Muchnick, who would succeed him. "Everyone seems to be in favor—(the majority is). In fact they feel thats [*sic*] a good way to control some of his actions by having him a member. Besides we'll need the doe."

Soon the NWA was "configured to include virtually every major promoter and wrestler from coast to coast," according to Tim Hornbaker, author of the definitive history of the organization, *National Wrestling Alliance: The Untold Story of the Monopoly that Strangled Pro Wrestling*. By 1951 the alliance consisted of thirty-six of the nation's top promoters, who on their own and through associates and affiliates controlled hundreds of venues across the country. They had succeeded in unifying the male heavyweight title with the ascension of Lou Thesz two years earlier and they now ran wrestling with an iron grip. "Recognition by the members of the National Wrestling Alliance as world heavyweight champion was acknowledged as the pinnacle of professional wrestling for more than 40 years," Hornbaker wrote.

The NWA never did recognize a women's title but the organization was still extremely valuable to Billy Wolfe. His women frequently appeared on cards with male wrestlers promoted by NWA members in the areas of the country where women were permitted. The NWA members acted as a national distribution network for his wrestlers, with his women being booked through twenty-six different promotional offices. Wolfe's position in the organization made him a member of an exclusive boys' club with the power to keep women wrestlers in line and stamp out competition. If one of his women tried to go "outlaw" and work on her own or for someone else, he could blacklist her throughout the nation.

The NWA started a monthly magazine, *Official Wrestling,* in April 1951. Wolfe's wrestlers immediately started appearing inside in cheesecake photo spreads and profiles. The magazine gave nearly equal coverage to the women. Their matches had captured the public imagination, and the sex appeal did not hurt. It was wrestling's golden age, with women like Mildred Burke, Nell Stewart, and June Byers sharing the spotlight with men like Lou Thesz, Gorgeous George, and Antonino Rocca.

Billy Wolfe reached his peak in the summer of 1951. The occasion was marked by a long story in, of all places, the *Wall Street Journal,* America's most respected business publication. Under the headline "Spruced-up Wrestlers Bring a New Boom to an Ancient Sport," the story pointed out that wrestling gate receipts had risen 180 percent since 1946, crediting television for giving "a lot of impetus to the wrestling revolution." Also credited were Gorgeous George, Lou Thesz, Antonino Rocca—and Billy Wolfe. "In addition to the 3,000 male professional wrestlers the country has about 200 women grapplers," the article said. "Almost all of these are graduates of a special school for women wrestlers which is operated by former wrestler Billy Wolfe in Columbus, Ohio." He was quoted in the article alongside such wrestling luminaries as Toots Mondt and Sam Muchnick, the new NWA president. Mildred Burke also made it into the story. She was listed among a half dozen wrestlers who earned $100,000 a year.

There was no one to challenge Billy Wolfe as the acknowledged master of women's wrestling. He held all the cards. "People were afraid of Billy Wolfe," remembered Ida May Martinez. "We did what Billy said. Whatever Billy said, we did."

There was no place to go but down.

12

Tragedy

By 1951 Billy Wolfe had been in the wrestling business for three decades. He and his women had been in thousands of matches and received innumerable injuries ranging from dislocated thumbs to broken noses, ribs, and collarbones. Still, nobody had died. That was about to change.

In the book Wolfe maintained to keep track of his business, he kept a list under the heading "Available Girls that May Make Good at Wrestling or Has Some Experience Already." On that list was Janet Boyer, 7188 Knollwood Drive, Minneapolis, Minnesota. Next to that entry, typed in red, were the words: "This little girl is the one that Tony Stecher wanted me to give a chance." Stecher was the chief promoter in Minneapolis and the brother of the famed Joe Stecher, a sterling champion who had emerged after World War I. Tony Stecher was a good judge of wrestling talent, and like Wolfe he was a member of the NWA. When Boyer was sixteen, she asked Wolfe for a tryout as he made a swing through Minneapolis. She was Mildred Burke-sized, five feet, three inches and 120 pounds, and she worked in a stocking factory and lived with her widowed mother. "You're too little and too small," Wolfe told her. But she was persistent, like Mildred. When she was seventeen, she asked again. "I can throw any girl I've ever seen up to 180 pounds, and a lot of men," she said. She was also growing. After she put on some weight, Wolfe gave in. "I guess you need a daddy," he said, "and we need a daughter."

He guided her training, waiting for the moment to make her his newest star. She also became a favorite of his, in a very special way. Because she was under eighteen, he later told the newspapers, he had to become her legal guardian in order to train her as a wrestler. Her mother signed the papers to allow it. From then on, Wolfe described Boyer as his adopted daughter, Janet Boyer Wolfe. They were photographed together sharing a nightclub table in the pages of the NWA magazine. Her career as an active wrestler lasted six weeks.

The stories of what happened to Janet Boyer are numerous, backlit by conspiracy theories and speculations, all obscured by the fog of memory. The known facts are that Boyer, then eighteen, died on Saturday, July 28, 1951, after falling ill during a tag-team benefit for the Shrine Club at Patterson Field Stadium in East Liverpool, Ohio. It was Boyer's second bout of the evening; earlier she had worked with Ella Waldek, perhaps the most powerful new wrestler in Wolfe's troupe. The muscular, 150-pound Waldek had defeated Boyer in seven minutes. In the dressing room afterward, Boyer complained of a "bursting headache." Waldek later recalled, "She kept complaining about this terrible pain in her head. I told her, 'You need to tell your future father that you're having trouble, that you may have a brain concussion.' Well, she was afraid to tell Billy that she was hurt." Nobody had seen her take a blow to the head. At 10:30 p.m. she went out for the tag-team match partnered with Eva Lee against Waldek and Johnnie Mae Young. In a tag-team match, two wrestlers fight in the ring, while their two partners watch outside the ropes, waiting to be tagged to enter as the tagger exits. Boyer worked a few minutes with Young, then signaled to Lee that she wanted to tag out. After Boyer exited she collapsed on the ring apron. The crowd gasped. "She put her hand to her head as if in pain," an onlooker said later. "Her knees seemed to buckle and she slid down, grasping for the ropes."

A doctor from the crowd found her unconscious. "This girl is in bad shape," he said. "Get her to the dressing room right away."

Oxygen was administered in the dressing room and in the ambulance that rushed her to East Liverpool Osteopathic Hospital. She never regained consciousness and was pronounced dead at 4 a.m.

Waldek, Young, and Lee were taken to the Travelers' Hotel in East Liverpool for questioning by the county sheriff. They were treated as criminal suspects. "They locked Mae Young, Eva, and me in a hotel room because they had no prison facilities for women," Waldek recalled. "And we were going to be accused of manslaughter in the first degree." The women said they "just couldn't understand" what had happened. No unusual "holds or twists" had been used. The police decided not to press charges.

Wolfe was devastated. "I loved her very much," he told the Columbus, Ohio, *Citizen*. "I hadn't brought her out into the public yet, but I was hoping Janet would be able to step into the title when Mildred dropped out."

The autopsy showed she had a "traumatic rupture" of the stomach and a subdural hematoma, a blood clot between the brain and its lining. Either injury was serious enough to cause death. Ringside fans thought she had been hurt during her bout with Waldek, who had body-slammed her to the mat. Wolfe told the Associated Press he thought a body slam had caused the brain hemorrhage. His wrestlers told him that Boyer had been complaining about headaches for several weeks. "Janet was so intent upon becoming the top woman wrestler in the country that she refused to let anyone tell me about her headaches for fear that I would cancel her bookings and it might take

Young and unworldly, Millie Bliss dropped out of high school in the ninth grade and embarked on a secretarial career after the stock market crash of 1929. Within a few years she was working in a diner in Kansas City (below) with her mother, Bertha, pictured. Two unidentified men sit at the counter. At eighteen, she was divorced and pregnant, and earning $4 a week as a waitress. *Courtesy of Joe Wolfe*

Mildred Burke taking her stance in March 1937, six weeks after becoming the first widely recognized world champion of women's professional wrestling. She stood five feet, two inches tall and weighed 128 pounds. *Courtesy of Joe Wolfe*

Wrestling drew Millie Bliss into the orbit of Billy Wolfe, the man who would train her, rename her Mildred Burke, marry her, and make her champion. She is standing (above) third from right at a gathering of Wolfe's family. Her son, Joe, sits in Wolfe's lap to her left. Wolfe's son, G. Bill, sits at far right. Wolfe was once the middleweight wrestling champion of Missouri (below right) and he became famous and prosperous as the boss of women's wrestling in America (below left). *Courtesy of Joe Wolfe*

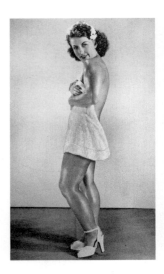

Wolfe promoted Burke as a sexy, powerful athlete with a carefully crafted image that was decades ahead of its time. In the early 1940s, he had her photographed in suggestive poses (above left) and sent them out in calendars. Through rigorous training, she developed defined muscles (above right) that she showcased in tight suits of white satin. *Courtesy of Joe Wolfe*

Her ring earnings allowed Burke in 1943 to buy her first home, a bungalow in Los Angeles where she could have the semblance of a normal life. She sits on the porch, Wolfe sitting behind her with her brother, Louis, and mother, Bertha, while her son, Joe, rides a pony. *Courtesy of Joe Wolfe*

The cornerstone of Mildred Burke and Billy Wolfe's success was their ability to get publicity in newspapers. Interviews with reporters (above) were a staple of their business. In her matches on the road, Burke was always treated as a celebrity and occasionally as a dignitary, as when she visited Cuba (left) and met the president at his seaside palace.
Courtesy of Joe Wolfe

Burke's strut to the ring from the dressing room was carefully orchestrated for maximum impact. She designed her own robes in brilliant colors such as fuchsia. Wolfe trails behind her as an awe-struck female fan looks on in 1943.

Myron Davis, Time LifePictures/Getty Images

Burke (above, left) wrestling at her height. Her skill allowed her to triumph over bigger women by bringing them to the mat and applying her leg holds. Here she topples Therese Theis. *Courtesy of Joe Wolfe*

She used her ring earnings, which reportedly had reached $50,000 annually by 1949, to buy diamonds, furs, and floral dresses that enhanced the feminine image she wanted to project. "Women's wrestling wasn't going to be any freak show while I was champion," she later wrote. "My resolve was to be a woman and a lady first, and a champion wrestler second."

Courtesy of Joe Wolfe

A triangle in business and in bed: Billy Wolfe, Mildred Burke, and G. Bill Wolfe. Burke was married to Wolfe, her manager, but sleeping with G. Bill, her driver and her step-son while her husband dallied with other women wrestlers, including Nell Stewart and June Byers. *Courtesy of Joe Wolfe*

Posing with the famous: a headlock for boxer/wrestler Two-Ton Tony Galento, in the ring with former heavyweight boxing champion Max Baer, and another headlock for entertainer Al Jolson. *Jack Pfefer Collection, University Libraries of Notre Dame*

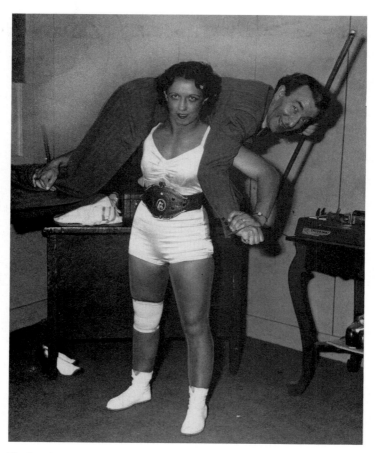

The female champion gives a lift to the irrepressible promoter Jack Pfefer around the time in 1940 that she opened up the New Jersey territory for him, making a big splash for women wrestlers on the East Coast.
Jack Pfefer Collection, University Libraries of Notre Dame

She worked out constantly to tone her muscles and to withstand the rigors of the ring. Here, she flexes before a mirror at her house in California. *Courtesy of Joe Wolfe*

The opponents (left to right): June Byers, the physical powerhouse who became champion after Burke, and married G. Bill; Gladys "Kill 'em" Gillem, Burke's first great foil; Johnnie Mae Young, the toughest of them all; and Karen Kellogg, Billy Wolfe's last champion and girlfriend. *Jack Pfefer Collection, University Libraries of Notre Dame*

June Byers   Gladys Gillem   Johnnie Mae Young   Karen Kellogg

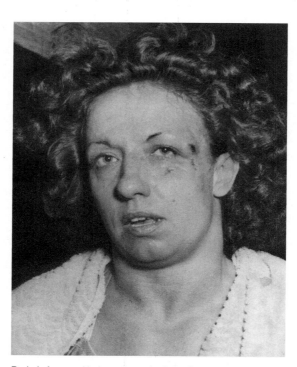

Burke's face and hair were roughed up after a tough match in August 1951 in Boston. Her years in the ring coarsened her features. *Boston Globe*

Burke's Chrysler Imperial was crushed after a near head-on collision in September 1951 with another driver on Highway 66 in the Mojave Desert. Her passenger, G. Bill Wolfe, was thrown clear and left with a fractured skull and broken bones throughout his body. He spent eight months in a body cast. Burke broke five ribs near her spine but was back in the ring four months later against Nell Stewart.
Courtesy of Joe Wolfe

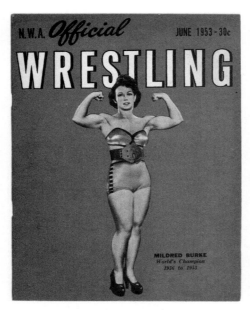

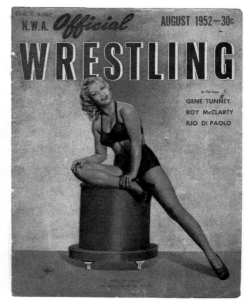

THE CHAMP COMES BACK

LAST spring when Mildred Burke was seriously injured in an automobile accident, many thought the amazing girl wrestling champion might never return to the mat, probably would lose her title in short order if she did.

Now they know better. The champ has returned to the wars and emerged victorious, albeit by the skin of her teeth and by virtue of a lucky time limit.

Even without the drama surrounding Mildred's return to the mat, the bout was one that will be talked about as long as men—and women—discuss wrestling.

Here's the picture. The finals had been reached in the WLW wrestling tournament for men and women in the Dayton, Ohio, Coliseum. Ruffy Silverstein and Buddy Rogers were the principals in the men's division, while Mildred was to battle Nell Stewart for distaff honors.

The 9,000 seats in the Coliseum were sold out three days before the matches were held. By ring time standing room was at a premium and thousands were turned away at the gate, which was altogether fitting and proper as proceeds of the bouts went to the Damon Runyon Cancer Fund.

Silverstein retained his Ohio State title when Rogers was disqualified in the third fall, after each had won a fall. Although the men put up a whale of a match, their contest was overshadowed by the drama provided by Mildred and Nell.

Nell Stewart demands return match with no time limit. "Any time, any conditions," agrees champion

The champion entered the ring looking as fit as ever and won the first fall rather handily. Apparently showing few effects from her accident, she disposed of Nell with grace and finesse and to the great delight of the audience, who had installed her a sentimental favorite on her return to action.

Nell electrified the crowd in the second fall by pinning the champion with a sleeper hold. Mildred apparently was not the same rugged, invincible wrestler she had been before the automobile smashup!

The third fall started with Nell again in high gear, clearly outclassing Mildred. Once again she clamped a sleeper hold—the same hold that won the second fall—on the champion and it seemed inevitable that Mildred was to suffer her first defeat on the mat. Then came the time limit bell—and the champion emerged with the crown still in her possession, although slightly tarnished by the first draw she had ever been held to.

Jack Dempsey, who refereed, and Bernarr Macfadden, famous physical culturist, both declared the contest the greatest they had ever seen between women wrestlers.

Immediately after the Dayton match promoters from all over the country began bidding for the right to stage a rematch for the title. Nell Stewart is demanding that the bout be held where there is no legal time limit placed on matches.

"Mildred was saved by the bell this time, but the next time she can't have that edge—and I'll be the new champion," she declared immediately after the tussle in Dayton.

"I was slightly stale after the long layoff I had to take because of my accident," Miss Burke said. "Give me another match or two under my belt and I'll take on Nell anywhere, under any conditions—and I'll give her a wrestling lesson she'll never forget."

The Dayton match was the third between Miss Burke and Miss Stewart. They first met in Cuernavaca, Mexico, six years ago. Their second encounter was in Dayton last year after Nell won the WLW tournament. Mildred won both matches in straight falls.

Miss Burke being the fighting champion that she is and Miss Stewart being the determined challenger that she is, it's a certainty they will meet at least once again in wide mat circles decisively. And it's a cinch the bout will set a new record for attendance for female grapplers, no matter where it is held.

Nell Stewart

19

In 1952, Millie Burke finally had her showdown with her great nemesis, Nell Stewart. Both of wrestling's cover girls coveted the title, and Wolfe wanted it for Stewart, his girlfriend who would become his third wife.
Jack Pfefer Collection, University Libraries of Notre Dame

Outfoxed by Wolfe in her struggle for the business, Burke turned to a powerful fan, Republican Sen. John Bricker of Ohio (left). Her son, Joe, remained the one constant in her life (right). *Courtesy of Joe Wolfe*

Billy Wolfe finally met his match in his fourth wife, the West Virginia wildcat LeeChona LaClaire (left, with her mother), who took his car to Florida and wrecked it after saying she was going for a swim in Ohio.

Jack Pfefer Collection, University Libraries of Notre Dame

Burke felt her greatest triumph was her successful tour of Japan in November 1954. But she was unnerved when the Japanese fans sat in polite silence at the matches.
Courtesy of Joe Wolfe

Joe give this one to Grandmother.

—

Darling Mother:
Had a wonderful trip over and a tremendous welcome but I'm lonely already.
Love.

Mildred.

Mildred (Burke) Younker posing before her Lincoln Continental in the 1980s. Her successful wrestling school and film business allowed her a small measure of her former riches.
Courtesy of Joe Wolfe

a few months longer for her to realize her ambition," Wolfe said the day after her death. "Had I only known, I might have saved her life."

The local paper stated Boyer was slated to make her debut the next week in Columbus at a tournament for a new junior championship that Wolfe was creating. To mark the event Wolfe had purchased a diamond ring for Boyer. Now, he said, he would give it to her mother. Boyer's mother didn't blame Wolfe. "My daughter's death was an accident that could have happened in any sport," said Selma Boyer in Minneapolis. "She was doing what she wanted, and what happened was God's will. Janet was always a strong, healthy girl, so I didn't stand in her way. If a girl wants to do something and really has her heart set on it there is no sense in standing in her way. It will only make her bitter."

The other women wrestlers blamed Billy Wolfe and Janet Boyer. "He was going to make her champion, he said," Young recalled years later in the documentary *Lipstick & Dynamite*. "He had her up in the gym all the time wrestling different people and getting hurt." Waldek might not have been charged, but she was stamped as a woman killer, since she had beaten Boyer in the earlier match. Decades later Waldek still bore the pain. "We were exonerated, but by then it was too late," she said. "I had already had publicity all over the United States and maybe further that I had caused Janet Wolfe's death. I went into the ring sometimes and everybody was calling me a murderer. I had to have guards, sometimes. But, boy, was I doing some houses. Everybody wanted to see this stupid blonde that killed Janet Wolfe."

Although Mildred was described as the dead girl's adopted or foster mother, she gave no newspaper interviews after Boyer's death and made no mention of it in her autobiography. Joe Wolfe said his mother never acted as mother to Billy Wolfe's "adopted" daughter. "That was just something Billy Wolfe did," Joe said. There is no record in Columbus that Wolfe formally adopted Boyer.

A dozen years after the death, the *Wrestling Revue* magazine, citing no medical authority, claimed Boyer died from the stomach rupture, not the brain hemorrhage, after overeating before her final matches. "Janet's stomach, bloated with beans, mashed potatoes and gassy Cokes, had apparently burst under the impact of a punishing kick to the body received during the bout," according to the magazine. "The stomach contents had spilled out, choking her insides." The article reported she was buried as Janet Boyer Wolfe. "Janet idolized Billy, and she would have wanted it that way," the magazine quoted her mother.

The tragedy stoked the backlash against women's wrestling that was never far from the surface. Cleveland councilman Harry T. Marshall asked the city's safety director to ban female wrestlers, saying Boyer's death "proves that the sport is much too hazardous for women." The *Post-Standard* in Syracuse, New York, editorialized against the women. "Perhaps we are just old fashioned and will think of all women as ideally on something of at least a little pedestal," the editorial stated. "But old fashioned or not we still find something deeply revolting about the spectacle of women slugging each other, just as we hated to see Jimmy Cagney squash a grapefruit in a lady's face years ago. With women mauling each other on the television screens and gangsters slapping glamorous blondes around in the movies, it's been several years since we've seen anyone hold open a door for a lady."

Janet Boyer's death was the first domino in a chain that led to the undoing of the sweet life the women wrestlers had been living. In the summer of 1951, as Boyer met her fate in Columbus, Mildred Burke was resting up with G. Bill in a new home Billy Wolfe had bought for the two lovers in the Woodland Hills area of Los Angeles. He paid cash for it, $20,500. Burke later wrote that Wolfe bought her the place because he owed her money from wrestling revenues and she had demanded payment in the form of a house. "By this time, between three and four million dollars had been taken into the Columbus office off my bookings," she wrote. "Naturally, I felt I had earned a home, that I had it coming." In a move that might look unusual in most families, Wolfe put the house in the name of his wife and son. The titling of the deed, Burke said, was simply a ploy on Wolfe's part. "The place was purchased by Wolfe for me," she wrote. "He kept control of the property by making G. Bill a joint tenant on the deed. This stratagem was to prevent my selling the place." At nearly four times the value of the Vermont Avenue house, the new residence befitted a champion. The 2,500-square-foot ranch-style house rested on an acre in the southwestern San Fernando Valley. It was built of stone and wood with glass-brick dividers, a swimming pool in back, and fourteen walnut trees. Millie was enormously pleased with it.

By this time she and G. Bill had been together eight years. Burke wrote that G. Bill had reached the point where he wanted their relationship to be out in the open. He had told her he intended to ask his father to divorce her so that he could marry her. "In those tender years of his life, G. Bill was still honest," she wrote. "His mind was still his own. He hated the things he saw his father doing to me in the business." Burke wrote that she was "horrified" at the thought of G. Bill going to Billy. She said she tried to talk him out of it, explaining repeatedly "how my marriage to his dad bound all our business together, both ways." It was no use; G. Bill thought it was a merely business deal, one he could negotiate with his father, she said. "G. Bill's sincerity was only exceeded by his persistence," Burke wrote. "He wouldn't give up his idea of marriage. To get some peace, I finally agreed to marry him, subject to Billy Wolfe's permission and a divorce." This passage in her autobiography is a good clue to Burke's true feelings for G. Bill. If she had not been in love with G. Bill, would she really have agreed to risk the wrath of her formidable husband just "to get some peace"?

Burke does not say when G. Bill went to Billy on his foolhardy and quixotic mission; she said only that it occurred in Billy's office at the Park Hotel. Most likely it happened shortly after Janet Boyer died. By coincidence, Wolfe had transferred the deed to the two lovers the day before Boyer's death; it is highly unlikely that he would have given an expensive new home to Burke and G. Bill after hearing that they wanted to marry. Considering that Billy Wolfe would have been grieving for his "adopted daughter," G. Bill's timing could not have been worse.

Romantic and noble as it might have been, G. Bill's approach to Billy was perilous in the extreme. It is hard to understand how either Millie or G. Bill could have thought there was the slightest chance of a happy outcome. The proposed game of musical marital chairs appears an especially unwise idea for people like Mildred Burke and Billy Wolfe, who lived their lives in the public press. It would have created a field day for the papers: Women's wrestling champion leaves husband for stepson. The scandal would have exposed the secret lives they had all been living, and it would have made all three laughingstocks in both the wrestling and the wider worlds. It would have especially humiliated Billy Wolfe, turning a man's man into a national symbol of cuckoldry at the hands of his own son. More than that, the moral opprobrium probably would have wrecked their business. That makes Billy Wolfe's reaction at least understandable. According to Mildred, he mocked his son's request, cussing him and painting her "in offensive, disgusting terms, foul enough to make his son cringe." She was "dirty," a "filthy bitch." Mildred reproduced this quote from Billy to G. Bill: "Bill, you son of a bitch, you ain't never gonna get Mildred. Me, I don't want her myself—just what I can get out of her. Hell, I'd rather have any of these bitches around here than her. No, I don't want her, but by Christ, no one else is getting her. Spread that around, and get the hell outta here."

The message was clear: Millie and G. Bill could have their little affair, Billy didn't care. But they could never marry. They could go on leading their dirty little life together as long as they stayed in the shadows. Millie was incensed at the double standard. A man could have everything he wanted, all the money and all the whoring, but a woman could have nothing but the title she had earned with her blood and sweat. "The lopsided injustice of this situation in my life seems odd by present standards, but then it was the norm," she wrote in the 1980s.

Millie and G. Bill stayed together but their relationship unraveled. "Inconsolable over not being able to marry me, G. Bill started drinking heavily," Burke wrote. Already a heavy drinker, he became a full-blown alcoholic, given to binges and blackouts. Joe Wolfe, who had returned after working much of the school year and summer for a jaundiced Billy, remembers finding G. Bill's hidden vodka bottles all over the house in Woodland Hills. G. Bill had been put into an impossible position, forced to chose between his father and his stepmother, his boss and his lover, and he was cracking under the pressure.

With the end of summer, Mildred's wrestling season began again. On September 27, 1951, she and G. Bill drove east. She was the driver now; she could not trust G. Bill in his current condition. At least they rode in style, in a beautiful new silver-on-gray Chrysler Imperial. The car had pulled slightly to the left coming from the dealer, putting extra wear on the left front tire; Burke meant to have it repaired before the trip. G. Bill was entrusted with getting the car serviced, but he was drunk coming back from the station, forcing them into a late start. In her rush Millie did not take the time to look at the tire.

They left so late they didn't even make it out of California before stopping for the evening. They put up for the night at a hotel in Barstow. When Burke got up in the morning she noticed that the left front tire was still bald. She planned on replacing it as soon as she could. They set out in the Chrysler followed by Joe, who had just turned seventeen, driving a brand-new ivory-yellow 1951 Mercury. Billy had bought the car as a thank-you for the work Joe had done that summer in the gym and for driving wrestlers for his stepfather. On September 28, they headed east on Route 66 through the Mojave Desert. G. Bill was passed out drunk on the front seat next to Millie. She later said she was driving about eighty miles an hour because she was late for her first booking, in Tulsa. They passed Ludlow, about thirty miles east of Barstow. Joe had a very good view for what happened next.

The Imperial's left front tire blew out, forcing the vehicle into a wild shimmy as the rim of the tire dug into the highway. The car fishtailed toward oncoming traffic. Millie made a split-second decision to turn hard left to avoid an approaching Chevrolet. She figured the other driver would also turn to his left, avoiding the head-on collision. She figured wrong. He turned right, T-boning the Imperial in midair off the steep shoulder of the raised highway.

Joe saw it all: the puff of air from the blown whitewall tire, his mother's car airborne, the onrushing Chevrolet slamming into it and crumpling the Imperial's rear-passenger door, the Imperial's front-passenger door bursting open, G. Bill flung from the car, the trunk popping up and ejecting a fluttering cloud of his mother's publicity material. The posters and the photographs of her posing in furs and flexing her biceps floated down and spread over the scene like confetti at a parade. It happened in an instant. Joe was convinced they were all dead.

He could see the Chevrolet's driver pinned in his seat by his car's pushed-in engine block. He was bleeding from the head. The Imperial rested atop some lava rocks on its passenger side, as if it had been carefully placed by a giant hand. As Joe sprinted toward the car he saw G. Bill lying on his back a distance away. Blood bubbled out of his mouth and his leg twisted in an unnatural position. The boy kept running toward his mother and the Imperial, its motor still cranking. The broken drive shaft thrashed on the rocks, pitching sparks into the air. Gasoline poured out of the ruptured tank and Joe feared a fire and explosion. For a moment he could picture his mother burned alive.

The Chrysler's smashed passenger side jutted about six feet into the air. He clambered on top of it, only to find the door jammed. He forced it open, reached in, and shut off the motor. He saw his mother rolled and bundled and stuffed up underneath the dashboard. She looked like a broken doll. Fingers moved on her left hand. But he couldn't get her out without help. The impact had squeezed the midsection of the car to the point that the rear doors were nearly touching.

Joe got in his car and drove at over a hundred miles per hour back to a gas station in Ludlow. Help came and they managed to get Millie out. As they carried her from the car she regained consciousness. Her first words: "How is G. Bill?" Joe decided to lie. "G. Bill is fine," Joe said. "You are the only one hurt." He did not want to give her the news that G. Bill was dead. Then they heard G. Bill moan, "My leg, my leg." Miraculously all three victims, were alive.

As Millie and G. Bill went off in separate ambulances, Joe watched bystanders gathering up his mother's publicity photos. Then he remembered the things in the glove compartment. He went back to the Imperial. The jewels and gun were still there.

Mildred had five ribs broken near the spine on her right side, a dislocated sternoclavicular joint, abrasions, lacerations, and a severe neck injury. G. Bill fared even worse; he had a fractured skull with broken bones from head to foot.

Billy Wolfe came to Barstow. At the hospital he managed to appear both concerned and unemotional. "I never really saw him get in any way, shape, or form emotional," Joe recalled. "That wasn't a really big thing in his character anyway."

G. Bill was encased in a full-body cast. Mildred, despite her injuries, left the hospital in a back brace after a week. She later said Billy Wolfe had insisted on her discharge with a "brutal ruthlessness." He rode with her back to Los Angeles, she said, forcing her to drive. "The pain was excruciating," she wrote. "Tears rolled down my cheeks.

When I asked him to drive, he looked straight ahead, expressionless. 'I don't know the way,' he said. 'You drive.'" He was angry about the injuries to his son. "During the trip, Wolfe reminded me again and again that his son was back there in the hospital, and that I was to blame," she wrote. "G. Bill couldn't be moved, or he would have been in the car with us. His father wanted me to feel guilty for a crash that his son's negligence made possible."

G. Bill's injuries required a long convalescence; he was in the body cast for more than eight months. He most likely recuperated at the home of his mother, Mickie Johnson, in Kansas City; Millie does not mention in her autobiography caring for G. Bill herself. Instead, she writes of sending a letter to G. Bill in care of his mother in Kansas City. She described it as an attempt to restore some of the old intimacy between them. She wrote of her feelings for him but also that they must accept their situation. "I told him of my love for him, and of my bitter regret that he had ever gone to his father about a divorce," she later wrote. "In sadly summarizing the affair, I said we would have to resign ourselves to separate lives as long as business bound me to his father." The attempt backfired. To her lasting regret, she said, Billy Wolfe happened to stop by his ex-wife's place the day the letter arrived and, recognizing Mildred's handwriting, he ripped the envelope open and read the contents. Burke said that Wolfe handed G. Bill the letter "with a malicious smile." The father let the son read it, then snatched it back and waved it under the younger man's nose. "You silly son of a bitch," Billy said.

Burke said Wolfe conducted an intense campaign to wean G. Bill away from her. Both men liked to drink, but while Billy could hold his liquor G. Bill could not. "His father poured the liquor to him to see if he could drink it faster than the distillery could make the stuff," Burke wrote. Billy also used sex against her. "Some of the wrestlers that Billy Wolfe controlled and who were eager to win his favor were paid to sleep with G. Bill," she later wrote. "His father introduced him to the sexual orgies that were staged at the Park Hotel." A least one other wrestler of Wolfe's confirms that the father tried to set up the son. "I think they sort of fixed him up with whatever girl they could," recalled Ruth Boatcallie, who said one of those was Carol Cook, a new and young addition to Wolfe's troupe. "According to Carol, he was very polite and good to her. She was seventeen when they sort of threw them together." Gradually, Burke said, Billy succeeded in turning G. Bill away from her and back toward him. "A clone of Billy Wolfe emerged from all this, an automaton able to do only his master's bidding," she wrote.

13

A Bout with Nell

The carefully crafted equilibrium that sustained the professional lives of Mildred Burke and Billy Wolfe, all the lies, evasions, and compromises, began to unravel after the automobile accident. With the champion injured and unable to perform, the future of the business was in doubt. Burke's injuries, of course, brought up the question of succession. Nell Stewart and June Byers had both been listed for years as the number one contender. Gloria Barattini, the beauty with the opera-trained voice, waited in the wings. It was during this period that Wolfe's allegiance to Stewart came to the fore. She had been his lover and his lady-wrestler-in-waiting for many years now. She had also become as big a draw as Burke.

Millie hated her. In her autobiography she said she heard from other wrestlers that Billy and Nell made fun of her behind her back. "One of his favorite sayings was that I was so dumb, all he had to do was throw me a hamburger or a fish and I would keep quiet," Burke wrote. "Nell Stewart once suggested that my expense allowance on the road be limited to $25 a week, since that would be more than enough." Burke said they also joked about her thirty-one-inch bust. "Although I had a near-perfect body for a female athlete, the family genes gave us all small breasts," she later wrote. "This was a source of huge humor for Billy Wolfe. He enjoyed citing the superior endowment of Nell Stewart in that category." One time, in the dressing room before a match in Atlanta, Nell cupped her thirty-eight-inch breasts and told Millie, "These are the real thing." Burke shot back: "My husband knows they're the real thing. But what's important is what's under them, the heart. When your heart gets to be the real thing, you'll have something to brag about." Millie said she then took revenge on Nell in the ring, "throwing her around like a bean bag and finishing her in two straight falls." Back in the dressing room Millie told her, "Nell, that's the *real* thing."

They had wrestled only a handful of times, when Nell was starting out and, later, when Wolfe needed last-minute substitutions. Millie, of course, always won in the worked matches. But she maintained that Stewart was a poor wrestler. "There was never an occasion on which I did not have to carry her," Burke wrote. "For the sake of the business, I made her look good before pinning her. Whatever her talents were outside the ring, wrestling was one thing that she just couldn't do." That flies in the face of what other observers, press accounts, and women wrestlers say about Stewart, and probably reflects the depths of Burke's bitterness more than anything else. Stewart was a younger woman on the rise behind Burke, touted for her beauty, who happened to be sleeping with Burke's husband. The press coverage makes it clear that Wolfe was grooming Stewart as Burke's successor. In May 1951 *Glance* magazine had posed the question: "Who is wrestling's beauty queen?" It answered with a full-page photograph of Stewart. "Blonde and buxom Nell Stewart, out turners Lana in all around beauty." A smaller, half-page photo of Mildred adorned the opposite page.

★   ★   ★

After the accident Billy Wolfe put his usual good public face on things. He wrote the editor of the NWA magazine in January 1952 that Burke was back in training. "Her wonderful muscles are starting to ripple as well as ever. Outside of cuts and bruises, the total extent of her injuries was five broken ribs." Burke later wrote that her doctors told her she needed six months to mend those ribs, but Wolfe pressured her to come back two months early. "Word's out that you're through," she said he told her. "We have to get you back in front of the public as soon as possible." She suspected it was part of his plot to replace her. "My misfortune was his big break," she wrote. "His plan was to have someone double-cross me while I was afflicted with healing ribs. He knew he would never have a better chance to get my title away from me—a goal he had been trying to achieve for years." Despite the turmoil, Wolfe would persist in sending out holiday greetings, papering over the feuds. He signed them on behalf of himself and "Mildred Burke, Nell Stewart, June Byers," and he wished his friends "a happy, peaceful and prosperous New Year."

The year 1952 would not be happy, peaceful, or prosperous for any of them. Preparations were made for Millie's first major comeback bout. Billy began by insisting that she needed to wrestle to a draw with Nell. Burke later said Wolfe told her that her constant winning was "ruining her gate." Burke was convinced he wanted the title to use for his own sexual gain. "My integrity in defending the title, and my scandal-free tenure of the championship, blocked Wolfe from all the sexual juggling and trading that he wished to do with the various women he had under contract," she wrote. "All of them were promised the championship at one time or another, and the next thing they knew they would be between the sheets."

To make things even more humiliating for Burke, Wolfe wanted her to lose a fall to Stewart in a sleeper hold, which would have forced the champion to feign passing out in the challenger's arms. They began to argue about it and it blew up into a terrific verbal row. They went after each other's perceived shortcomings. He lashed into her about her breasts: "You should take a look at Nell Stewart and some of the other girls and see what real tits are like." Burke said she shot back: "What I lack, I can make up for by buying a padded bra. What you're small on, you can't do anything for." She didn't stop there. She told him that the word was out in his harem that he was a lousy lay. "He fancied himself a great lover, but he was like a drunken sailor reeling from one prostitute to another, and the girls laughed at him in secret," she later wrote. "For years he had been buying every sexual favor he enjoyed, one way or another. His manly attraction for a womanly woman in freedom was absolutely zero, and I told him so." At this, Burke wrote, Wolfe seemed to come unhinged. "Again he went through those ghastly, Jekyll-and-Hyde convulsions that I had first seen when we crossed from Missouri into Kansas to join the carnival. . . . His fury was demonic and total."

She finally agreed to the worked draw with Nell, however. "Arguing all afternoon with Billy Wolfe would grind down anyone," she later wrote. "His willpower was like a bludgeon."

Wolfe staged a prematch publicity session that was so thick with irony, undercurrents, and campy patter that it seems of a piece with the coming Pop Art movement that would break out in the culture citadels of the nation several years later. On February 7, 1952, the Ohio *State Journal* ran a large picture with the caption, "A Wolfe and Two Ladies." It showed Billy Wolfe sitting between Stewart and Burke at a lunch table in the Southern Hotel, the upscale hotel Millie used as her base when she came into Columbus. The sports columnist gave over his entire column to hype their upcoming match. "Two natural wild minks coats were hung gently on hooks by four lovely hands covered with headlight diamonds, the gorgeous blue-eyed blonde and the dazzling green-eyed redhead sat down to our left and right, and men diners all over the Southern Hotel dining room worked desperately to get the eyes back in their heads."

The columnist engaged them in a conversation about their upcoming match at the Coliseum, a Saturday night benefit for the Damon Runyon Cancer Fund. The repartee was as worked as any wrestling match, but the cattily ostentatious sniping also provided a glimpse of the cold loathing just beneath the surface.

Burke: "Oh, that's two days off yet—I'd much rather tell you about my new home up in Woodland Hills, Los Angeles. It adjoins Betty Grable's and Harry James' place, has a wonderful swimming pool, and a modernistic kitchen where I can cook fried chicken to my heart's content."

Stewart: "That's exactly what I want one of these days. My mother taught me to cook when I was just 10 years old; I've got a lovely hotel apartment, but there's hardly enough room for myself and my little Chihuahua."

Burke: "I have a cute boxer pup that I've named 'Champ.' When I was hurt in that auto accident four months ago he wouldn't leave my bedside. He's simply dear, and oh how he likes fried chicken."

Stewart then said she envied Burke because she could not yet afford to feed her dog Sheila fried chicken on $12,000 a year; by the time she got to be Burke's age, she said, she, too, would be pulling down $50,000 a year with neighbors like Grable and James.

Burke: "What was that you said about my age? I'm only 36, you know. What age are you using now?"

Stewart: "I'm just 25—began wrestling when I was 15. I was just thinking, Mildred, you broke in way back when there weren't any girl wrestlers. I remember that you were matched with almost 200 men before you could get any lady competition."

Burke: "Yes, and I beat all 200 of them, too. And I don't know that I've *ever* had any 'lady' competition."

Nell reminded her that they had wrestled once before.

Burke: "I repeat the statement."

The columnist tried to change the subject. He asked Nell if it was true that she gave up being a waitress in Birmingham to make more money wrestling to support her widowed mother and two brothers.

Burke stepped in with an answer that was a shot at Stewart: "She gave up being a waitress. I gave up being an interior decorator."

Stewart fired back: "Mildred, did I tell you I now drive a 180–horsepower automobile, that they are now billing me as 'Wrestling's Betty Grable,' and that I am the popular choice to soon take away your championship?"

The fidgety columnist again tried to change the subject. He asked Burke to name her two favorite hobbies.

Burke: "Diamonds and mink coats." The columnist then reported that she smiled sweetly at Stewart and a waiter across the room dropped a tray after being blinded by the glare from Burke's five-carat ring.

The columnist asked Burke if she had any new holds for the match.

Burke: "No. I'll probably employ the same holds I used to beat Nell last year in our only other match. I can tell you that I, myself, am a lady in the ring and very seldom use a 'give up' hold. I prefer to use the alligator clutch, for instance—merely an uncomfortable maneuver."

Stewart: "The body backdrop is still my favorite. That's the one I accidentally broke my sister's leg with in her backyard in Birmingham last summer. But I've got a new one I'm going to test on you Saturday night, Mildred. And by the way, did you know that Gladys Gillem, who taught me most of what I know about wrestling, now has an animal act with five lions?"

Burke: "You better bring some of the lions in with you Saturday night."

Stewart: "I can't understand why you named that hound 'Champ.' I hope it doesn't inconvenience you to have to change its name after Saturday night."

Burke: "I've got his name spelled out in uncut diamonds on the collar. But they are just a few I had left over anyway."

For Stewart, the moment appeared to have arrived. Wolfe ensured that she got the buildup over Burke in the local papers. It was Nell who received the Mildred Burke treatment now. The reporters wrote of her many ring injuries—broken collarbone, ribs, kneecaps, ankle, torn ligaments, and sprained fingers—and her self-designed ring robes, wrestling suits, and boots. "Her choicest robe is princess styled American Beauty velvet with startling cuffs and back panel of wedding stain hand embroidered in red, blue, orchid, rust and peach silks outlined in brilliants," the Columbus *Star* noted. "The panel alone cost $300." Stewart's ambition burst from the page. "I have my hopes pinned on the world championship," she said. "When I get that I'll retire and become a promoter and stop living out of a suitcase."

Millie got into the ring with Nell on February 9, 1952, before a huge crowd of 9,500 at the Fairgrounds Coliseum in Columbus, Ohio. The match was declared a draw, with each woman having won a single fall when the sixty-minute time limit expired. In wrestling parlance, such an extended draw was known as putting on "a Broadway," or a really good show. In an article in the NWA magazine that was no doubt Billy Wolfe's handiwork the bout was described as an instant classic. "Jack Dempsey, who refereed, and Bernarr Macfadden, famous physical culturist, both declared the contest the greatest they had ever seen between women wrestlers," the NWA coverage stated. "Any doubts anyone might have had about who was someday going to be the boss of the lady wrestlers were dispelled when Nell Stewart held Champion Mildred Burke to a draw in their classic tangle . . . It was the first time the Mauling Mildred had failed to win a match since she won the Ladies' Wrestling Championship. The result—which came after Nell had taken the second fall and was on the verge of victory in the decisive third when the time limit bell clanked—clearly established the gorgeous Nell as the heir apparent to the crown."

The quotes attributed to Nell herself were confident and cocky. "The more I think about it, the more I know I should have won the match," she said. "Frankly, I got so wrapped up in wrestling and was so excited over the knowledge I had Mildred beaten, I forgot all about the time limit . . . Mildred was saved by the bell this time, but next time she can't have that edge—and I'll be the new champion." Mildred must have been piqued by Stewart's bubbly confidence but her own comments reflected her stoical and practical nature. "Titles are won— and lost—in the ring," she said. "At the proper time and in the proper place I'll give Nell another shot at my crown . . . I'm tickled pink that there's such a worthy opponent around. It's good for the game—and my pocketbook." She promised to take care of Stewart in a rematch. "I was slightly stale after the long layoff I had to take because of my accident. I'll take on Nell anywhere, under any conditions—and I'll give her a wrestling lesson she'll never forget."

Burke later wrote that the match had repulsed her. "In the ring, the bout went against my principles entirely, because Nell Stewart was such a feeble competitor. Making her look good and not stinking out the arena was a hard task. My healing ribs hurt like the devil."

She did not have to wait long to get her revenge. Although Burke and Stewart were his two biggest draws, Wolfe usually kept his wife and mistress from wrestling each other, for obvious reasons. After having a few matches when Nell was starting out during the war, they had faced each other only a few times in the ensuing seven years. Now illness and injuries to other wrestlers forced Wolfe to book Stewart and Burke into a series of matches around the country. Millie and Nell wrestled in Little Rock, Joplin, Memphis, Chattanooga, Albuquerque, El Paso, and Tucson. His hands full running the business in Columbus, Wolfe sent them on the road alone. "Wolfe would not be along to ramrod the results," Burke wrote. "This was like putting your pet pussycat outside and closing the door, when you know there is a German shepherd on the prowl." Burke said she relished what came next. "In Albuquerque and three other cities I gave Nell Stewart the royal treatment. Every time, I beat her two straight falls in a total of not more than five minutes for each match." Burke then clipped the newspaper accounts of the bouts— "They all recounted how rapidly Nell Stewart had been slammed and pinned and 'completely outclassed'"—and sent them to Wolfe and promoters and sports editors. "This destroyed Billy Wolfe's plan to put her over as the new champion on the basis of that phony draw in Columbus," Burke wrote. The surviving newspaper accounts don't quite match Mildred's memory of the bouts. None of them was over in less than five minutes, and they were clearly worked matches where the wrestlers dragged out the action and traded falls. In Memphis, they wrestled to another one-hour draw. In Joplin, they put on a three-fall, twenty-minute match won by Burke that featured her "wearing a nifty-looking, perforated black suit, black shoes and striking chartreuse trim," and Stewart in an "aqua-blue job, accentuated by silver and red shoes." At the end of the day Burke could claim nine defenses of her title against Stewart with no defeats.

Yet Nell was clearly on the rise. In August 1952 the influential NWA magazine put her on the cover in a revealing two-piece bathing suit and called her "Crown Princess Nell."

A few weeks later it all came to a head in Los Angeles. Everyone had come into town for the NWA's annual convention in Santa Monica in the first week of September. Billy Wolfe chose this occasion to take Mildred to a dinner at a "really high-class" restaurant on Ventura Boulevard with G. Bill and Joe. "My heart sank," she later wrote. "He loved nothing more in this world than to get into classy restaurants and then let fly at me with his filthy mouth at bullhorn volume. People would stare at us as though we were scum, and I would nearly die of embarrassment."

In the restaurant, Wolfe told her it was time to lose to Nell. This must have seemed entirely reasonable to Wolfe. Millie had held the title for fourteen years, longer than any champion up to that point, male or female. Even Strangler Lewis had given up the title for the good of the business. Millie had been badly hurt and she was aging just as Nell was coming into her own. Wolfe must have thought the time had come for the title to be traded among his women; the attendant drama no doubt would have boosted business. It also would have helped Wolfe with his girlfriends. Instead of gracefully bowing out, though, Burke had returned to what she considered her rightful place, beating Nell and all the others in matches all over the country. Wolfe must have felt that this woman who had helped build his business was now holding that business hostage. For Burke, there was nothing reasonable about giving up the title; it was her only power over Wolfe. She simply refused to lose to Nell. "If you think she's good enough to beat me, just let her do it," she told Wolfe. "I'll wrestle her anywhere, anytime you say. If she beats me she gets the title. But that's the only way she's getting it." Joe Wolfe recalled that things escalated from there. "They said, 'Okay, it's going to be me against you,'" he remembered fifty-five years later. With G. Bill on his side, Billy began to berate Mildred in his loud voice that everyone could hear.

She fled the table in tears.

Joe came out to console her.

"If I lose to Nell Stewart, he'll kick me out without a dime," she said she told Joe. "He'll see I never get another title match in my life. He's got all my money. The title is all I've got, Joe."

The Wolfes came out into the parking lot. Everyone sullenly got into the car and the argument continued, with G. Bill driving, Billy in the front seat, Millie and Joe in the back. "When G. Bill stopped at his favorite liquor store for some cactus juice, Billy Wolfe leaned back over the front seat and punched me in the face with all his force," she wrote. "Sparks and stars danced before my eyes."

"You dumb son of a bitch," Wolfe told her, she wrote, "when I tell you to lose to Nell Stewart, you lose to Nell Stewart. You lie down when I tell you!"

"'Nothing doing,' I cried. 'You can sit there and punch all day, but I'm not losing to Nell Stewart.'"

She and Joe got out of the car. The clerk in the liquor store serving G. Bill was staring at them. Billy Wolfe ran to the door and stuck his head inside. "Just a little family quarrel," he told the clerk. "Don't pay attention to the lady. Thanks." Joe was shoved back in the car.

G. Bill came out of the store carrying his bottle, stashed it in the trunk, and came to his father's aid, Burke wrote. She said G. Bill blocked her path of retreat into the liquor store, allowing his father to catch her from behind. "What now ensued was like one of those beautifully choreographed Hollywood beatings that you see in movies, where everything is perfectly timed by stuntmen," she wrote. "This was starkly and painfully real."

She said the two men worked her over as a team. "First they punched me back and forth between them," she said. "Only my devotion to training and my washboard abdominal muscles saved me from permanent injury. Punches slammed into my ribs, my kidneys, solar plexus and breasts. The two men hit everywhere as hard as they could. Warding off such a rain of blows was impossible. G. Bill grabbed me in a hammerlock. His father relentlessly punched me in the face and chest while I was pinioned. Punching, slugging, smashing at me while teenage Joe yelled helplessly at them to stop, the two of them dragged and shoved me across the sidewalk. They were going to stuff me in the car. When my head wouldn't lower under the door, Billy Wolfe slammed my face again and again into the car roof. The noise was like a body and fender man pounding out a dent. Blood pouring out of the cuts went all over me and splashed on the sidewalk in a crimson pool."

It is safe to say that something happened that night. We have Mildred's account of the incident but not the Wolfes'. It is difficult to believe that G. Bill joined in the beating with any particular vigor. He had just spent nearly a year in a body cast, recovering from injuries that would leave him with a permanent limp. Three weeks earlier, a newspaper article had pointed out that G. Bill was still too badly injured to attend one of Burke's matches. Perhaps G. Bill merely stood by and allowed Billy to strike the blows. Perhaps he tried to intervene, ineffectually, and she took that as complicity. In any case, Burke viewed his actions that night as extreme cowardice and betrayal. Joe, who had just turned eighteen at the time, does not have a clear memory fifty-six years after the occurrence, other than that the fight had started with Billy insisting that Millie lose to Nell. Joe said his vantage point in the car did not allow him to see much. "I don't remember the blows, but I remember some of the pushing and shoving before that," Joe recalled. "Maybe they shoved me in the car for a reason. I saw the beginning of it. I remember them putting me in the car and watching a scuffle." He does remember that his mother was injured, but not the pools of blood. "All I remember is saying something about the bruising on her face," he said. "If I was in that car and that happened somewhere outside the car, I don't have a clear recollection of that."

She said they finally got exhausted from hitting her and trying to force her into the car. "They were arm weary, and didn't have the strength to punch any more," she said. "They started talking, while I bled profusely from cuts over my eyes, on my cheeks and forehead. My face looked like fresh hamburger." In the interlude, she said, she was able to run into the liquor store and appeal to the clerk, who threatened to call the police. Then, she said, the Wolfes tried to placate her and make peace. "Let's go home and talk it over. Get a shower and clean up. Relax a bit. Everything will be okay, Millie." But she was reeling from the worst beating of her life, "in or out of the ring," and in no mood to make up. She refused their offer, instead waiting for her mother and brother to come for her and Joe. "The agony in my mother's heart came welling out of her face," Burke wrote. "She said nothing. She didn't have to. Rather did she do what was important, taking me immediately to a hospital in Pasadena, where she put me under her own doctor." Burke had a lacerated face and cracked ribs. Her mother had the injuries photographed and urged her to go to the NWA and the Los Angeles police.

"What dissuaded me from it when I viewed the whole thing with a calm heart was that I would destroy the star status I had built," she later wrote. "The legal action would undoubtedly ruin Billy Wolfe, and probably land him in prison. He deserved much worse in the eyes of many. Whatever satisfaction that might give me, I would emerge from such a struggle unavoidably tarnished, diminished in the eyes of the thousands of fans who looked up to me as a champion. . . . Any time the private problems of any kind of star become public knowledge, a little part of her glitter dies. How also could I avoid appearing as anything but a 21-carat idiot for remaining tied to a man who beat me to a pulp?"

Her relationship with G. Bill at this point is even harder to fathom. She is vague about G. Bill and how they split apart, suggesting in her later writings that they were never really a couple and that things just petered out. Joe's memory was that the restaurant beating marked the point at which the great, long-simmering battle with Billy broke out into the open. But even Joe is uncertain about what happened with G. Bill, beginning after the auto accident. "The one thing that has always puzzled me is her closeness and relationship with G. Bill and how he felt about what happened after that accident, because that kind of really tipped off the end of Millie and Billy Wolfe," Joe recalled. "I never knew. Was G. Bill put into a position where he had to make a decision at that point?"

Burke was supposed to make an appearance at the NWA convention but the injuries to her face wouldn't allow that. She said all the promoters wondered where she was because they knew she lived in Los Angeles and she had talked about bringing them out to see her new home. She later learned that Billy Wolfe told them she had cancer and that her career was over. "The cancer lie was a cunning stroke that typified Billy Wolfe," she wrote. One promoter and old friend, Salvador Lutteroth of Mexico City, insisted on seeing her. When he showed up, the room was darkened and heavy makeup hid her injuries. "When he came into my room, despite the shadows I could see his look of deep sorrow," she wrote. "I didn't understand then that he thought he was saying farewell to a cancer terminal. He held my hand, patted my arm and his dark eyes were moist." She said he told her, "Please get well. We all love you."

Sometime after the beating in LA, Mildred moved out of the Woodland Hills ranch house. At first, she refused to let Wolfe handle any more of her bookings. But when she approached NWA members such as Morris Sigel in Houston and Leroy McGuirk in Tulsa, she was turned away. Sigel told her he could book her only through her husband. She was forced to return to him. When she got back out on the road, she found that he had been telling people either that she was dying of cancer or that she was rich and headed toward retirement. In any case, he booked her into only a handful matches and her money soon began to run out.

The California beating gave her the impetus to finally break with him. It "had changed me fundamentally," Mildred wrote. "I wanted to be done with this rotten individual with the same intensity that I had first wanted to be a wrestler." She hired lawyers and a private detective, who tailed Wolfe and caught him in the act with Nell. "Subject and Nell Stewart arrived at Nell's apartment, 1742 East Broad St., at 9:20 p.m. on Friday, December 5, 1952. Nell was driving the car. They removed much clothing from the trunk. Nell carrying the clothing and subject carrying a suit case . . . No one entered or left the apartment after their arrival . . . Saturday morning December 6,

1952, at 10:20 a.m. Nell came out and went to the grocery at Nelson & Broad Streets." The mundane details captured the cheating that had been occurring for years. The detective sent along his report and a caution about money. "We will wait for further instructions from you as to how much more information you need," the detective wrote. "You know time means money and we have spent a lot of time."

Oddly, ordinary business got done. With G. Bill out of the picture, Billy Wolfe lined up a new driver for Millie. On December 11, 1952, a Mrs. Margaret Williams of Los Angeles signed a document giving consent for her seventeen-year-old son, Bert Leroy Younker, to travel with Mildred Burke "to help drive and assist in her management and her to be his temporary guardian. This is at the request of her husband, William H. Wolfe."

Burke still had her position in the wrestling world. *Boxing and Wrestling* magazine still listed Burke as champion and Stewart as top challenger. "Mildred Burke still reigns supreme, and looks like doing so until she chooses to step down and quit the game." But Wolfe still controlled the bookings, the money, and the publicity. The NWA magazine, undoubtedly mouthing his position, gave an ominous indication of what lay ahead. "Beauteous Nell Stewart, shown here in flight, made the biggest noise in women's division during Miss Burke's enforced idleness," the magazine's editors wrote in their December 1952 issue summing up the year in wrestling. "Many think Nell will be the next champion, possibly defeating hitherto unbeaten Mildred."

Money became the most pressing problem. Burke and Wolfe had never been as flush with cash as their publicity proclaimed. They lived high and flashy but that was as much for show as anything else. The claims about Millie's earnings were no doubt exaggerated somewhat, another bit of hype to build the gate. Since most of the records are lost, it is hard to gauge exactly how much she and Wolfe made. In 1943, the first time she talked to a reporter about her earnings, she said that in the previous year she had paid taxes on $22,000, a considerable sum during the war years and the equivalent of a top baseball player's salary. Most likely that figure was for Wolfe's entire business; they were married, after all, and their taxes would have been jointly filed. The number claimed for Mildred's own earnings went up to $25,000 in 1944, $50,000 in 1949, and $100,000 in 1951, the last figure reported by the venerable *Wall Street Journal*. By comparison, Babe Didrikson Zaharias, the top female golfer of the era, earned $15,087 in 1951.

Such figures provided by wrestlers always have to be taken with a grain of salt. Hype about money was one of the hallmarks of the carny ethos from which Burke and Wolfe had emerged. Where detailed records exist, the true numbers are always lower. For example, Nature Boy Buddy Rogers, a top male star on par with Burke, netted $19,231 in 1948, according to detailed payment records kept by Jack Pfefer. Mildred wrote in her unpublished autobiography that an IRS agent called her in Los Angeles to tell told her that her husband claimed a gross of $250,000 for his entire business in 1951, when he was at his height and had thirty women wrestling for him; this figure also shows up in a detailed magazine profile of Wolfe written that year, giving it a measure of credence. Three years later, amid a downturn in the wrestling business, Wolfe's yearly revenue for his entire business was $30,073.15, generating a profit of $5,304.66, his surviving records show. Burke wrote that she brought in more than $150,000 in 1953–54.

"Certainly, I was the first million-dollar athlete in history," and she added that she may have earned more than $4 million in the course of her career, which seems high. "The true tally of my earnings will never be known," she wrote. "The accurate numbers were buried in Billy Wolfe's labyrinthine bookkeeping, and his financial secrets died with him."

In any case, Wolfe's total control of the money left her nearly destitute within months. With few funds coming in she found herself in December 1952 living in an ordinary tract house in Canoga Park.

As expenses mounted, she cabled her old friend Jack Pfefer, perhaps for business advice, perhaps to get new bookings, perhaps for money. "Dear Jack, it is most urgent and confidential that you call me tonight," she said on December 20, 1952. At the end of the month she wrote again: "It is very important that I get my divorce right away. As soon as I get that I will contact you. Thanks for everything."

The real battle was about to begin.

14

A Bout with Billy

By Mildred Burke's account it was she who asked Billy Wolfe for the divorce in late 1952. She said he was stunned. "He never expected me to come and demand what was rightfully mine—bought and paid for with blood and bruises," she wrote in her autobiography. "He actually thought that he could throw me a fish and I would be happy."

This would be no simple divorce. More important than the marriage was the business, but the two were so inextricably entwined that unraveling one could not be done without unraveling the other. Now everything was put into play.

Wolfe recovered quickly from his shock. "We went round and round verbally just like a couple of wrestlers looking for an opening," Burke wrote. "His control of the business was absolute, and it was plain that he wasn't going to give me my share unless I fought him at law." She may have thought of the struggle in wrestling terms; it was anything but. It was a battle of wits, and Billy Wolfe easily outmatched her.

If she was intent on fighting Wolfe via the law, the way she went about it showed how confused and ill-equipped she was for such a contest. Instead of suing him for divorce in Los Angeles and accusing him of infidelity with Nell Stewart, she gave in to his demand to have the whole thing handled by lawyers he knew in Missouri. Perhaps she was constrained by her own infidelity with G. Bill.

In any case, she allowed Billy to sue her for divorce in the county seat of Hickory County, Missouri, not far from where Wolfe maintained his longtime mail drop at the telephone exchange run by his older brother George in Wheatland. On December 30, 1952, Billy Wolfe filed a petition for divorce against "Mildred Bliss Wolfe" in the Hickory County circuit court. The grounds: desertion. While he had been faithful and treated her "at all times with kindness and affection," she had "wholly disregarded her duties as the wife," leaving "the home of the parties in the month of July, 1951." Given that he and Mildred had not lived together for at least eight years, one wonders why he chose July 1951; the only outward significance of that date is that it was the month Janet Boyer died, and most probably around the time when G. Bill had asked Billy for Millie's hand in marriage. Perhaps he chose the date because he felt that was the moment when his wife had violated the agreement that held their sham marriage together.

Even so, the charge of desertion was a shockingly brazen claim. And demonstrably false. First off, the homes of the parties were in Los Angeles and Columbus, not Wheatland, where Wolfe now claimed to have been a resident for "one whole year." In his representations to the Missouri court Wolfe was telling lies under oath.

Instead of challenging him, Burke acquiesced. In a document filed by Wolfe's Missouri lawyer along with the divorce petition, Burke signed her legal name, "Mildred Bliss Wolfe," and agreed to allow the divorce to go through without a hearing. She asked for no property or alimony. It is unclear why she willingly gave up so much leverage in the divorce battle that might have helped her later in the business dispute. In her unpublished autobiography, she makes clear that she wanted to avoid a protracted legal battle. "In my mood of determination to be rid of him," fighting Wolfe legally "made no sense to me," she wrote. She was walking away without a dime from the marriage, because "only on this basis would Billy Wolfe part with me legally. That is the way the divorce was set up and run through the Missouri courts by Wolfe's cunning lawyer and tax expert. I was free, but had paid a hell of a price: my total earnings from twenty years of professional wrestling. Never for a moment did I think that it wasn't worth the millions that it took to cleanse myself of the vicious man with whom I had become enmeshed for the sake of my ambition."

If that is how she saw things, she was allowing herself to be ruled by her heart rather than her head. And she was acting on some very bad legal advice. One clue to what happened may lie with the lawyer who represented Burke in the Missouri divorce. He was George R. Hedges, a Columbus attorney who subsequent events and records later revealed to have a far greater allegiance to Wolfe than to his soon-to-be ex-wife.

She didn't care about the marriage; the only thing she wanted from Wolfe was her freedom to wrestle on her own as champion. After all was said and done that championship belt was the most valuable item in the business. The agreement over the divorce merely set the stage for the far more important resolution of the business dispute.

Burke's fortitude and work ethic allowed her to keep functioning as a wrestler during this time. She was still a draw. "Record Crowd Sees Burke Win," headlined the paper in Tucson, where she entertained 3,000 on January 7, 1953. Four days after that match, as the divorce wended its way through the Missouri courts, Burke traveled to St. Louis to ask the National Wrestling Alliance to resolve the business dispute. Now that the divorce terms had been agreed upon, the business terms needed to be set. Since neither Wolfe nor Burke trusted the other, the NWA, the powerful ruling body of wrestling, was needed by both to act as mediator. On a cold Sunday morning that found a large portion of the heavily Catholic city in church, Millie appeared outside an NWA meeting at the plush Claridge Hotel, where Sam Muchnick maintained his offices. Wolfe, an NWA member, was allowed into the meeting. But Mildred was forced to sit in the lobby and await the alliance's decision regarding her fate. She caught NWA members on the way in, buttonholing anyone who would listen about her troubles with Wolfe.

A committee of five NWA members immediately was assigned to sit with the couple and arbitrate. Millie picked two of the members, Leroy McGuirk, the blind Tulsa promoter and onetime collegiate wrestling champion who she knew hated Wolfe, and Ray Welch, the promoter in Tennessee; Wolfe also picked two, the Houston promoter Morris Sigel and New Orleans promoter Joe Gunther. Eddie Quinn, the Montreal promoter, was added as a neutral member. The committee met with Burke and Wolfe that day and resolved that the solution was for one to buy the other out. Millie said she would sell for $50,000. Billy Wolfe threw up his hands and said that was too much. He then offered to sell to her for $30,000. Although she was broke she accepted his terms.

"He immediately agreed to get out of the managing and booking business, and this should have made me suspicious," Burke later wrote. She should have been suspicious about a lot of things, starting with the NWA itself, which within a year would be under federal investigation as an illegal monopoly that blackballed wrestlers and promoters on behalf of its members. With regard to the Burke-Wolfe dispute, the organization's true sympathies and allegiance were with protecting the interests of its member Wolfe. In St. Louis, as the NWA meeting continued the next day on to a host of other matters, Muchnick felt the need to bring up the dispute behind closed doors with the members, Wolfe among them. Burke, of course, had no idea about what was transpiring. "Another problem faces us," said Muchnick, then the most powerful man in wrestling. "Personally, I think that the trouble between Mildred Burke and Billy Wolfe is strictly a marital matter and not for us to get involved in, but Mildred has sent me a wire applying for membership in the alliance and stating that she is going to open a booking office for girls. Billy Wolfe had been a member of this group, has paid his dues, and has always been willing to cooperate with alliance members. Whatever Billy and Mildred do regarding their personal affairs is their own business."

A written version of Muchnick's speech later fell into the hands of the feds investigating the NWA. It contained two crossed-out passages that revealed where Muchnick really stood. On Burke's application for NWA membership Muchnick wrote, "I cannot concur in that. Firstly, I believe that this is a man's organization and am not in favor of women being admitted." As for who the NWA should support in the dispute, Muchnick left no doubt: "Insofar as wrestling is concerned, I think we have a good booker for girl wrestlers and should all stick with him. There is no law in the world that says that we cannot pick our talent from whomsoever we choose."

Needless to say, Burke was unsuccessful in her attempt to become the NWA's first female member.

Now that Burke had agreed to Wolfe's price she had to find the money. She turned to Ray Welch and Leonard Schwartz, a Chicago promoter, who agreed to back her. But then both men backed out. It came out later that Schwartz had put in a call to NWA member Al Haft, Wolfe's close confederate, to tell him about the investment he was about to make with Burke. "You're buying something I wouldn't buy," Haft told Schwartz, according to someone who was in Haft's office when the call came in.

Desperate, Millie had to scrounge up the money from a motley collection of Columbus investors. She got $5,000 from George Hedges, the attorney who had failed to challenge Wolfe's false assertions in the Missouri divorce. She got another $2,500 from James L. Moats, the detective who had caught Billy Wolfe with Nell Stewart, then warned Burke about spending too much money on the case. She also received $12,000 from attorney Curtis H. Porter, who would go on to represent Billy Wolfe in subsequent legal matters. The money was accompanied by notes personally guaranteeing repayment by Burke on behalf of a corporation Porter and Hedges were setting up with her called Attractions, Inc. Burke's "sweat equity" would give her ownership of 50 percent of the corporation's stock, while the rest went to the partners who had lent the money to buy out Wolfe. But the notes also transferred all of the risk for the deal onto Burke. They contained an unusual and highly draconian provision that made her extremely vulnerable in the event the corporation missed a single one of the twice-a-year payments of principal and interest. The provision was a "confession of judgment" by Attractions, Inc., which allowed any attorney to go into court without notifying Burke, put the corporation in receivership under the administration of a judge, and obtain a judgment for payment in full. The corporation waived all rights to appeal. It is almost certain that Burke, a ninth-grade dropout, had little idea of what she was signing.

She delivered the $30,000, in cash, in an attaché case at another meeting with Wolfe in St. Louis brokered by the NWA on January 26, 1953. She considered the proceedings bizarre and rushed—barely two weeks had passed since she had agreed to buy Wolfe out. She didn't understand why the payment had to be in cash, but she was relying on the advice of Hedges and Porter. Looking on were G. Bill, Muchnick, and Lou Thesz, the reigning NWA heavyweight wrestling champion. Billy Wolfe agreed in writing to refrain from promoting women's wrestling in the United States for five years. Burke reiterated her agreement, already stated in the Missouri divorce papers, to give up all claims to alimony and property. Muchnick told her the NWA would "stand behind the contract" to prevent Wolfe from competing with her, she later recalled.

After the meeting wrapped up she was approached by Lou Thesz. As the heavyweight champion of wrestling's ruling monopoly, he was not just a major draw but also the most respected man in the business. Thesz was a "hooker," the last of the champions who could really wrestle. Gorgeous George may have made wrestling more popular with his outrageous antics, but Lou Thesz was an honored link to wrestling's storied past, a reminder that the sport had once held men like Frank Gotch, Joe Stecher, and Ed Lewis. Eschewing fancy outfits or silly gimmicks, Thesz preferred to wrestle in simple black trunks and boots. In the ring he was a tiger-muscled man with catlike quickness and grace, a tough master of wrestling holds who could shoot when the occasion called for it. Fast and exciting to watch, Thesz never failed to draw fans. Old-style promoters who might be embarrassed by having to put Gorgeous George or women wrestlers on their cards were proud and honored to host Thesz. Thesz, the traditionalist, was himself no fan of women's wrestling. The NWA would even come up with the "Thesz rule," an instruction to its members not to put the male champion on cards with women. Still, he had posed in publicity pictures squeezing Burke's biceps and he had wrestled on cards with her that drew headlines and huge crowds in Kansas City and elsewhere. After the St. Louis meeting Thesz, an honorable man, felt the need to warn Burke about Wolfe. As Millie left Muchnick's suite of offices, Thesz told her, "Watch yourself in the clinches, Mildred," she later recalled.

Two weeks later Wolfe was granted a divorce. It had taken a mere forty-three days. Burke, upon failing to appear for a hearing, was found in default and Wolfe was judged to be "an innocent and injured party." He made sure that the news made it into the papers, along with the desertion claim. He got his divorce, and Burke got nothing but a divorce. However, she now had the business, and that was what was important to her. Eight days after her divorce was final Burke wrestled black challenger Babs Wingo in Kansas City before a crowd of 8,972 in what was billed as "the first interracial wrestling championship." But Burke's moments of triumph would be fleeting. She had walked into Wolfe's trap.

Billy Wolfe had always run the business without contracts, so secure was he in his control of the women who worked for him. He had a firm grip on the title through Burke and the backing of the NWA monopoly. No major promoter could book women in any big city without running up against Wolfe and the NWA. No female claimant to the title received any traction while Burke, the unassailable champion, was active in the ring.

In buying the business from Wolfe, Burke was really paying him to allow her to use her title and the relationships they had built with the twenty-six NWA members whose offices put women's wrestling matches on cards in hundreds of venues throughout the nation. Burke may have had the title but she was not an NWA member; soon her relationships with the major promoters would be tested. Her relationships with the women wrestlers would be tested as well. Burke may have been free to go off and start wrestling for herself and booking women into matches, but all the female wrestlers, none of whom were under contract to either Wolfe or Burke, were now free agents, too. Standing aloof as the pampered champion, Burke did not have the bond with the other women wrestlers that Wolfe did; they did not fear her as they did him. He may have been their tyrant, but he was also their father figure. Still, in a sign that many were disaffected with Wolfe and saw a new era dawning, three dozen women agreed at the outset to wrestle for Burke.

On March 4, 1953, less than three weeks after the divorce was final, Wolfe struck. Three things occurred that day that reveal that

Wolfe was putting his house in order for the coming battle with Burke. First, Burke and G. Bill signed off on the sale of the Woodland Hills house, which went for $19,000, a loss; this severed Burke's legal ties to the Wolfes and took away the last legal leverage she had against them. Second, G. Bill transferred the deed to a house at 1315 Franklin Avenue in Columbus to his father for $1, clear evidence that they were working together; most likely Billy and G. Bill were arranging things as they saw fit between themselves prior to the third maneuver happening that day: a new wrestling business was incorporated, Girl Wrestling Enterprises, Inc., with Nell Stewart, secretary, and June Byers, treasurer, as the legal front for the operation. It is easy to see what happened. As soon as the sale of the Woodland Hills house went through and Burke could no longer block it, the Wolfes were free to mount a business offensive against her, under the cover of Stewart and Byers.

Girl Wrestling Enterprises was really just Stewart and Byers, in league with a few other women closely tied to Wolfe. In case the connections needed to be made any clearer, the new business listed its address at 261 South High Street, the site of Haft's Gym, where Wolfe had kept an office for years. To add insult to injury, G. Bill married Byers a few weeks later. "Billy always had the girlfriends and when he finished with them G. Bill had them," recalled Kathleen Wimbley, one of Wolfe's black wrestlers. "G. Bill had her and he married her." G. Bill and June took up residence at the Columbus house that G. Bill had just transferred to Billy.

Since the new enterprise was run by his girlfriend and his daughter-in-law and not Billy Wolfe himself, the arrangement nominally appeared to get around his noncompete agreement with Burke. But it was obvious to everybody what was really happening. "Mildred and those attorneys should have been smart enough to know that [the Wolfes] were going to stay in the business," Ida May Martinez said. "That was just silly."

The NWA, instead of enforcing Burke's agreement with Wolfe, appeared to bless the new competition. "So now there will be two rival major leagues in women's wrestling," proclaimed the April 1953 issue of the NWA magazine. "At the start there may be a struggle for supremacy between them, just as there was in professional baseball at the turn of the century when the American League was formed in competition with the National League . . . Let us hope things will work out equally as well with the futures of these women wrestlers." That went beyond wishful thinking. The crowds had fallen off and everyone knew there wasn't enough business to go around. To Millie, it must have seemed a cruel joke, drenched in Billy Wolfe's particular brand of mendacity.

The next month, full-scale war was declared with competing full-page ads in the NWA magazine from the two women's wrestling groups, both based in Columbus. Mildred's group boasted that it was the "Successors to Billy Wolfe" and had "35 top-notch women wrestlers." In an obvious shot at Nell Stewart, Burke's ad called Terry Majors, a new entrant to the game just getting traction, "wrestling's most beautiful girl." The ad for the other group featured far fewer women—just eight. It focused on Stewart, who was described as "the Queen of Them All, Greatest Boxoffice Attraction of Girl Wrestlers." A photograph in the back of the magazine offered a clue as to what Burke was up against. It showed Wolfe and Stewart in evening clothes seated with the editor of the NWA magazine at a table at Manhattan's famed Stork Club.

Burke rightly felt doubled crossed. But the surviving NWA records do not show that she made a formal protest or any other attempt to get the NWA to hold Wolfe to his agreement. Perhaps she thought that she could beat Wolfe at his own game because she owned the title. If so, she was mistaken. The battle soon became a war of attrition over money. As with any free-market competition, the wrestlers themselves soon felt the benefit in their pocketbooks. Wolfe had always taken a hefty 50 percent of his wrestlers' earnings as his commission; by comparison, Jack Pfefer's records show he took 30 percent from his male wrestlers. Burke began to offer contracts to women wrestlers that lowered the commission to 40 percent. Girl Wrestling Enterprises struck back by dropping its commission to 25 percent. Ida May Martinez was one of the women who went with Stewart, Byers, and the Wolfes. "I just didn't like hopping around," she recalled. "I didn't know Mildred that well. The one thing I knew was that Billy was more stable. And because of Nell. Nell and I were friends." Cora Combs, the Kentucky wildcat and Wolfe's "Hadacol Kid," was one of the wrestlers that went with Burke, who had helped Combs when she was coming up. "She just told me how to act, how to get in the ring and listen to the people," Combs said years later. "They call you every kind of names that there were. She said just don't get mad because they had paid their money to see you, so you've got to get up there and perform. She told me that. She told me a lot. We talked a lot."

The sentiment that the two wrestling groups could coexist soon collided with hard financial realities. The wrestling boom brought on by television was busting. The signs had been in the air for some time. "The fans are content to stay home and restrict their attendance to the front room," *Ring* magazine said in late 1950. "This new attitude is cutting deeply into the pocketbooks of the wrestlers." Two years later, the magazine reported that wrestling had "slowed down in its drawing power with the exception of a few big cities." In addition, the country was heading into a recession that began in the second quarter of 1953 and would ultimately cost the economy $56 billion. All this couldn't have come at a worse moment for Mildred Burke. She wasn't much of a businesswoman in the best of times. "Billy Wolfe handled all the business, and had all the business knowledge, contacts and influence," she wrote. "When

I decided to book and handle girls myself, I was starting from ground zero in a phase of the wrestling business of which I had only a sketchy grasp."

The one thing Mildred Burke had was the title. And then a move was made to take that away. A Baltimore promoter announced a tournament to crown a new women's world champion in his city. The promoter, Ed Contos, was close to Wolfe's friend Al Haft. Contos, no doubt with the help of Wolfe, found an ingenious way to undermine Burke's claim on the title in a letter written to NWA president Muchnick seeking approval for the Baltimore tournament. Contos pointed out to Muchnick that the NWA had never recognized a women's champion; Burke's title had always resided with Al Haft's smaller Midwest Wrestling Association. Contos argued that the NWA should help clear up the women's title picture, which currently had several women claiming to be champion, among them Lillian Ellison, now wrestling for Jack Pfefer under the name Slave Girl Moolah. Contos also pointed out that Burke had years earlier lost her title to one of those other claimants. "Clara Mortensen did what nobody is supposed to have done: defeated Miss Burke," Contos wrote. "It was a few years back, in Chattanooga 'right in the middle of the ring,' and the sports departments of the Chattanooga papers are called on to verify it." The inside information about this match, which had occurred shortly after Burke had defeated Mortensen for the first time, could have come only from Billy Wolfe. It was part of the confusing legacy left by the Burke-Mortensen matches, but Contos was able to use it to get mileage with the press. There was no doubt about Wolfe's hand in the matter. "Mr. Contos would like to stage a women's world championship tournament in Baltimore, and he seems to have the approval of both Muchnick and Billy Wolfe, Wolfe being the main booking agent for gals (including his wife, Mildred Burke)," wrote Dave Feldman, a sports columnist with the Tucson *Daily Citizen*. Feldman did not see fit to mention that Wolfe and Burke were now divorced and that Wolfe was no longer Burke's booking agent.

The Baltimore tournament would claim legitimacy as the only title to receive official recognition from a government body, in this case the Maryland State Athletic Commission. The organizers claimed that Burke had been invited; she claimed that she had not. In any case, she most certainly could not have won the tournament, controlled as it was by Wolfe and the women of Girl Wrestling Enterprises. Instead, she wired the newspapers in Baltimore, protesting that the tournament was a sham without her there to defend her title. Burke saw the hidden hand of Billy Wolfe behind it, and she applied her own hand openly to counter him. "Congratulations to Ed Contos for promoting a tournament in which Nell Stewart is to win from nobody," Burke wrote in a cable to Jesse A. Linthicum, sports editor of the *Baltimore Sun,* on the day of the tournament. "I wrestled Nell Stewart last year in seven matches for the title and defeated her seven straight falls. These were the last matches she wrestled me. No champion in history has ever defended his title that many times in succession against one opponent. This wire is dated and timed before the Baltimore Tournament."

Burke created a furor in Baltimore and almost certainly succeeded in changing the outcome of the tournament. The one-night, single-elimination event involved ten women, essentially the entire roster of Girl Wrestling Enterprises at the time. In the final bout, June Byers beat Nell Stewart to become the new champion. It was a shocking upset. "Almost everyone, it seems, thought Miss Stewart would wear the belt, but the Houston (Texas) gal with the light brown hair and the hazel eyes walked off with the laurels," the *Sun* reported.

It must have been heartbreaking for Stewart, who had waited so long to replace Burke. The match had lasted only five minutes, by far the shortest of the tournament. That said it all. Stewart no doubt had no stomach to put on a lengthy worked match with Byers and had opted to limit the torture by getting things over as quickly as possible.

The story about the match that Billy Wolfe had planted in the NWA magazine was almost comical in its attempt to paper over all the bad feelings swirling around the tournament. "When the big moment came and Miss Byers faced Miss Stewart, the crowd saw only five minutes of wrestling, but they long will remember those five minutes! June, fresh as if this was the first match of the evening, went after her opponent from the tap of the bell and didn't let up for a second. In just five minutes she had Nell Stewart pinned with an arm lock and body press in as neat a fall as any one would wish to see. For a moment the vast crowd was stunned but realizing what happened they gave the new champion the biggest ovation a woman wrestler ever received in any ring." Stewart, a chatterbox after her draw the previous year with Burke, was nearly mute about what must have been one of the bitterest nights of her life. "Nell Stewart, good sport that she is, had little to say after the match except first to give full credit to June Byers for her Victory and second to express the hope that she would give her a crack at the championship and belt at an early date," according to the article. "She did say however that she felt she hadn't had the best of luck in the drawings and that her opposition in the eliminations was tougher than June's."

Burke took a kind of victory from Stewart's defeat. Millie later wrote that her wires to the newspapers had "put Billy Wolfe's back to the wall and he could not now put over Nell Stewart as champion. He had to allow June Byers to chew her up in the finals, which wasn't any great trouble for the big gal from Texas." In retrospect, Burke's intervention against Stewart had the unintended consequence for Burke of elevating a woman who would be a far more formidable opponent if they ever met in the ring.

Ida May Martinez, the young wrestler who had become Stewart's best friend, confirmed that Stewart's planned ascension to the title was derailed by Burke's publicity blitz. "She called everybody and told them that Nell Stewart was going to be the next champion," Martinez, who participated in the Baltimore tournament, recalled decades later. "So they switched it to June. That's how June got it. Either Billy or Nell told me that. And they were really ticked off because Nell was supposed to be the champion. Many times, when I think about it, I wish she had been, because her life went downhill after that." Stewart later said "it was Byers who robbed her of the championship match she was to have had against Mildred Burke," according to Penny Banner, who worked as Stewart's tag-team partner in the mid-1950s. "What happened?" Banner asked. "It's a long story," Stewart said, never to elaborate.

Wolfe gave Stewart two consolation prizes. Two weeks after the Baltimore tourney, on May 1, 1953, he married her in Clovis, New Mexico. There was not much time for a honeymoon; the wedding came four days after Stewart and Byers wrestled in Abilene, Texas, and three days before Stewart traveled to another match in Ogden, Utah. Nell was also given the prize of defeating Ida May Martinez to win her third annual WLW-TV championship on May 16, before a record crowd of 15,000 at the Cincinnati Gardens. She got $2,000, a percentage of the gate receipts, and a gold belt. But it was clearly second place. "June Byers is the lady champion recognized by the Maryland State Athletic Commission which officially sanctioned the title tournament won by June Byers," the NWA magazine stated, in words that were probably dictated by Billy Wolfe. "The fact that Nell Stewart for the ladies and Buddy Rogers for the men won the WLW-TV tournament respectively, doesn't make them world's champions."

Even though she had stymied Billy's title plans for Nell, Burke's worst fears about her own belt were being realized. The cover of the June 1953 NWA magazine was another direct strike at her position: Burke was posed in a pink suit on a green background below the headline "World's Champion, 1936 to 1953." The most powerful publication in wrestling was printing the tombstone for her career. Inside the magazine, there was no mention of her in an article about June Byers's victory in Baltimore. The Houston woman now held "the official world's championship belt," the article proclaimed, as awarded by the Maryland State Athletic Commission. There was no attempt to explain how a state commission could award a "world" title. The cover was obviously orchestrated by Wolfe. As if to leave no doubt about who was pulling the strings, the article announced that Byers was immediately booked "solid through the month of June in Canada, which was arranged by Billy Wolfe." He had relinquished his bookings in the United States, the article helpfully pointed out, and was now devoting his entire time to foreign bookings.

The magazine cover hit like a bomb in the publicity war between the two rival female wrestling groups, a clear signal of which horse the NWA was backing. Burke was incensed and threatened a lawsuit against the magazine. To make matters worse she was losing the business battle at the box office. Traveling on the road all the time to wrestle in her own matches, Burke found it impossible to arrange the bookings for her wrestlers. At first her partners, the lawyers in Columbus, tried to manage the bookings. But they had little success, thanks to Wolfe. When the lawyers tried to make bookings, Wolfe would contact the wrestlers in question and try to unbook them. "Billy would call and say, 'Don't do it, honey,'" recalled Ethel Brown, the young Columbus wrestler. "Billy would say, 'Don't go, please.' He was in the process of trying to take over completely." Brown was one of those who viewed Wolfe as a father figure, so she did what he said. So did many of the others.

To counteract this problem, Burke convinced her partners to bring in a new man, Tulsa promoter Leroy McGuirk, a former NWA junior heavyweight champion who could use his connections in the business and his standing with the NWA to ensure that Burke got a fair shake. She picked McGuirk, who had retired from wrestling after losing his sight in an auto accident, in part because he despised Wolfe.

Still, her business continued to slide, and even wrestlers who had been loyal to her started defecting to Girl Wrestling Enterprises. During this time, in a sign of her desperation, Burke accepted a booking in New Jersey from a promoter who was not affiliated with the NWA. New Jersey was NWA member Toots Mondt's territory, and he complained to Muchnick, who relayed the complaint to McGuirk, who told Burke she had to cancel the booking or she'd "get herself in bad" with the NWA. She canceled.

As business worsened, she continued to blame Wolfe. "A pattern began to emerge," Burke later wrote. "On several successive occasions, Billy Wolfe provided promoters in the territory with girl wrestlers free of charge—provided the promoter would kill my bookings." McGuirk told her that Billy Wolfe had offered him a $10,000 bribe to double-cross her; she began to think that McGuirk had taken the money. Soon Burke and McGuirk separated and she went in search of a new partner in her war with Billy Wolfe.

He may have been giving Burke fits on the business front, but Wolfe's efforts were less successful in the wrestling ring. Other than the NWA magazine, he had failed to convince the wrestling world at large that Byers should replace Burke as the new champion. The influential *Ring* magazine lamented the dismal state of affairs. In an unusual write-up, the magazine went up against the NWA power structure and editorialized against Girl Wrestling Enterprises without naming the group. "The world being what it is Nell Stewart, calling herself Queen of them all, acts as the front for a new organization," wrote Nat Loubet, *Ring*'s longtime editor. "It's none of our biz but it would seem that one champ is enough. . . . It would seem that the promotion of women needs all the strength and solidarity within its own ranks without splitting up."

Boxing and Wrestling magazine came out strongly in favor of Burke in an another unusual editorial. "One of the best conditioned and trained female athletes who ever lived, is Mildred Burke, internationally recognized as the World's Champion Lady Wrestler," wrestling editor Charles A. Smith wrote in the August 1953. "But some group got the idea that we should have another champion so they set about arranging a tournament among a picked group of girls, to determine the World's Lady Champion and selected a certain spot in the East near the Nation's capital for this." Smith wrote carefully, naming no names other than Burke's. But he made clear that he considered the Baltimore tourney a sham. "Surely enough, there *was* a winner of the tournament but we venture to suggest that all who took part, *including* the winner, were victimized, for *no tournament can ever determine who is champion unless the title has been vacated by death or retirement,* or unless *the winner of any tournament meets the champion* . . . In our book, *Mildred Burke* is the world's champion lady wrestler until she is defeated or retires or gives up the title."

But in the same issue, in a sign of the divisions the Burke-Wolfe battle had created, *Boxing and Wrestling*'s own ratings of women wrestlers seemed to presage Burke's downfall. "Mildred Burke has been the champion of the Women Wrestlers for more years than some of us have lived, and it is our opinion that her sun is setting," the magazine's unnamed editors wrote. "If she is still champion when the last day of 1953 is here, we'll be the most surprised people there are. . . . Gazing into our crystal ball has revealed several interesting things we are not at liberty to disclose at present. Look for a *new World's Champion gal grappler . . . perhaps before this appears in print.* We predict."

On August 16, 1953, June Byers appeared on national television in the popular game show *What's My Line?* Sitting between two immense men, Byers wore her enigmatic smile as a panel that included TV personality Steve Allen and Random House publisher Bennett Cerf fired questions and attempted to guess which of the three was the world champion wrestler. Cerf correctly guessed Byers. The next day, Mildred Burke's partners—Hedges, Porter, and Moats—called in the $30,000 debt, forcing her business into receivership. Burke received no notification and was completely in the dark. As her business came crashing down she was appearing before 3,600 fans on a card with Gorgeous George in Tucson. She beat Cora Combs in two falls and got the headline over George, even though he came into the ring preceded by his perfume-spraying valet and wearing an extremely colorful new sequined robe that he called "Sunset Over Old Arizona."

A judge would now decide how Burke's business should be managed to pay her debts to her partners. In her autobiography, Burke claimed Wolfe had gotten to them by offering access to his women at the Park Hotel, then photographing the men in compromising situations. "Before my lawyers knew what was happening, Bill laid on a bevy of his prettiest young women wrestlers, and laid all the lawyers," she wrote. "He had pictures taken of the lawyers, in the clenched ecstasy of orgasms and laid these pictures on the lawyers." She offers no evidence to back this up. Porter, who was also the treasurer of the business, entered an affidavit with the court saying the corporation had $18.16 on hand and outstanding debts of $750.00. Further, he said, an accounting with "Mildred B. Wolfe," president and manager of the corporation, "will probably show that she is indebted to said corporation in the amount of several thousand dollars in commissions."

The swiftness and timing of events showed that everything had been worked out in advance with Wolfe. The court of common pleas judge in Columbus appointed a receiver, who with the approval of Hedges and Porter immediately recommended bringing Wolfe back in to run the business he had sold less than six months earlier. The receiver said this unusual step was necessary because the business was "a unique and highly special one" and Wolfe was "highly qualified" to manage it. It left Burke with nothing. Even worse, she was on the hook for the $30,975 in notes. The whole matter was handled in three days. "Mildred Burke in $30,000 default, Wolfe to Run Ex-Wife's Agency," read the headline in the Ohio State Journal for a story that

Wolfe clearly had planted. The brief article went beyond the facts in the lawsuit to describe Burke as "ex-World's Champion Woman Wrestler."

Wolfe wasted no time in proclaiming his victory to the wrestling world. On August 20, 1953, the very day that he was appointed business manager of Attractions, Inc., he sent out a general letter to wrestling promoters announcing his return to the booking business in the United States. Wolfe offered that he had had a "splendid vacation" for the past few months, making very profitable foreign bookings. He reminded everyone that in early 1953 he had "turned over his booking rights of girl wrestlers in the United States to Mildred Burke and her associates for a period of five years." Now, however, he was taking over Burke's failing company with the court's approval. Wolfe announced that he was now the sole booker for the twenty-eight women who had been working for Mildred, as well as for Stewart, Byers, and four others who had been booked through Girl Wrestling Enterprises.

The court had in effect restored Wolfe's monopoly, and the list of women under his management and control now encompassed virtually every prominent female wrestler in the country, including Burke herself. If she wanted to work she would have to work for him. His victory appeared complete.

Six days after Wolfe sent out his letter Burke responded in a cold fury in a letter to the NWA written from Dallas. "You received a letter from Billy Wolfe dated August 20 to which he finally got up enough nerve to sign his own name instead of Ed Contos or the Maryland Commission. One thing I want to make clear is that Billy Wolfe is not and never will run me or any agency of mine." She then detailed her ex-husband's subterfuges. "Our dear Mr. Wolfe says he has been enjoying a splendid vacation. What a laugh that is. He never worked harder in his life than he has in the past months blasting me. This you all know for a fact." Although she admitted she had "plenty of personal debts," she denied that her business was bankrupt. She said she had been "sold down the river by people who like Champagne. . . . A big double cross was trying to be pulled on me by lawyers I made the mistake of trusting." She vowed to continue in business and fight in court. She then played her strongest card. She challenged Byers's legitimacy as champion. "In the newspaper clipping attached to the letter, it states that June Byers has taken my title. What I want to know is where and when. I have defeated her a hundred or more times. She has never defeated me."

Burke made a final plea to the men of the NWA to do right by her at the alliance meeting coming up the next month. "I could have caused a big scandle [sic], but to protect the game I came to you, the Alliance," she wrote. "We agreed to go by the committee's decision. It was agreed I buy Bill out. I kept my agreement, paid his price, but he has fought me with every cent he could beg, borrow or steal. I have kept the business running under opposition that Billy Wolfe never had. I am a woman alone fighting to do what is right and to be right." She outlined the scandal she could create if she chose to go public. "Please keep in mind that I gave Bill, or let him keep everything we ever made together as joint pardners [sic]. I waived all alimony and I could have gotten plenty. I took a beating from two brave men, Billy Wolfe, Jr. and Billy Wolfe, Sr., because I wouldn't lose the title to Nell Stewart. I have witnesses that she even bragged about this. Bill took my money and hung mink coats and diamonds on her until she looked like a Christmas tree."

As a coup de grâce, Mildred enclosed a sworn statement she had obtained from her friend Cora Combs. "I personally witnessed on several occasions Billy Wolfe and Nell Stewart in bed together when he was still married to Mildred Burke," Combs wrote. She brought the Wolfe-Stewart-Byers triangle out into the open for the first time, stating that she had known the three of them for three years and "personally know and will testify he has lived with Nell Stewart and June

Byers for the full three years and have heard many girls testify to the fact that they had lived together for years before I knew them." Wolfe had even told her that himself, Combs wrote.

Combs further stated that Wolfe was involved in bribery and sexual procuring. "Billy Wolfe ran his business entirely on an immoral basis and tried to get me to participate in immoral conduct with his lawyer during the time I worked for him," she said. Wolfe had offered her 85 percent to quit working for Burke and "return to him under cover of Nell Stewart and June Byers Girl Wrestling Enterprises," Combs stated. "He has made this same offer to practically every girl in the business."

With nowhere else to turn, Mildred Burke reached out to a powerful fan. John Bricker had been the governor of Ohio when she was at her height. In 1948 he was Thomas Dewey's running mate as vice president on the Republican ticket in the famed "Dewey Defeats Truman" presidential race. Bricker was now a U.S. senator. Desperate, she put in a call to his office. "Senator Bricker is conducting hearings of the Atomic Energy Committee today, but he has spoken of you so often, Miss Burke, and so highly, that I feel as though I know you," she recalled being told by one of Bricker's aides. "I'm going to go in and tell him how badly you need his help."

Ten minutes later Bricker himself was on the phone. "Listen, Mildred," he said, "what those lawyers have done could get them disbarred. It's absolutely illegal. We'll fix them." Bricker referred her to Robert L. Barton, the senator's closest associate and the most powerful lawyer in Columbus. A young man with slicked-back hair and a trimmed mustache, Bob Barton had been Bricker's secretary when the older man was Ohio's governor. After Bricker left office, they became law partners, and Barton ran the firm while Bricker went on to the U.S. Senate. A leading Republican, Barton was so prominent locally and so renowned for his courtroom skills that the firm became known as the

"Barton firm." He immediately took over Mildred Burke's case and accompanied her to the NWA's annual convention on September 6, 1953, in the Hubbard Room at the Blackstone Hotel in Chicago.

Once again, Burke had to wait outside, but this time she was waiting with Barton. Now the dispute was the first order of business on the agenda of the convention's third day. Another deal was brokered. Billy Wolfe would take over Attractions, Inc., but he would also assume the $30,000 in debt that had been hung on Burke, as well as several thousand more that Burke owed to Tulsa promoter Sam Avey, Leroy McGuirk's boss. Burke had to agree to continue working for Attractions, Inc., and thus Wolfe. She would be booked as the world champion and would retire in two years. Considering her circumstances, Burke viewed the deal as a triumph. "The old con man had outsmarted himself," she later wrote. "Defeat had been snatched from the jaws of victory." Burke finally got to see the inside of an NWA meeting room when she and Barton, along with the partners who had betrayed her, were ushered into the Hubbard Room to ratify the deal. "When I walked in with Senator Bricker's law partner, instead of limping in with my tail in a sling, the effects were close to comic," she wrote. "I have read in books about men wetting their pants under stress, but this was the closest I ever came to seeing it happen in real life, and to several men at once."

After the deal was done a motion was made that "the NWA divorce itself from girl wrestling." Wrestling's old-boy network had had enough of Wolfe's marital discord. The motion carried unanimously.

Mildred may have had her moment of triumph but it was just that: a moment. She was still competing in one form or another against Billy Wolfe, who remained an NWA member in good standing. In early November 1953 Burke wrote another letter to the alliance, this time to dispel talk that she was finished and would work only with one other woman wrestler. She believed Wolfe was behind it. She listed the names of a dozen women she would be "very happy to work with," starting with "No. 1 June Byers" and "No. 2 Nell Stewart." She promised to keep fighting. "Billy Wolfe has told in various places that he is washing me up the first of the year. I raised thirty thousand and bought him out. I let him back in for nothing. I am still spending all I make to keep him from killing me." She became convinced Wolfe was trying to kill her professionally by booking her against second-class wrestlers or scheduling competing matches in close proximity to hers. A week before she was to wrestle in Chattanooga at the end of 1953, Wolfe stole her fire by staging a seven-woman battle royal in the same city, featuring June Byers and his newest protégé, LeeChona LaClaire.

Burke had had enough. She sent out a letter to wrestling promoters announcing yet another split. She was leaving Attractions, Inc., and would henceforth handle her own bookings. She also offered to get out of wrestling entirely if Wolfe would pay her $30,000. "Please do not contact Billy Wolfe for any further bookings for me as he has completely abused his right as a booking agent," she wrote on November 25, 1953. "No court would ask me to work under conditions I can prove exist and if he tries to stop me he will be forcing a monopoly. I sincerely hope he will buy me out and I will be woman enough to stay out as I do not want to fight with him or anyone else. But I will fight him as long as I live or until he makes a proper settlement but no one will ever talk me into doing business with him again, three double crossings in a row are just too much for anyone."

15

A Bout with June

As her fight with Billy Wolfe stretched into 1954, Mildred Burke had to sell her diamonds. Her collection, the one famously promoted as being worth $50,000, brought her only $4,000 at fire sale prices. She had battled with Wolfe for nearly two years and had nothing to show for it but mounting debt. "Mom ended up almost destitute after the attorneys got everything," Joe recalled. "I had to give her my car so she could get some money out of that."

Visiting with Gorgeous George during a break between their matches in Cleveland, Burke combed out his golden hair in his dressing room and poured out her troubles with Billy. George handed her an envelope stuffed with $5,000. "Now you take that and you beat that son of a bitch," she said he told her. She had to give up even her modest house in Canoga Park and move in with her brother and mother in Reseda. A wire she sent to Jack Pfefer shows her distress. "Dear Jack, I have been in a desperate fight as you know with Bill and have lost a fortune. I am now stranded at home and desperately would like to borrow five hundred dollars." Sam Menacker, the El

Paso promoter, booked her in January 1954, then canceled; she was convinced Wolfe was behind it.

June Byers, meanwhile, was essentially living Burke's old life, touring the country with G. Bill in a "mile-long" Lincoln giving the interviews Burke used to give. Byers showed off the belt from the Baltimore tournament and claimed she was the true champion. "Mildred Burke was tops in her day, but she's been wrestling for 20 years now," Byers told A. C. Becker Jr. of the *Galveston News* in February 1954. "She ought to retire and give the young girls a chance."

At the end of the interview G. Bill asked June to perform the old ritual, one he had seen his father do with Burke and dozens of reporters. "Show Mr. Becker your neck and shoulder muscles."

June flexed. "Go ahead and feel," she said to the reporter.

To the women in Billy Wolfe's stable, G. Bill was a pale imitation of the man who ran their lives. Ida May Martinez recalled that he was "kind of sappy" and overly attentive to his appearance, combing his eyebrows and going over his thin mustache with a grease pencil as June drove the car. "He tried to emulate his father but he wasn't successful as far as being tough and trying to tell people what to do," Martinez recalled. "I don't think he had it in him." Gloria Barattini recalled that "G. Bill couldn't live up to his father. His father, he was the king of the girl wrestlers, that's for sure." To Kathleen Wimbley, G. Bill was "a weak person. When his father talked to him on the phone, he sounded like he was talking to a kid. I don't think he had a name in the wrestling business." June Byers's relationship with G. Bill amounted to another compromise for the sake of the business. "I don't think they were in love," Martinez said. "It was companionship."

The same month June Byers called on her to retire, Mildred Burke was redoubling her efforts to run her own booking business. She formed another group of a dozen women wrestlers and lined up two NWA members as the bookers, C. P. "Cowboy" Luttrall in Tampa and Don McIntyre in Paul Jones's office in Atlanta. To fight Wolfe, she would use her most important weapon, control of the title.

"The title was the master key to high earnings," she wrote. "I had the title, I knew many fine promoters and I knew the game. There was no reason why I could not book myself, and book other girls as well. In short, I was going into direct competition with Billy Wolfe and the girls he controlled." She was convinced she could beat him, that she could prove that it was her skill and not his maneuvering that had made the business in the first place. "My title, and what I brought and gave to that title, was what kept Billy Wolfe in business—not his abilities as a manager and businessman. Believing this in my heart was what led me to challenge him directly, as a rival booker and manager of women wrestlers. This was really the greatest 'shooting match' of my career as a woman, rather than as a wrestler." She called it the Great Booking War.

Despite Wolfe's machinations most of the country still recognized Burke as the champion. "Mildred is still champ, bless her," wrote the Tucson *Daily Citizen*'s David Feldman, who just six months earlier had carried the news of Contos's challenge to Burke's title. The Kingsport, Tennessee, *Times* called her "once again the only nationally recognized champ."

She started to get bookings from a subgroup of the NWA known as the Southern Wrestling Alliance—in Florida, Georgia, Texas, New Mexico, and Arizona. But she was caught in the same tailspin as the rest of the wrestling business. In Tampa, she drew only 1,062 fans in April 1954, a far cry from the 4,371 she had brought in five years earlier. Wolfe still dogged her. Paul Bowser, an NWA member and the most powerful promoter in New England, booked her into Boston, then told her that Billy Wolfe had written him a letter complaining about it.

Wolfe's business was hurting, too. Byers's championship in Maryland was just not good enough. "June, however, will have to meet and defeat Mildred Burke before she can obtain universal title recognition," noted the Joplin, Missouri, *Globe*. *Boxing and Wrestling* magazine wrote, "It is not our intention to cause trouble or make enemies but we are sticking by Mildred Burke as the genuine, World's Ladies Wrestling Champion because she has never been beaten for her title, because she has met every challenge in the ring, because she has never refused a challenger a shot at her crown." Burke issued her own challenge through the magazine. "I am ready and willing to meet any two of the present contenders in one evening, and that includes Miss Byers, NO HOLDS BARRED, WINNER TAKE ALL." The magazine added, "Wherever the 'Burke-versus-Byers' bout is held, it will be a sellout, that much is certain and we are confident support of the fans will be with the pint size smiling girl who made Gal Grappling the million dollar business that it is today." For whatever reason, though, the match did not get made.

Wolfe could not afford the competition. In the month after he took control of Attractions, Inc., commissions for all his wrestlers totaled $2,764.33 and, after expenses, profits amounted to $959.82. But after Wolfe paid all the debts associated with his settlement with Burke he was left with little to put in his pocket: "$29.76," he wrote in the ledger in which he recorded the commissions. "My First Profit with Attractions, Inc., Oct. 21, 1953."

June Byers's failure to draw like a champion was a big part of the problem. Her commission amounted to $33.60 on a September 28 match in Columbus, while Nell Stewart and Ida May Martinez raked in $145.70 on the same day for a match in Tulsa. In December 1953 Wolfe's profit dwindled to 44 cents and in the spring he started losing money, $1,074.55 in May alone. The deal Robert Barton had negotiated with Wolfe on Mildred Burke's behalf was starting to look like a very bad one for him.

He was still a master at presenting a shimmering image to the public. *Boxing and Wrestling* magazine compared him to Billy Mitchell, the army general who had the foresight to argue in the 1930s that the airplane was the weapon of the future. The magazine portrayed the old master in his lair, fully in control and flashing his diamond rings and belt buckle. "Today, Billy, in his luxurious suite in the Park Hotel, Columbus, Ohio, can settle himself comfortably in his leather club chair, light up a fragrant Havana Perfecto, and reflect that during the coming hours of the evening, there'll be at least 30 of his lady athletes hurling each other across the Nation's wrestling mats, while the arena turnstiles twirl merrily to jingling cash registers . . . Despite a recent stormy passage, he's come back stronger than ever, and now controls 99.9 percent of all the Gal Grappling bookings in the Nation."

Wolfe incurred another loss: his golden girl. Apparently the man without the title had not been enough for Nell Stewart. By July 1954 she was talking about going to Hollywood. "Paramount is going to make a picture on girl wrestling and it will be based on my life," she told a reporter. "I'm going to take a screen test on August 17. I sure hope I photograph good and can act good enough to get the lead role. I'm scared to death I won't make it." She also talked about a biography of her that was being written, "a 250-page thriller." But the movie was never made, the book never appeared, and Stewart and Wolfe called it quits.

It must not have been a surprise. Although Stewart had always had a special bond with Wolfe, she was never truly in love with him. She had been fifteen when they met, thirty years younger than he was. She had appreciated what he had done for her—he had transformed her into the Betty Grable of wrestling. She had ministered to his sexual needs and his crotchety stomach, helped run his business from the road. But she gave her heart to someone else, Joe Gunther, the NWA member from New Orleans, according to her best friend, Ida May Martinez. Gunther was the true love of Nell's life but he happened to be married. "She was in love with him from the very beginning and everybody knew it," Martinez recalled. "But she went her merry way with Billy and did what she had to do. She always loved Joe. She always dreamed of ending her life with Joe." In the end, Nell Stewart made the same compromises that Mildred Burke had made. But unlike Burke she never had the championship belt as consolation.

Instead, she occupied a jail of her own making. Stewart continued to wrestle for Wolfe even as they separated and made preparations for a divorce. And Wolfe, not one to lack for female companionship, simply moved on to younger women in his wrestling troupe. But to the end of his life Wolfe retained a special fondness for Stewart. Years later, when he learned that Jack Pfefer was going to be in the same town as Nell, Wolfe wrote asking him to "please do me a very special favor and personally give Nell a very big hug for me." Stewart, however, did not feel the same way about Wolfe. According to Terry Patterson, Stewart's niece, Billy Wolfe had Nell's tubes tied while she was under anesthesia for an appendectomy. When Stewart found out, Patterson said, she never forgave him for taking away her chance to have children.

Wolfe's new girlfriend was eighteen-year-old LeeChona LaClaire, the latest teenage wrestling sensation. A vivacious girl from coal mining country in Huntington, West Virginia, she was described in the press as five feet, four inches tall, "140 pounds of luscious dynamite," and "as full of life and mischievous potential as a yearling mink." LaClaire was seventeen when she asked Wolfe to give her a shot in the ring. "My gosh, he even checked my teeth like he was buying a horse," she said. She liked to party and she reveled in being young. When she took off the expensive gowns Wolfe bought for her, she let them drop to the floor and walked on them. "She was beautiful," recalled Sherrie Lee, a young woman who started working as Wolfe's secretary when she was seventeen and later wrestled for him. "Frankly, the most beautiful of all the girls. A lot of people think Nell Stewart was, but I thought LeeChona was."

★ ★ ★

As the business declined around them, Billy Wolfe and Mildred Burke still had one thing of great value, if they could put aside their differences: Burke-versus-Byers. The buildup had been manifesting for months. The timing and circumstances of the match would be key. Byers later said Billy Wolfe had been trying to get Burke to agree to the match for more than a year. Perhaps Burke did not trust Wolfe enough to get into the ring with Byers, no matter what she had said in her public challenges. But for Wolfe the money that could be made and the need to clear up the title picture made the match imperative.

Burke's partners, McIntyre in Atlanta and Cowboy Luttrall in Tampa, also wanted to get a piece of the money that could be made from such a match, according to Herbie Freeman, a onetime wrestler who worked as a matchmaker in Luttrall's office. Luttrall and McIntyre had "thought of the idea for Mildred and June to get together and work all over the country for the title," Freeman wrote in a letter to Jack Pfefer, the only surviving contemporaneous inside account of how the match came together. This meant that they would be going into business with Wolfe, and Burke would have to agree to trade the title back and forth with Byers. This she would not do. "If Billy Wolfe wanted to control the title, he could have one of his girls beat me in the ring," Burke later wrote. "Any time I was going to face someone from the Wolfe stable it would have to be a shooting match." It is understandable at this point why Burke did not trust Wolfe enough to engage in worked matches around the country with Byers, even though that would have meant more money for everyone. In Burke's mind all the business double crosses were merely the prelude to Wolfe's true goal. "Bill never relinquished his dream of having me beaten," she wrote. "This was more important to him than having me killed, because somehow deep down he wanted to see me humiliated under the lights."

In the end, Burke agreed to the Byers match only because she was broke and "owed everybody money," Freeman wrote, adding that the partners threw up their hands and agreed to Burke's demand of a shooting match. "However Mildred is a screwball, so Billie Wolfe and Cowboy decided to let them shoot just to see how good Mildred is," Freeman wrote.

Burke gives a more detailed account of how the match was made. She said the events leading to it began when she aggravated her old knee injury, which caused the joint to slip out of its socket. In her autobiography, written decades after the events, Burke said she reinjured the knee in a bout in Birmingham and had to cancel her next match in Nashville. "A huge swelling developed, and it was all I could do to struggle to Nashville," she wrote. She said a doctor in Nashville X-rayed the knee and told her she needed surgery. Instead, she had the knee drained and wrapped and she continued with the matches she had scheduled after Nashville. During this period, she said, her partners conspired with her enemies to use her injury against her. Burke claimed that the promoter in Nashville called her Atlanta office, which contacted Wolfe to arrange a match with Byers in two weeks' time in Atlanta. "I've got you booked in a big championship match with June Byers in Atlanta in two weeks," Burke said McIntyre told her. "A shoot." Burke said she didn't think could make it but then agreed to the match. "My acceptance of such a match at two weeks' notice, when I was lame and flirting with permanent injury, indicates how dull-witted I had become as a result of the frantic life I had been leading," she wrote.

Surviving records indicate the injury most likely occurred three months before the Atlanta match; she missed a match in Chattanooga in late May 1954 due to a knee injury. Burke did continue to wrestle after that injury, in more than a dozen matches, including one in Augusta eleven days before the Atlanta match. But she was clearly hurting and frazzled from the endless days on the road. Bert Younker, the nineteen-year-old friend of Joe Wolfe's who had taken over as Burke's driver two years earlier, recalled decades later that she was given little choice by Wolfe and her latest partners. "He forced her to take this match with June Byers," Younker said. "I think the partner tricked her into it." Burke also said her office booked her into a match in Rome, Georgia, the night before the Byers match, forcing her to drive seventy miles the next day for a full round of radio and TV interviews beginning at eight in the morning. But the Rome newspaper has no record of such a match.

The big match was set for August 20, 1954. Despite her condition Burke was confident she could beat Byers in a shooting match. "Strongly influencing my decision to go through with the booking was my lack of any fear of June Byers," Burke later wrote. "I was one of her original trainers. Through the years since, I had beaten her dozens of times. June Byers was not a particularly good wrestler in the legitimate sense, but she was rough. You always had to watch the dirty punch, dirty knee and other sharp shots that she took when the chance came. In an attempted double-cross once, she deliberately stomped me in the mouth on the mat. I remembered this incident well, because the dental bill was $2,000 to fix my loosened front teeth."

Burke was in the dark about a number of things, however. While she kept up her schedule of matches on the road, unbeknownst to her Byers had gone into serious training under Wolfe in Columbus. Penny Banner, the nineteen-year-old prospect from St. Louis who went on to a stellar wrestling career of her own, saw the preparations firsthand. She arrived to try out for Wolfe's troupe a couple of weeks before the big match. "I remember how powerful June looked with her clothes on and then I saw that she was even more powerful-looking in her wrestling suit," Banner later wrote in her autobiography, *Banner Days*. "I guessed that she was 5'6" and about 170 pounds." At Haft's Gym, Byers was taking on all comers, male or female, offering $50 to anyone who could stay with her for ten minutes. A man challenged her and she "beat him with a pin after taking him down, real fast," Banner recalled.

The idea of a shooting match was certainly screwball in 1954. There had not been such a match for a pro wrestling title in nearly forty years. On July 4, 1916, Strangler Lewis had allegedly shot with Joe Stecher, the successor to Frank Gotch, before 20,000 fans at the fairgrounds in Omaha, Nebraska. Lewis and Stecher wrestled a five-hour defensive battle with Lewis backing up and avoiding holds nearly the whole time. Neither man gained a single fall, and the disappointed crowded jeered and pelted the wrestlers with seat cushions. The next year in the same town, the still-undefeated Stecher took on former AAU amateur champion Earl Caddock. Stecher and Caddock, two of the finest wrestlers the country had ever seen, spent most of the three-hour match lying on the mat with their limbs entwined like lovers. They had recorded one pinfall each when the match was called for the 187-pound Caddock after the 205-pound Stecher refused to return to the ring following a ten-minute break. Although Mildred Burke often employed many of the mat-wrestling holds of Caddock and Stecher—the body and head scissors, for example—she had spent her entire career wrestling in the stand-up worked style that had saved wrestling in the 1920s. No one knew how a shooting match would play in the television age.

In handicapping the Burke-Byers match it helps to hear the perspective of the woman who probably wrestled more matches with the two women than anyone else: Johnnie Mae Young. The leading heel of Wolfe's troupe was so excited about the prospect of seeing Burke and Byers in a shoot that she and her friend Gloria Barattini had driven down for the match from Baltimore. Acknowledged by nearly all as the toughest woman in Wolfe's stable, Young has her own criticisms of both Burke and Byers, colored no doubt by the perspective of someone who always had to "put over" the champion. Discounting the bitterness and braggadocio, Young's view is instructive. "I don't know how tough Mildred was because I never had a shooting match with her and I never saw her shoot with anybody," Young said in an interview decades later. "I trained June Byers to wrestle. Billy tried to teach her how to shoot. You can't teach a girl to shoot who doesn't have guts. As much as I loved June and thought the world of her, she didn't have that extra thing to knock you back, that certain kind of guts to take on all comers, that confidence in yourself."

In Atlanta, Joe arrived from California to be with his mother for the most important match of her career. "She hadn't been able to train," Joe recalled. "She hadn't been able to get her full strength back or speed. She would talk about the pain in her ribs and neck." While they were awaiting the start of the match, Burke recalled, Bert Younker left the locker room and returned with a troubling story. Walking past the male wrestlers in their locker room he had overheard some of their talk. He caught only snatches. June Byers had been specially trained for the match by Ralph "Ruffy" Silverstein, a tough male wrestler who had been a collegiate champion in Illinois. He had never been a star in the pro ranks because he lacked showmanship, but he was known among wrestlers as a master of technique. "As professionals do, they talked about a clever ploy that Silverstein used in his bouts to beat his opponents," Burke wrote. "The key move was to push them into the ropes." But Bert didn't get any more than that. After that opening maneuver, he didn't know what the finishing hold was. "Ruffy's taught that one to June Byers?" Bert overheard the male wrestlers say. "Yeah. She's as good at it now as he is. That's what she's gonna use to beat Mildred Burke."

That was it. Burke didn't know what they were talking about. But at least she knew to stay off the ropes.

When she entered the ring Mildred Burke saw Billy Wolfe sitting near June Byers's corner with LeeChona LaClaire, who looked to Burke to be about fifteen years old. Millie was disgusted but her glimpse of Wolfe also gave her something to savor. There wasn't a diamond on him anywhere. The destructive struggle had stripped them both.

The ring announcer gave the weights. In Burke's account, she was announced at 140 and Byers at 180. She said she thought Byers's announced weight was a mistake until Byers took off her robe and Burke could see the packed-on muscle. "I was absolutely astounded at the difference in her body," Burke later recalled.

Alarmed by Byers's powerful body, Burke said, she turned to Joe, who was in her corner with her.

"Joe, I can't believe that is the same girl we knew as June Byers."

Byers's weight in her career had always been about 150 and her fitness in the ring was one of her hallmarks. No record of a weigh-in for the Atlanta match survives, and it is possible and no doubt likely that Byers bulked up considerably for the match. It is also easy to see how Mildred's perception was colored by Byers's fit appearance and training program. Still, it is hard to believe that Byers actually put on thirty pounds for the match.

Even though the occasion stands as a historic landmark in the history of pro wrestling in the twentieth century, there is no film footage and only one brief contemporaneous newspaper account of the bout survives. The leading Atlanta newspapers ran short advance pieces promoting it, but nothing on the match itself. Re-creating an account requires stitching together portions from Burke's unpublished autobiography, a long letter Burke wrote to a British physical culture magazine, a four-paragraph Associated Press story, the memories of a few surviving eyewitnesses, a telegram Wolfe wrote afterward, and the fleeting and incomplete postmatch references that have made it into various publications. All witnesses essentially agree on the character of the bout and how it transpired, although they disagree about the significance of what they saw. The descriptions of the action and the outcome support that it was a true shooting match, for it looked nothing like the fast, choreographed, slam-bang style of the worked bouts of the day. In her autobiography, Burke explained how the differences between a work and a shoot would be immediately apparent to any audience. "Working wrestlers need to trust each other," she wrote. "If they don't, then the open, free-wheeling style of modern matches becomes impossible. The spectacular is replaced with the dull."

That is what happened in Atlanta.

With the bell, the women immediately locked up in the classic collar-and-elbow stance, with each wrestler standing and facing the other, one hand gripping an elbow, the other held fast to the neck or collar bone of the opponent. In that position, they circled and probed for an opening.

In Burke's account, Byers resorted to the tactics that Bert Younker had overheard in the locker room. "All June's efforts were directed to pushing, shoving or spinning me backwards into the ropes," Burke wrote. "Being prepared for this was a big advantage. . . . Every time she tried to shove me backwards into the ropes, I always managed to turn her around and use her momentum against her. She was the one who went back into the ropes. She wore a surprised expression as it happened again and again."

For half a dozen minutes, Byers tried without success to get Burke onto the ropes. Neither woman attempted any hold other than the collar-and-elbow. Burke, fearing for her weak knee, refrained from diving at Byers's legs. Both felt the immense pressure of their opponent and the crowd. "Under the brilliant ring lights and before that huge audience, I quietly prayed to God to give me the strength to get through this battle," Burke wrote.

Joe recalled that the match started out well for his mother. "At the beginning, I thought, 'Well, this is going to turn out pretty good,' because Mom started out pretty strong. I think June Byers was apprehensive. But after a few minutes Byers started working on her ribs and the areas of weakness. My mom started drawing back and drawing back and I remember thinking, 'Man, this is not going well.'" At times, the back-peddling Burke would break from the clinch with Byers, trying to catch her breath amid the onslaught.

Then, at the sixteen-minute mark, disaster struck. Burke went down and Byers pounced. "She trips Mildred and Mildred takes a fall back and June jumps on top of her for one count of three," said Johnnie Mae Young, giving one of the rare eyewitness accounts.

Burke and Joe recalled it differently. As she backed away from Byers, Burke later wrote, she felt her bad knee slip out its socket and she went down in a heap. Byers immediately leaped on her trying for a pin. Burke said she managed to turn her body sideways to avoid the pin, but with her knee out she needed time to adjust it before she could move. "She couldn't get up and get in her stance or anything," Joe recalled. "I mean, that's a disabling thing, but the other things, the ribs and the neck, were more painful. The knee would pop in and out of the socket." To buy time Burke shouted to the referee, "Give her the fall." The referee did so, and Burke believed she had at least robbed Byers of the satisfaction of pinning her.

The match was two out of three falls, and Byers would have to win another one to become the champion.

As Byers walked back to her corner after the first fall, Burke, still prone on the mat, glimpsed Billy Wolfe behind Byers "leaping in savage glee. He knew all about my right knee, from the time it happened that night on the carnival twenty years previously. Now here was the great Mildred Burke, his nemesis, lying on the mat crippled. Triumph was within his grasp."

Burke rallied. "Struggling around on the mat, I managed to work with the knee so that it went back into its socket. Kneading with my hands, I straightened out the cartilage as best I could, then limped back to my corner."

Joe recalled decades later how badly his mother was hurting in the corner. "Oh, God, the pain," she had told him. It hurt when she breathed. She complained about her ribs, neck, and knee.

He remembered thinking, How in the hell is she going to do this? If she had decided to quit right then he would have been fine with it.

But she wouldn't quit. She saw the look in his face and tried to reassure him. "Don't worry, Joe," she told him. "It won't happen again. She's not getting anything else, even if both knees come out of their sockets."

The bell sounded for the second fall and Millie once again hooked up with June in the collar-and-elbow stance. "June Byers was in exceptional condition, but so was I in every way except for my leg," Burke wrote. They proceeded to block each other as the minutes ticked off. They were covered now in sheets of sweat. To the spectators, the action was minimal, but to the wrestlers the strain was enormous. "All the time, she was trying to shove me backwards into the ropes, and I was preventing that," Burke wrote. It was as if she had been transported back to the carnival, wrestling defensively, blocking her opponent, the entire goal being to avoid getting pinned and losing the second and determining fall. The two women stayed on their feet, their hands locked around each other's necks and elbows, straining and pushing all over the ring in an awkward dance for the smallest advantage, a momentary loss of balance, a tiny shift of weight, a slow ebbing of strength. Byers was still in the lead, the aggressor pushing Burke backward, trying to trap her against the ropes, trying to rock her off balance and force her down. In time Burke began to regain her equilibrium, relying on her stout legs and the intuitive balance that had always been her greatest asset in the ring. She began to feel better. The match passed the half hour mark.

As she wrestled, Burke silently prayed. Though not religious, she had always believed in a divine presence. She believed it was with her now. She called it the Power. Tired, slick with sweat, fighting the pain in her knee and struggling to stay on her feet, Mildred Burke fought on. An hour in the ring in full struggle is an eternity; wrestlers who train all their lives can exhaust themselves in nine minutes of the hardest action. Burke and Byers were burning at full flame. Unlike in a worked match, there was no leisurely strolling through the choreographed moves, no histrionic moments where a tired wrestler could snatch a quick rest while her opponent slapped the referee and argued with the crowd. Unlike in boxing, there were no one-minute stool breaks for the competitors to catch their breath after each three-minute round; the break after the first fall was the only one either women would see.

The match had little differentiation, just two women locked together in the relentless logic of forward and retreat, push and pull, a clenched two-step all over the ring. The legs moved, the muscles strained. Neither could gain an edge. Byers was unable to use her weight and strength to steamroll Burke and Burke was unable to use her wrestling skill to pin Byers. The bigger woman could only expend her energy pulling and tugging on the immovable rock that Burke had become.

It came down to will. Burke's against Byers's. Who would break first? "I was continuing to get stronger as the match progressed," Burke wrote. "Byers's heavy breathing could be heard in the balcony."

Joe noticed the shift in the match. "Maybe something happened after the loss of that first fall," he later recalled. "From some place, Mom got the strength to overcome it all. I don't know how in the hell she did it. I know June Byers wasn't giving her a second . . . Millie was really coming on strong. As time went on, maybe because she was exerting herself, she actually started improving."

In the smoky, unair-conditioned arena, under the hot ring lights, as the sweat flowed down her body and pooled in the socks of her white leather boots, Mildred Burke collected herself. She had a plan for victory now. The match had no time limit. The clock was her ally. "June Byers was starting to wheeze down in the pit of her stomach. I now felt better than when the match started, and ready to go with Byers until she reached exhaustion—a point that was obviously close. From disadvantage and imminent defeat, I had turned the bout around." Joe Wolfe could not believe what he was seeing. "June Byers started giving up the ghost," he recalled. Bert Younker remembered seeing blood in Byers's nostrils.

It was not going the way Billy Wolfe had planned. He must have hoped for a quick victory, with all the physical advantages on the side of his champion. He must have become concerned the longer the match lasted and the longer he watched his sleek, powerful new race horse of a champion pulling and pushing without any discernible result at his small, crippled, washed-up donkey of an ex-wife. He knew both women intimately, in every sense of the word, as wrestlers, partners on the road, bedmates. He knew their strengths and their weaknesses. As a man who worked all the angles constantly, he knew their psychology down to the depths of their beings. As the minutes passed concern must have passed to anxiety, then finally to something like fear. His future was on the line as much as Burke's.

The reaction of the crowd was another matter. The fans were actually bored and unsatisfied with the slow and deliberate shooting match, the significance of which was lost on many who thought they were there just to see another world title bout. Burke later called their silence as rapt attention. "Under normal circumstances, people would walk out on a match of this kind," Burke wrote. "Something of the deep personal drama that the struggle in the ring exemplified communicated itself to that crowd. The tension in the air had the whole arena electrified." But that just wasn't so. The crowd was deeply disappointed in the lack of showmanship. In the greatest of ironies, the most inwardly dramatic and direst of struggles, true wrestling gold in an era of fool's gold and fakery, was completely lost on the crowd. "People at the match didn't understand what was going on," Bert Younker recalled. "They were looking at history. There was no funny stuff. Mildred and June were just grunting and groaning. There was no showmanship. It was old-fashioned wrestling." Joe Wolfe felt similarly about the crowd's reaction. "They had the match of the century and didn't know it." There were boos and catcalls. "The audience commenced clapping and making noise, and the referee and judges said they would have to end the match," Burke later told the federal prosecutors who were investigating the NWA.

With the one-hour mark approaching, the referee told the two wrestlers that he was on the verge of calling the match. "If you don't have a fall in the next five minutes, the commissioner says he's stopping the match," the referee said. Burke cried out in protest. But after the next few minutes transpired without a second fall the match was called. It had lasted one hour and three minutes.

As Byers sucked in her breath, Burke grabbed the microphone from the ring announcer's grasp. "Ladies and gentlemen, I refuse to leave this ring," she said. "I'm ready to wrestle all night for my title."

The crowd roared its approval. Billy Wolfe sulked at ringside.

"Either we continue the match, or you announce that I'm still champion," Burke told the referee. Byers still needed the second fall to decide the match; unless Burke quit, Byers could not be awarded the match on one fall. It had never happened in the history of wrestling. Gotch had beaten Hackenschmidt short of a deciding fall, but only because Hack had quit. Caddock had beaten Stecher short of a deciding fall, but only because Stecher had quit. Mildred Burke would not quit.

After some discussion the ring announcer said, "Commissioner stops the bout. Mildred Burke is still officially champion of the world."

She left the ring in triumph, the title still hers at age thirty-nine. She had held her own in a shooting match against a much bigger opponent who was in her prime and who many to this day consider the most formidable female pro wrestler of all time. But Burke, bad knee and all, was still the champion. "That's the way I left the ring in Atlanta on that unforgettable night, and a release to that effect went out of the Associated Press worldwide," she later wrote. She was right about that, even though the AP story's headline was "June Byers Gets 'Moral' Victory Over Miss Burke." The story reported that the city athletic commissioner had halted the match and "ruled it a no decision, which means that whatever advantage Miss Byers had it was purely a moral victory." Paul Jones, the promoter of the match and the NWA power in Atlanta, told the AP that "the tussle was growing a little dull and the commissioner thought best to stop it to allow the rest of the program to go on."

Dull or not, Mildred Burke considered it the greatest match of her career. So did June Byers.

"As a legitimate, shooting match, I regard this bout as my greatest achievement," Burke wrote. "The weight of planning and preparation on the other side should have been overwhelming, but I had God in my corner. That gave me the edge. I will never forget praying under the lights while I wrestled that night in Atlanta, and feeling that surge of power in response." Joe said they celebrated that night secure in the knowledge that his mother had triumphed over great odds. "I was so goddamn proud after that match you wouldn't believe it." For all those who considered her a fake and pampered champion, nothing but a creation of Billy Wolfe, she had provided the most convincing answer that she could.

Johnnie Mae Young and Gloria Barattini, two of the best female wrestlers in the business, who had driven nearly seven hundred miles to see the match, didn't appreciate what they saw despite all of their inside knowledge of wrestling. "It was stinko," Barattini recalled more than fifty years later. Young, also recalling the match decades later, said that even though it was a shoot Burke and Byers could have tried to work a few moves into it, for the sake of the fans. "It was a big joke," Young said. "The match stank. They stank to high heaven. Neither one of them showed any skill at all as far as wrestling or showmanship. Just stumbled around out there." But Young insisted that the match in no way amounted to a victory for Byers, moral or otherwise. "June never did beat Mildred," Young said. "Mildred stumbled on her feet and June beat her for one fall, then they went through the time limit. It was really a joke. June never beat Mildred."

Herbie Freeman, the former wrestler who had an unique view of things from his perch in Cowboy Luttrall's operation, gave his account in a letter to Jack Pfefer written four days after the bout. Freeman promised "the inside story of the Burke Byers Match." He wrote that "June won the first, then they just stood and pulled necks, it stunk bad so the Comm and Paul Jones had it stopped." Freeman blamed Burke and said the match had "proved that she is not so hot either, she can't wrestle, was a Billie Wolfe buildup over a long period of years." Though he had described the match accurately, Freeman had missed the point. To dismiss Burke as "a Billie Wolfe buildup" is one thing. But Freeman failed to explain how a "not so hot screwball" who "can't wrestle" had given up seven years in age and a significant number of pounds and still managed to hold at bay for one hour an obvious powerhouse like Byers.

The outcome of the Atlanta bout birthed an unending controversy. Billy Wolfe thought June Byers the clear winner. With all his trademark energy he quickly went to work to convince others.

"June Byers won the one and only fall in sixteen minutes," Wolfe wrote in a telegram sent at 5:56 a.m. the morning after the match to Toots Mondt in New York City. "June Byers defeated Mildred Burke decisively right in the center of the ring." In the telegram, Wolfe gives the most detailed contemporaneous account of the match that has surfaced so far. "At the end of one hour wrestling, Paul Jones, the promoter, and the state commission inspector jumped in the ring and stopped the match, and called it no contest, which, in my opinion, definitely saved Mildred from being defeated in two straight falls, as never once in the entire one hour of wrestling did Mildred get behind or on top of June Byers for one second." Both women had been introduced in the ring as title claimants. In winning the only fall Byers had settled the claims, Wolfe argued. "This definitely gives June Byers the rightful claim to the world's title," he wrote.

Wolfe had his version printed on high-quality paper stock with a picture of June Byers and mailed around the country. He also obtained a telegram from Howard Haire, secretary of the Atlanta Athletic Commission. "Am abiding by referee's decision declaring June Byers the winner over Mildred Burke for the women's championship, held in Atlanta, Ga., on Aug. 20. Byers won only fall of match. Congratulations to the new champion!" Haire's telegram, though dubious in origin, intent, and authority, gave an official imprimatur to Wolfe's crusade. He quickly put the wire to work, circulating it to the wrestling world as proof that Byers had won the match. But the referee's decision had been to declare Byers the winner of only a single fall, not the match itself, as the AP account clearly shows. The records of the Atlanta Athletic Commission have been lost. It is unknown what, if anything, Billy Wolfe did to obtain the telegram from Haire.

Two days after the match Wolfe got his version of events into the local paper back in Columbus. "Miss Byers, who claimed the title when Miss Burke failed to show up for a world tourney at Baltimore a year ago, is the queen of the mat, according to her manager, Billy Wolfe. 'She scored the only fall and must be regarded as the champ,' stormed Wolfe."

Wolfe, the master of publicity, was effective, as usual. A month after the match, the new *Wrestling World* magazine printed Wolfe's account and simply added to the bottom of it, "Well, now you know what happened." The men who ran *Wrestling World* were Wolfe's old friends Ned Brown and Al Mayer from the NWA magazine. For good measure, they put a picture of June Byers in a bikini and high heels on the rear cover of the magazine with the words, "New Undisputed Women's World Wrestling Champion."

Burke had no way to counter Wolfe's elaborate campaign. She said that the Atlanta promoter Paul Jones was so angry with the outcome of the match that he refused to pay her, even though he was one of her booking partners. "Tremendous plans and programs were in train at the time of the Atlanta bout, aimed at exploiting the status of the new champion," Burke wrote. "All this was derailed, and the promoter's fury was vented at payoff time. He refused to pay me a dime for packing his arena with the world title bout just concluded. I left the arena without enough money to get Joe and myself back to California." To raise the fare home, she said, Joe had to hock his serpent-head diamond ring and she had to wrestle matches in New Orleans for Joe Gunther, Nell Stewart's lover.

Burke's other partner at the time, Florida promoter Cowboy Luttrall, was also unhappy with how things had turned out. "Luttrall commented that the match was 'dull but should have been completed,'" according to the AP story. Luttrall wanted to get Burke and Byers to meet in a rematch in Tampa, but it never came off and Luttrall cut his losses. Four days after the Atlanta match Luttrall announced "Florida Recognizes June Byers as Champion of the World" in the souvenir program he controlled as part of his Tampa promotion. It was a huge blow to Burke's remaining claim on her title. "A newspaper report about the match said that Miss Byers won a 'moral victory' when the match was stopped when neither could get the upper hand in the second fall after nearly an hour of wrestling," the program notes stated. "But Miss Byers won the first and only fall decided in the match and that gave her the title, according to Promoter Luttrall. The genial Tampa promoter had signed the winner to meet an opponent in a title match here on Aug. 31 and it will be Miss Byers against a selected opponent."

Luttrall was now clearly in the other camp. "Miss Byers is every inch a champion," he told reporters. "She is in the best shape of her career and I am firmly convinced that she could have beaten Mildred in straight falls if the match had continued."

Luttrall's support was decisive in convincing those promoters who had not been swayed by the Baltimore tourment. "With the decision over Miss Burke in Atlanta, Miss Byers becomes the only recognized women's wrestling champion," according to Luttrall's program. "A dozen states recognized the Maryland decision, but Southern and Far West Wrestling Alliances still recognized Miss Burke. Now Florida and 25 other states have named Miss Byers the world's champion."

With New York and California off-limits and the Midwest locked up by Wolfe and Haft, Burke could not afford to lose the South and far West. Her support had dwindled down to pockets here and there. "There are many persons who do not agree with the ultimatum that Miss Byers is the champion," the Abilene, Texas, *Reporter-News* stated three months after the match. But Burke was now in the position of Clara Mortensen; the champion was the one whose claim received the most respectful attention in the press. That distinction now went to Byers.

The argument over the match would last for decades, with Burke protesting that she was still champion and Byers claiming she had won fair and square.

Byers gave a highly embellished account of the match to a British wrestling magazine in 1965. "We kept up a blistering pace, and the fans loved it, roaring approval every time one of us got socked or floored. But as the bout wore on, I realized that Mildred was slowing up," Byers said. "I had won the first fall with a series of crushing body slams." Byers went on to claim that she beat Burke for the decisive second fall. "I caught her bouncing off the ropes, smashed her into position for my Byers Bridge, in which I bend an opponent backward, and took the second and deciding fall," Byers said. "Well, you never saw such a stunned reaction from the audience. They couldn't believe that the great Mildred Burke had finally lost her title . . . A sad moment for Mildred . . . but a deliriously happy one for me. I should have been shouting with joy. But when I looked over at Mildred, shoulders sagging with defeat, all I felt like doing was bawling."

None of it was true.

Whatever else it was, the Atlanta match does not appear to have been a big moneymaker for Billy Wolfe. His records do not show any commissions for the match. Perhaps the Atlanta promoter refused also to pay him. Or maybe he had agreed to take nothing for the opportunity to have Byers shoot with Burke. For the month of August 1954 he showed a loss of $43.04. He had pulled off the greatest women's match in history and he had lost money. He ended the year with $5,304.66 in profits, half of which went toward the debt left over from Attractions, Inc. Half of the rest went to pay Mildred's debt to Sam Avey, the Tulsa promoter. Wolfe ended up making just $1,326.17 for the entire year.

June Byers and G. Bill did not have long to enjoy the triumph that Billy Wolfe had engineered for her. Two months after the Atlanta match June and G. Bill were robbed outside Stewartsville, Missouri, the very part of the country where Mildred Burke had begun her career as an arena wrestler in mixed matches with men eighteen years earlier.

June had wrestled in St. Joseph the night before, and the couple was heading back to Columbus on U.S. Highway 36 along with Betty Jo Floyd, another female wrestler. A car with a red light and siren pulled them over. Three gunmen with white handkerchiefs over their faces demanded their diamond jewelry. Two of the men got into the victims' car and drove them to a gravel road. G. Bill tried to hide two of his rings but the gunmen seemed to know exactly what they were looking for. G. Bill later told police that one of the robbers said the holdup had been planned for a long time. One struck Floyd on the head and G. Bill and Byers were beaten. June successfully hid her most valuable possession, however, the five-carat ring from Wolfe that she always flashed in front of the other girls back in Columbus. It was worth $10,000, the newspaper reported. When one of the robbers asked where it was, she told him it was being repaired in St. Joseph. The gunmen did get three of G. Bill's rings valued at a total of $12,500, his watch fob valued at $3,000, a stickpin and tie clasp worth $1,000, and a $500 collar pin. Byers surrendered a $4,000 watch, a $3,500 ring, and earrings worth $2,000. G. Bill also gave up $375 in cash, although the robbers gave back $140 after Byers said they needed the money to get home. The robbers tied up their three victims and disabled the car by puncturing a tire and pulling out the ignition wires. When they were alone Byers wriggled out of her bounds and freed the others. Then they walked along the highway until they came to a farmhouse.

The debate over who was the better wrestler continues to this day. In 1963 *Ring Wrestling,* then the leading wrestling publication, ran the famous picture of Mildred Burke posing in the zebra-striped two-piece and high heels, her muscles oiled and rippling. "After all is said and done, after all of the candidates for top consideration are paraded, we are left with Mildred Cyclone Burke, the greatest yet." The next year, the magazine's editor in chief asked Jack Pfefer, who had seen them all, for his opinion. "I would no more dare settle the Burke–Byers battle than I would tell my wife that she is wasting all that dough she spends weekly in her so-called beauty parlor," Pfefer said. "Live and let live. Does Byers have tricks Burke did not use? Yeah, a few of the rougher ones. Did Burke have holds which Byers has not developed so expertly? Yeah. Just so long as you ain't using my name. I would say Burke has the edge. But again—off the record. If you use my moniker I will deny the whole business."

Billy Wolfe's opinion changed over the years. A few years after the match, when Stewart was back in his good graces, he called her the "greatest female wrestler I've ever seen. We've never had a better athlete nor a bigger drawing card than Nell." Some years later, with more perspective, something closer to the truth came out. "I would rate Mildred Burke and June Byers as the finest, with Nell Stewart right on their heels," Wolfe said in an interview for Al Haft's souvenir program in 1960.

16

Millie without Billy

Two months after the Atlanta match, Mildred Burke wrote Jack Pfefer that she was at loose ends. "I am going to stay home for a while and get a much needed rest as I have been double-crossed so much I just got sick of the business," she wrote. "I broke Billy Wolfe which is what I set out to do, however that doesn't mean I am quitting." She also said she was getting married to Bert Younker, her nineteen-year-old driver. "The fellow traveling with me and I are getting married in February for three reasons," she wrote. "I love him very much, to stop Bill's foul mouth and to keep a bunch of jerks in the business from bothering me also I just can't travel alone."

Younker had met Burke when he was seventeen and she thirty-seven, through Joe Wolfe, his high school buddy. He had been stunned when she told him that she was the world champion lady wrester. "I'll tell you she was a real woman," Younker recalled fifty years later. "Very feminine, very loving, very good to me. She was very, very kind to her friends. But she was deadly to her enemies." Like G. Bill, he had bonded with Burke during the long hours on the road, beginning in early 1953. He drove her as much as eight hundred miles in a single day and watched the sad decline of her business from the front seat. "It was awful hard on her, trying to wrestle, contracts, the fifteen or sixteen girls working for her," he recalled. "She was just going hot and heavy all the time."

She was about to take one of the biggest trips of her life. In November 1954 Burke led the first contingent of American female wrestlers on a tour of Japan. Burke assembled several others who had come up through the Wolfe stable, Johnnie Mae Young, Gloria Barattini, Ruth Boatcallie. The tour was put together by some Honolulu promoters and backed by the Sankei Shinbun newspapers. Burke was still billed as the world champion. On November 10, 1954, the women were met with a tumultuous reception when they landed at Haneda international airport in Tokyo. "Thousands of Japanese greeters thronged the airport and its approaches, climbing fences, standing on top of cars and trucks, smiling and waving little American flags," Burke wrote. "When the stewardess opened the airliner door and I stepped out on the little platform, there was a roar of welcome from thousands of fans. . . . Rows of beautiful little Japanese girls, wearing their traditional kimonos, formed an aisle from the foot of the airline steps. Each of these delightful Japanese females carried a bouquet of flowers, and they pressed these into our hands with charming enthusiasm and warm smiles. Never had I ever been given such a reception in twenty years as world champion."

Billboards and posters plastered her face all over downtown Tokyo. Burke was thrilled but she was also worried about her bad knee, which ached as a result of the chilly Japanese weather. Burke's troupe wrestled twenty-six matches before U.S. troops at various military bases. Several of the matches were televised live by Nippon TV. In Burke's first bout the twenty-one-year-old Boatcallie stuck a finger in the thirty-nine-year-old champion's eye, Burke later wrote. The young girl's untrimmed and unusually long thumbnail sent a searing pain through

Burke's head. Millie thought it was deliberate and she sensed it was another Wolfe plot. "My immediate urge was to tear Ruth Boatcallie's head right off," she wrote. "I wanted to kill her." But realizing she was being watched by the Japanese promoters, Burke wrestled through an exciting, professional match. She then threatened to make Boatcallie "the sorriest human being that ever lived" if she did "one more crooked thing on this tour."

From that shaky beginning the tour went on to unimaginable success. In Tokyo, the women sold out three shows at the brand-new Kuramae Kokugikan Hall, the mecca of sumo, Japan's traditional style of wrestling. The preliminary bouts involved female Japanese amateurs. Burke noticed that the crowd was very different from the U.S. military audiences. The Japanese sat and watched in absolute silence. This was the Japanese way, a promoter told her, yet it did not sit well with her. "As the main event, my match, came closer and the Japanese crowd maintained its stolid silence, I became a little unnerved. I started to perspire." She later called it "the biggest moment of my life." She felt like a pioneer again, like little Millie Bliss setting out from Mom's Café. Only this felt much bigger.

"I was pioneering women's wrestling in Japan, breaking through centuries of tradition instead of the simple prejudice that I had beaten in my own country," she later wrote. "This was a booking that I had made myself, without the services or the sabotage of the old Columbus con man. Forty thousand fans had paid to see me and were waiting. All my life, it seemed to me as I walked down that longest of all aisles, had been a preparation for this one stupendous moment."

And it was about to happen in total silence. After she and Boatcallie entered the ring, a young Japanese boy handed each woman a bouquet of red roses. There had been no reaction, not even a patter of applause, as they made their entrance. Burke grabbed the Japanese flower boy and gave him a kiss, a spontaneous gesture of gratitude for the flowers. The vast crowd convulsed in cheering, yelling, bellowing, and whistling. Programs, papers, and hats rained into the ring. "I had really woken them up, in more ways than one," Burke wrote. "I was told that kissing in public was forbidden in Japan. Within fifteen seconds of my first appearance in public in Japan, I had cut down one of their cherished customs."

The match began. Now the crowd, its emotions aroused, broke its silence with periodic cheering and hollering. Once again, she had broken through. She believed it to be her finest moment in the ring. "A pinnacle of achievement had been reached after a twenty-year climb up from the carnivals," she later wrote. Since she was a child she had dreamed of flying over a large crowd, levitated by applause, and the overwhelming response in Japan once again brought home that she was living the dream.

The tour continued, selling out auditoriums throughout Japan, and then on into Hong Kong and the Philippines. During the matches the wayward Boatcallie struck again, Burke said, bending her over the ring ropes and savagely punching her in the solar plexus during a match in Kobe, a blow Burke called "one of the hardest I ever took." Once again, she smelled treachery. "She was trying to knock me out for a pin—to take the title on a double cross." This time Burke didn't hold back. She bounced off the ropes and punched Boatcallie in the face, repeatedly. Boatcallie crouched down to avoid the blows. Burke picked her up and body-slammed her. After the dazed Boatcallie had risen off the mat, Burke bounced her off the ropes and flattened her with a shoulder block that was followed by two more body slams and an Irish whip that flung Boatcallie across the ring. Finally, Burke clamped on the pièce de résistance, her most painful and devastating hold, the crooked-leg head scissors that had been the demise of the giantess twenty years earlier at that carnival in Kansas, where it had all begun. Boatcallie started yelping.

"I give up!" Boatcallie yelled. "I give up!"

In an interview decades later Boatcallie challenged Burke's account. "Mildred was hard to work with, you know," Boatcallie recalled. "I worked with Carol Cook for three years. It was like a dance. She was good. She was a baby face and she could really take the bumps. Mildred was sort of muscle-bound and harder to work with." Boatcallie said that she did get into it with Mildred in Japan. "She hit me across the nose, a miss," Boatcallie recalled. "I just came back at her. I got her up against the ropes and told her to watch it. We weren't used to working together."

Burke also said that she and Johnnie Mae Young also almost came to blows in a dressing room in Japan.

"How come *you're* always the main event and we're not?" Burke said Young had asked her.

"What do you think a world champion should be, a preliminary to *you*?"

Burke said Young drew back her fist.

"I've got a notion to knock your teeth right down your throat," Young said.

"Johnnie, before you swing that fist, let me tell you that you'd better be prepared to eat it, because I'm going to shove it right back in your mouth."

Young took fifteen seconds and finally lowered her fist. "There was no more mutiny from Mae Young," Burke wrote.

Burke said she thought Wolfe put Young up to it. "Whatever the real background to Mae Young's threat, she didn't frighten me. We had wrestled untold dozens of times through the years. She knew she couldn't beat me on the best day she ever saw."

In any case, Mildred Burke had given a lasting boost to women's wrestling in Japan. The next year, the All Japan Women's Pro-Wrestling Association formed in response to the interest generated by Burke's tour. For the next three years the business would thrive, then it would diminish. In the 1960s there would be a second and more lasting bloom, also propelled in part by Burke. Japan would grow into the world center of women's wrestling, both professional and amateur, a position the country maintains to this day.

Back in the United States Mildred Burke had a hard time finding her place in life. She later wrote that she should have retired after Japan. For weeks after the trip she had basked in a rosy glow, but she knew she was now at a crossroads. She realized she would not be able to top Japan, and she did not want a sad fade into obscurity. "Despite my bad knee, I knew I could carry on for many years in the ring. I also knew that my performances would slowly decline. My thirty-ninth birthday had passed, and I don't want to join Jack Benny in making it last as long as possible, because in wrestling it wouldn't be funny. My respected public would not enjoy seeing an 'old woman' in her forties in the wrestling ring."

The truth was that she was being forced into retirement. The Japan triumph did little to solve her money problems. She complained that her bookers had agreed to pay her in advance, then failed to do so. Her check of $500 for her last week of work had the payment stopped on it. The trip had not gone through bookers associated with the NWA, and once again this brought her into conflict with pro wrestling's ruling monopoly. The NWA member in Honolulu who considered Japan his province was furious. Al Karasick wrote to NWA president Sam Muchnick while Burke's trip was in progress. "I am sure that no member of the NWA has cooperated with them, but at the same time would appreciate it if in a bulletin you might mention the matter, for future, should anyone be approached to go to Japan and wrestle, under any other office but mine," Karasick wrote.

Burke was dead broke and desperate for work but found few takers. On March 9, 1955, she wrote to Toots Mondt, the dean of wrestling promoters who still commanded enormous respect in NWA circles. She wanted to know if he could get her bookings and a tour of South America. "It will certainly be appreciated from the bottom of my heart as I have many debts hanging over my head and no other way of paying them," she wrote. But Toots himself had fallen on hard times, including a bankruptcy a year earlier that forced the sale of his venerable Manhattan Booking Agency for $200. He knew a lot of history and a lot of people in the wrestling business but his ability to mount the kind of tour she needed was nonexistent at this point. In two years, Mondt would hook up with Vince McMahon Sr., the D.C. promoter who was the coming power in pro wrestling. McMahon would use his control of the TV wrestling broadcasts in New York City to create the Capitol Wrestling Corporation, a D.C.-based promotion that eventually controlled Boston and Philadelphia as well. Under the auspices of McMahon, Mondt got back into the game. It was McMahon's help that Burke needed, not Mondt's, and within a year McMahon would put his weight behind Lillian Ellison.

In her letter to Mondt, Burke apologized for the incident involving the non-NWA booking in Toots's territory in New Jersey. "For any misunderstandings we have had in the past I am truly sorry as in my fight against Bill I done things that hurt other people and only wish I could undue [sic] them," she wrote. "I will be looking forward to hearing from you soon as my situation is urgent."

Two weeks after writing to Toots, she sat down with the Justice Department attorneys who had just revitalized an antitrust investigation of the NWA. The Justice Department had frist received complaints in 1953 in Los Angeles from wrestlers and promoters that the NWA had a stranglehold on the sport. Burke told the feds the story of her recent battles with Billy Wolfe and added everything she knew about the NWA trying to control wrestlers and squelch competition. To the allegations of Wolfe's business double-dealing, she added information that the IRS was investigating him over his 1951 return. She also told the feds that on two occasions he had tried to get women to work her over "or to kill her" in the ring. "She also believes that he is responsible for the death of a girl wrestler whom he booked as his adopted daughter, Janet Wolfe," the Justice Department memo on the interview states. Burke said it was a classic case of overtraining. "She believes Wolfe was training Janet to defeat her," the memo stated.

Millie had been living with her brother and mother in Reseda in the San Fernando Valley. After getting married in Oakland she and Bert moved across the bay to an apartment in San Francisco. She tried to reestablish herself as a wrestler, hooking up with Bill Newman, a non-NWA promoter in the city. In June 1955 Newman's office put out new promotional material for her using several of the old lines from the Billy Wolfe publicity sheet: "Mildred Burke, world's wrestling champion, can best be described as the Pin-Up Girl who pins 'em down—at $50,000 a year." She had "a waist of a musical comedy star and the build of a female Atlas."

The $50,000 was now wishful thinking, a vestige of a golden age that was long gone.

Her new publicity blitz got her nothing but more trouble from her NWA enemies. Even though she was past forty, she said that she planned on wrestling for quite some time. "Lou Thesz is 10 years older than I and the champ is still wrestling," she told a reporter for the Long Beach, California, *Press-Telegram*. Thesz, the beloved NWA champ, was in fact a year younger than Burke. Billy Wolfe, quick to spot an opportunity to score a point on an adversary, made note of the outrage to NWA president Muchnick. "Please notice, in quotations, she declares Thesz ten years older than she is, and most of the promoters of the entire Nation know or believe Mildred to be forty-three years of age." Wolfe was so angry that he resorted to using all capital letters:

"JUST HOW DIRTY AND UNFAIR, WITHOUT ANY REA-SON WHATSOEVER, CAN A WOMAN BE?"

On July 18, 1955, Mildred Burke wrestled her last match in the United States. She met Ruth Boatcallie in Reno, Nevada. A record crowd of 2,300, the largest ever to see a wrestling match in the state, turned out at Reno's Moana Ball Park. Burke pinned Boatcallie for the third fall after the two engaged in an out-of-the-ring melee, a feature that had long ago become a standard part of the act. The story in the Nevada *State Journal* provides the final image of Burke in the ring. "The champion entered the ring in a silver-white two-pieced garment, a mop of auburn hair and wearing her $10,000 bejeweled champion's belt. The latter she removed, bringing her weight to 145." The article neglected to mention that the jewels had been removed from the belt and hocked; the shiny baubles that remained were fakes.

The next day she recieved one last burst of publicity as an active wrestler, a column on the local sports pages. She used it to announce that she had opened a gym in San Francisco with $20,000 worth of equipment to train women to wrestle. "The housewife has taken a beating, both physically and mentally, long enough," she said. "I want her to stand up and assert herself."

She was whistling in the dark. Her association with Newman brought her no other business. In September 1955, she called the Justice Department to check on its NWA investigation. "She said that in San Francisco she had tried to open up booking girl wrestlers; that she had sent out announcements to over 300 promoters in the country, and had not received a single answer—showing how tightly the NWA had things tied up," the Justice Department memo on her phone call states. Burke also reported that Ruth Boatcallie had called Houston promoter Morris Sigel to get a booking for her and Burke only to be turned down and told, "You know how Billy Wolfe is."

★   ★   ★

Millie and Bert eventually moved to San Diego, to accommodate Bert's new job, not hers. Younker had joined the Coast Guard—he and Joe Wolfe went together and signed up on the same day in 1955. But Joe and Bert had gone their separate ways after Bert became Joe's new stepfather. "I think it became a little bit of an embarrassment because we were close and the same age," Joe recalled. "Even though Bert and I ran around together and were the best of friends, that just kind of did it for us." Joe gave the couple a wide berth and went through a period of time where he didn't know what his mother was doing. Bert started work as an aviation technician at the Coast Guard Air Station in San Diego.

At first, Burke kept away from wrestling. The pain was too fresh. "If anyone met me, even in the street, and mentioned wrestling, I would weep uncontrollably," she later wrote. "Any event, scene or magazine illustration that had anything to do with wrestling affected me similarly. Just hearing the word eventually sufficed to trigger tears." Gradually, the bad feelings faded and the old interest returned. She tried to train a new group of women wrestlers that she could manage and book into matches. To help make ends meet, she put her stenography training to work and got a job the next year as a clerk for the Atlas Rocket Division of Convair Astronautics. But the bills mounted and she was forced to file for bankruptcy protection in 1958. She listed debts totaling $15,555.51, including $3,500 to the Zales jewelry stores in Albuquerque and El Paso, $2,300 still owed to Gorgeous George for his help in the Billy Wolfe battle, $1,618.62 to Polly's Women's Apparel in Van Nuys, and $600 still owed to her lawyer Bob Barton for the Attractions, Inc., debacle. Against that mountain of debt she listed assets of $350: furniture, appliances, clothes, pictures, family portraits and frames, one radio, and one television.

When *Ring Wrestling* magazine caught up with her that year, the writer found her putting on her best face. She said she was happily married to Younker—she posed in an apron cooking him breakfast—

and planning another comeback as a booker of wrestlers in the San Diego area. She intended to manage women—even though California still banned them from wrestling in the state—as well as a male heavyweight contender named Jess Johnson. She also said she was working on her autobiography, to be called "The Third Fall," which "will go to the presses sometime this summer."

The book did not appear that summer. Jess Johnson faded into obscurity. Her new troupe of women wrestlers was no more successful than any of the others. Bert, trained in electronics, left the Coast Guard in 1959 and began working for a defense contractor that did work on submarines in Glendale. They divorced in 1962, after nearly eight years of marriage. The parting was amicable. "I just didn't believe in the things she was doing," he said. "She went one way and I went another. She liked money. She liked to spend a lot of money. And I'm a frugal guy. It was money that was the biggest reason." They remained friends, and as he rose in business to attain a top secret clearance and become the supervisor of the fire control system for the U.S. Navy's Seawolf submarine, he remembered what he had learned from her. "Mildred taught me a lot," he said. "Most of my success was her logic and her thinking. Her get-up-and-go. She was quite a gal. I'll never forget her."

Mildred again became close to Joe, who had left the Coast Guard and found a good job with the Culligan water company. Millie worked as a registrar at the Los Angeles Chiropractic College. She kept her hand in wrestling, even if only part-time, renting space at a small gym on Roscoe Boulevard in Northridge and advertising for prospects in the *Los Angeles Times:* "Girl Wrestlers. Girls wanted to learn wrestling, a fabulous well paying career, under supervision of world champion Mildred Burke. Requirements are age 18 thru 21, 5'2" to 5'8". Attractive, healthy and free to travel." To Pfefer in October 1962 she wrote, "I am divorced and not connected with anyone personally. I have some truly beautiful girls in training and when I think they are ready I will send them on tour."

That year she got a job as fitness director for the La Quinta Shangri-La resort in Indio, California, and extolled the resort as "a new adventure in living and the ultimate in physical fitness" in letters to friends in the wrestling business. She also let them know she had not given up on wrestling. "I am training the finest stable of professional lady wrestlers to ever be presented," she wrote. "In the near future you will receive publicity on them."

Women were still banned from wrestling in California and she found no bookings elsewhere. The resort job didn't last long, and her son got her work as a saleswoman for Culligan, going door to door. "I got many a chuckle out of people who would open their doors, recognize me from the old days, and point at me saying, 'Didn't you used to be Mildred Burke, the rassler?'"

Joe also bought her a small chili parlor in LA, Millie's Chili, which she operated with her friend and fellow former wrestler Mae Weston. Burke used a recipe from Mom's Café and proudly displayed a large color poster of herself posing in her wrestling togs, wearing the gold belt with her biceps flexed. She was back where she had started, working in a small restaurant serving her mother's chili.

17

Billy without Millie

The championship match in Atlanta did little to improve Billy Wolfe's prospects. As Mildred Burke left the stage pro wrestling continued its decline. Wrestling coverage moved off the networks and onto local stations. "We are now in the midst of a depression, judging by the dropoff in business most everywhere," Sam Muchnick wrote to the NWA membership.

Wolfe finalized his divorce from Nell Stewart in October 1954, once again entirely on his terms. The paperwork was handled for Wolfe by Curtis H. Porter, one of the lawyers who had invested with Mildred Burke and then forced her business into receivership. Stewart did not contest the filing and Wolfe received a default judgment on the grounds that Stewart was "guilty of gross neglect of duty." She also received no alimony. She did keep the title to her car, a 1954 Oldsmobile. Wolfe kept his 1950 Lincoln, all the household furniture, and his real estate, which included the home at 1315 Franklin Avenue in Columbus where G. Bill and June Byers now lived.

Byers continued to travel with G. Bill and he continued to drink. At one point, she checked him into a clinic to dry out. Billy Wolfe had to go to Missouri to fetch him. But then G. Bill joined Alcoholics Anonymous, got sober, and changed his life. Using one of Billy's lawyers, Byers divorced G. Bill in March 1956 and he quickly married eighteen-year-old Betsy Ross, a beautiful girl from West Virginia. Ross had left a girls' home to work as Billy Wolfe's secretary while still in her early teens before becoming a wrestler for him. G. Bill retired from the wrestling business and started selling life insurance. Betsy retired from the wrestling ring and started having children. They settled down in the small town of Newark outside Columbus and began living the middle-class American dream. They documented their home life in a series of Kodak moments that reveal children at play and adults goofing around—an apparently genuine happiness.

Billy Wolfe kept at the wrestling game. Business was bad but his press remained stellar. "Grand Vizier of Gal Grappling throughout the entire world is William Wolfe, better know to pals as Billy," proclaimed *Boxing and Wrestling* magazine. He continued to seek sexual recompense from his wrestlers. On July 10, 1956, Wolfe married LeeChona LaClaire. She was twenty years old. He had turned sixty six days earlier. LaClaire went on to win the TV wrestling championship, the lesser title that had been one of Nell's claims to fame. "If there is any better way for a girl wrestler to become a champion than by being trained by Billy Wolfe and married to him, it doesn't present itself at the moment," reporter Joe R. Mills wrote in the Columbus, Ohio, *Star* on September 15, 1956. A week after the story Wolfe filed for divorce. "The ink wasn't cool on the story of the love of Billy Wolfe and LeeChona LaClair [*sic*] last week before that great and consuming passion had chilled," the *Star* noted. "Who knows?" Wolfe said. "We may be married again before another paper comes out."

Wolfe had found out that LaClaire was more than he could handle. A few days after the *Star* story touting his happy home life, he came into his office at the Park Hotel looking very dour. LaClaire had taken off in the Chevy Bel Aire convertible that Wolfe had given her as a wedding present and had not come home. Later in the day, Wolfe took a call from the Florida Highway Patrol; his wife had had an accident and was in the hospital. She wasn't too badly hurt. They put her on the phone. "But, honey, you didn't tell me you were going swimming in *Florida*," Billy said. When LaClaire got back to Ohio, Billy had her served with divorce papers during dinner. "I thought you said you wanted me to come back?" she said to Wolfe. "I did," he told her. "The car's not in your name yet."

Once again, the divorce was on his terms. LaClaire was found in default and "guilty of extreme cruelty." She got no alimony or property. This time the divorce was handled by George Hedges, another of the lawyers who had sunk Burke's business. Like Stewart and Byers, LaClaire kept wrestling for Wolfe after their divorce. "He still treated her like a queen," recalled his secretary Sherrie Lee. "He was very generous with his wives." Despite what the divorce decree says, Lee said Wolfe let LaClaire keep the Bel Aire convertible.

A month later the Department of Justice settled its antitrust suit against the National Wrestling Alliance. To resolve the matter, the NWA had agreed to rewrite its bylaws and change its monopolistic ways. Billy Wolfe was one of the thirty-four promoters and bookers who signed the settlement for the NWA. Wolfe was interviewed about his role in the NWA by none other than Jimmy Breslin, then a cub reporter for a wire service. "I'm still puzzled," Wolfe said. "What in the world would the government want to bother June Byers for? Don't they know how tough she is?"

The government's great investigation of the NWA, the organization that had upheld Mildred Burke's bitterest enemy and helped destroy her career, had closed with a quip. Still, the NWA went into decline after the consent decree and never again wielded the same power. After all, who needed to belong to an illegal monopoly that promised no longer to act as an illegal monopoly?

Wolfe's luck in business, as in love, appeared to have run out. He had lost money in each of the last eight months of 1956 and ended the year with a profit of only $345.47, hampered in part by his obligation to keep paying down the debt owed by Attractions, Inc. He remained on a ceaseless search for the next Mildred Burke, a new prospect he could develop into a champion and use to restore the business. An article in the Columbus *Star* in April 1957 reported Wolfe thought twenty-one-year-old Joyce Bragg was "one of the hottest finds ever." But she did not go on to a notable career, much less become the next Mildred Burke. With Bragg there was no romance, Wolfe emphasized, going out of his way to cut down on the tongue wagging about his harem. "I'm a very happily married man."

The new Mrs. Billy Wolfe, the fifth one, was seventeen-year-old Lola Laray, another of his wrestlers. The marriage lasted two months. Once again the ex-wife got nothing. Laray was found in default and "guilty of extreme cruelty and gross neglect of duty."

Like Millie Bliss, Laray had been a single woman with a baby when she married Wolfe. "I needed a way to support me and my child . . . Not only did I get into professional wrestling, but I also married Billy," she reminisced years later. Like LaClaire, Laray had no hard feelings for Wolfe. "I was simply too young at that point in my life and Billy was considerably older than me. We parted but remained very good friends up to the day he died."

Nell Stewart returned to Wolfe, professionally at least, after a two-year absence. He was overjoyed. "I believe Nell is better than ever," an excited Wolfe wrote Pfefer in July 1957. "The two-years rest she had, seems to have done her good . . . A few months back, Nell allowed herself to get a little heavy, but she has lost that extra weight, and possitively [*sic*], and absolutely looks like a million dollars in the ring and out of the ring." A week later, in a match between two of Wolfe's ex-wives, Stewart defeated LaClaire at Haft's Acre in Columbus to regain the Ohio women's championship.

Stewart went out on the road with one group of Wolfe's wrestlers while Byers led another. "I am working with about 12 girls and 4 cars, and with this smaller outfit, I'm in more personal touch with each girl and getting better results on each girls [sic] dependability," he wrote Pfefer. "When I had 30 girls and 10 cars everything went crazy in all directions." He was philosophical about it. "A few years back, I did have a big business but I worked day and night and I want to take it a little easier now. I am working less hours and making enough money to be happy and I don't want a big outfit again." The big outfit was now run by Vincent J. McMahon, whose Capitol Wrestling promotion was starting on its path toward wrestling domination. With McMahon's support, Slave Girl Moolah won a tournament in September 1956 in Baltimore that did not include Byers and thus laid claim to yet another version of the title.

Wolfe wrote Pfefer that he was "showing a reasonable profit," but his surviving records show a loss of $2,160.27 for 1957. That year, no longer in need of a big national organization to watch his back, he dropped out of the NWA.

The audience for female wrestlers had dried up.

The dynamics of Wolfe's harem were changing. The girls had gotten younger and less experienced, and he was more and more the sugar daddy trying to keep up. As his earnings dwindled he spent the cash he had accumulated when he was the czar of women's wrestling. He needed to spread his money around to keep his wrestlers around; he no longer had glamour and riches and fame to offer them. "The girls would borrow money and give him IOUs and for Christmas he would tear them up and say, 'Merry Christmas,'" recalled Sherrie Lee. He bought them gifts and treated them at Carollo's, a fancy steak house on North High Street in Columbus. "Most of the girls called him 'Papa,'" Lee recalled. "Most of the girls were party girls. They liked nightclubs. Most of the girls married him because he had money. It was what he could do for them."

But the money was running out. In 1958, he had to give up the house on Franklin Avenue and move back into the Park Hotel. In two years, his revenues had dropped from $18,000 to $3,810. A friend visited him at the hotel and found that he kept his filing cabinet with his publicity photos and records in the bathtub.

Increasingly, his wrestlers were leaving him. June Byers left to wrestle as champion for the new man in her life, Frank "Sam" Menacker, a forty-four-year-old TV wrestling announcer and former promoter in El Paso. Wolfe was conciliatory. "Anything that Sammy and June do, is all right with me," he wrote to Pfefer. "Like Mildred Burke, they both have money troubles because it costs a lot of money on the road for them and they both have children at home to support." Nell Stewart returned to New Orleans and Joe Gunther. As her career dwindled she had been required to "put over" LeeChona LaClaire, who was younger and on the rise. "Beating Nell was a little sad," LaClaire recalled. "She'd always been my idol. It was like Rocky Marciano knocking out Joe Louis, I imagine, or some eighteen-year-old kid beating the great Jim Londos." Eventually LaClaire also left; she got married and had a baby.

LaClaire returned to wrestle for him in 1960, with the permission of her husband. She won an elimination tournament staged by Wolfe at the Ohio State Fairgrounds Coliseum. He tried to argue that she deserved the title over Burke, Byers, and Moolah but he no longer controlled the business, and he had little ability to put LaClaire over. When he wrote to Penny Banner a month later to congratulate her on having a baby, the sentiment was marred by self-pity. "You will remember when you came to me that June Byers was then in the championship picture," Wolfe wrote. "When Mildred Burke pulled away from me I immediately established June Byers as the champion. You left my booking office before June Byers and Sammy Menacker had pulled away from me but had you still been with me when they pulled away, I would have spent my time and money to help you become the greatest of all girl champions."

Someone finally reported him to authorities for doing what people behind his back had been hinting he'd been doing all along, pimping out his women to powerful promoters. The informant, a male wrestler whose identity is still secret, admitted that he had no information to substantiate his allegation; the FBI never found any reason to charge Wolfe.

The next year, 1961, Wolfe became excited by yet another prospect, eighteen-year-old Karen Kellogg. One newspaper reporter described her as "an unmistakably attractive blue-eyed blond weighing 118 pounds." She was pretty but unschooled, a sweet corn-fed girl who was a bit of a country bumpkin, born and raised in Charles City, Iowa. Kellogg, the oldest of five children, had ditched a secretarial career after seeing women's wrestling on the family's first TV set.

Kellogg was not just his newest prospect; she was, like Burke, Stewart, Byers, LaClaire, and Laray before her, his newest paramour. The Kodak-moment pictures taken by G. Bill and Betsy Ross show Billy Wolfe and Karen Kellogg celebrating the holidays together, with the old man planting a passionate kiss on the mouth of the teenage girl. There was a forty-seven year difference in their ages. "He said they couldn't marry until she turned twenty-one," Sherrie Lee, his secretary, recalled. "He didn't want her parents to have to sign for her."

He tried to work the old promotional magic, invoking the name of his most famous champion to sell his newest one. "Karen is dazzling fast, very strong and she has learned the finer points of the sport faster than any girl I've ever developed with the possible exception of my famous all-time champion, the great Mildred Burke," Wolfe wrote to the *Wrestling Revue*. "It wouldn't be long before the whole world knows about Karen Kellogg, and calling her another Mildred Burke, which is the highest tribute any female wrestler can hope to get." But the headlines he ended up getting were in publications like the *Hartley Eastern Review*, a small newspaper in the suburbs of Columbus: "Great as Mildred? Karen Kellogg Seen as Lady Wrestling Champ."

In April 1962 Wolfe wrote to Jack Pfefer to thank him for sending him a box of neckties. "The note you put in with the neckties is real encouraging to me," Wolfe wrote. "When such men as you have confidence in my future success it helps me a lot to have confidence in myself." But the future was ebbing before him. His tax return for the previous year showed business income of $1,156.38 and expenses of $3,264.21, a loss of more than $2,000. He said he was delayed in writing because he had to find a new place to live. The Park Hotel was being torn down. When Pfefer next came to Columbus, Wolfe offered to show him "my little five room living quarters."

Wolfe coronated Kellogg on November 3, 1962, at Bluefield, West Virginia, a hardscrabble coal mining town. They drove 230 miles to get there from Columbus, Wolfe behind the wheel, Karen resting in the backseat. When Wolfe's powder-blue Mercury sedan pulled into Bluefield, he got out and opened the door for her. "If you get the breaks tonight," he told her, "the next time you get into this car you'll be champion." Wolfe's newest girlfriend won the lightweight title in a match against his most recent ex-wife, Lola Laray.

Billy Wolfe lived four more months. On March 6, 1963, he suffered a heart attack while he was on the road with his wrestlers heading home after matches in Richmond. He had been fighting the flu and had felt poorly all day. Karen wanted him to see a doctor but he refused. In

Opal, Virginia, they stopped at a restaurant so he could get a drink and take some aspirins. Karen accompanied him inside. They sat at the counter and a waitress brought him a glass of water. As soon as he had taken the aspirins he said, "I feel like I'm going to faint." Then he fell backward off the stool. He was taken to Fauquier Hospital in Warrenton, where he was pronounced dead at about 1 a.m. He was sixty-six.

A month later, Al Haft wrote to Jack Pfefer. "I am very sorry that I cannot send you clippings on Billy Wolfe's funeral. He was not buried in Columbus. I was at the funeral which was at Newark Ohio. So it was not carried in the Columbus papers." Haft said G. Bill had given his father a "wonderful funeral . . . Many of the girls wrestlers, both white & black, were there. Other folks among the wrestling fraternity were also on hand." A few days later a Columbus *Citizen* columnist did a short appreciation for the "masterful showman," recalling their first meeting. "The year was 1937, the place Wheeling, W.Va., and I had only a few months of sports writing under my belt," the columnist wrote. "Billy was handling a well-muscled gal named Mildred Burke, the queen of the mat. I was at the press table ringside when Billy, assisting Mildred into the ring, paused and called Miss Burke to my side. There, a red-faced 20-year-old rookie sports editor had to squeeze the muscles of Billy's champion . . . before a packed house."

G. Bill was named the administrator of his father's estate. At forty-one, G. Bill bore no resemblance to the young man who had worked for Billy Wolfe. Sober now, he drank Squirt and buttermilk out of the bottle. He loved his children, relishing the time he spent with them and his pretty young wife, Betsy. He was on the road a lot, selling insurance, but the weekends were cherished. "Every weekend when he came home, he cooked, he grilled," recalled his daughter, Mickie Johnson. "My dad was really tender and really affectionate. He became a Christian through Alcoholics Anonymous. He was a gentle man. He used to say, 'I love you as big as the sky.'"

Nearly a year after his father died G. Bill was sitting in his favorite spot, a kidney-colored leather easy chair, watching Jackie Gleason on the television. He suddenly grabbed his chest. He, too, suffered a heart attack. He lived eleven days in an oxygen tent at the hospital. He was forty-two. In addition to his family, his obituary mentioned his insurance company, his church, and that "he was associated with his father as a wrestling promoter until 1956." G. Bill's estate was modest: $925 in personal goods and $3,500 in real estate. It was slightly less in value than the watch fob, tie clasp, and stickpin he had lost in the robbery with June Byers a decade earlier.

William Harrison Wolfe and George William Wolfe are buried near each other at the Maple Grove Cemetery in Granville, Ohio. None of the seven women they married are buried near them.

Betsy Ross struggled to support herself and her four children after losing the two most important men in her life in a little more than a year. "Billy was her salvation, G. Bill was the love of her life," said her daughter, Mickie Johnson. "The most important thing about her life was Billy Wolfe. He took this little girl and made her beautiful and glamorous." She suffered a nervous breakdown and was institutionalized. After some time, she recovered and got the children back. She worked for a while as an exotic dancer. Eventually, she settled into a life of taking in laundry and typing papers for students at Ohio State University.

Nell Stewart continued wrestling into the 1960s, but without the glamour or the diamonds. Ida May Martinez visited her around this time and found her living in an apartment in New Orleans with Joe Gunther. By the 1980s Stewart was working as a hostess at Pat O'Brien's, a lounge in the French Quarter. She lived out her life alone in a trailer outside of Gardendale, Alabama, working as a clerk at a liquor store. Nobody remembered that she had once been the so-called Betty Grable of wrestling. In 2001 she died of cancer of the throat. Penny

Banner and Ida May Martinez spearheaded a fund-raising drive for the $3,000 needed to provide Stewart with a decent burial.

June Byers continued to wrestle as champion throughout the 1950s, but she worked increasingly in Moolah's shadow. In 1959 she married Sam Menacker. She talked in every interview about beating Mildred Burke in Atlanta. In 1963 Byers had a serious automobile accident in Indiana, where she and Menacker had started a wrestling school for women. "She was going down a winding road and she swerved to miss a little dog," recalled her daughter, Jewel Olivas. "She lost control and hit a tree." Her right leg was crushed, her right knee cap shattered. A pin was put in the leg and she never wrestled again. Byers and Menacker divorced and she remarried and divorced again and again. In the end, none of her seven marriages would prove successful. In the 1980s she hocked the big diamond ring that Billy Wolfe had given her to help her brother open a restaurant in Las Vegas. The venture failed and she never saw the ring again. Byers, who now went by the name DeAlva Snyder, became a real estate agent outside Houston. When she died in 1998 her family took out an obituary saying she retired as "the only Woman's World Wrestling Champion of the World."

Karen Kellogg wrestled a few more times but, without Wolfe behind her, she was lost. While they were together Wolfe and Kellogg had a child. He was born in 1961. The child was given up for adoption, and his new family gave him the name Tim Kelly. After he grew to adulthood he traced his birth parents. He found the name Karen Kellogg on his birth certificate. Her address was listed as the Park Hotel in Columbus. Through the Internet Kelly learned that Kellogg had once been a famous lady wrestler for Billy Wolfe. Tim Kelly put two and two together. He traced Karen Kellogg, who had suffered several strokes, to a nursing home in Iowa. "When I asked her who my dad was, she told me in a heartbeat: 'It was Billy Wolfe, I wasn't with anybody else.'" A DNA test with Marie Laverne, the daughter of the wrestler Ann Laverne and who has long been thought to be Billy Wolfe's out-of-wedlock daughter, confirmed the truth of it. "I'm Billy Wolfe's last son as far as I can tell," Kelly said. During his visit with Kellogg he was struck by "the twinkle in her eye" when she talked about Wolfe. "I believe she was still in love with him," Kelly said. He asked his mother why his birth certificate indicated that he had been delivered by the county coroner. "He was good friends with Billy Wolfe," she told him. "He did it as a favor. You were delivered in the morgue."

18

Mildred Burke Productions

California finally repealed its ban on female professional wrestlers in 1966. This was the opening Mildred Burke needed, and she threw herself into promoting the women she was training. Her circumstances were humble; she was now working out of a gym located inside an arcade on Van Nuys Boulevard in Los Angeles. But she soon found an eager venue for her wrestlers in Japan, where she had planted the seed of women's wrestling more than a decade earlier. She established a new women's title, the World Wide Women's Wrestling Association championship, and her girls traded it among themselves and with female Japanese pros, helping to create a second revival of the women's side of the sport in that nation. In Japan, the WWWWA belt became a coveted title known as "the red belt." It would be contested there for thirty-five years.

Gradually, Burke's fortunes started to improve in the United States as well. "I now have my own gym and a number of good girls with more in the making," she wrote to Jack Pfefer in December 1968. She was still living with her brother and mother in Reseda, but the wrestling magazines announced that she was back, with a stable of twenty women. Still, Burke found little success promoting matches outside of Japan. It was the Fabulous Moolah who reigned as world champion, with the backing of the new power in wrestling, Vince McMahon. Moolah promoted her own troupe of women wrestlers and did not want to share the business with Burke. In the view of some wrestling purists, Moolah had extremely limited wrestling ability and had made a mockery out of the women's end of the business. "Anybody can beat Moolah," Ida May Martinez said.

Burke was home watching wrestling on television one night when she heard Moolah announced as the world champion who had taken the title from Mildred Burke. She complained to the newspapers. "I've never even met Moolah in street clothes," Burke said. A wrestling magazine made the same claim. She got them to print a retraction. But she was fighting the tide.

The woman who was now the wrestling queen had been a nonentity when Burke was at her peak. When they were both wrestling for Billy Wolfe, Burke had been the remote champion, always on the road, and Moolah one of many neophytes who had not yet risen to the point of being credible opponents for Burke. They had met only once, in the dressing room after a Burke match. Moolah still retained some of the awe she had felt for Burke from the time she was a teenager who had been mesmerized by the sight of the champion in the ring in South Carolina. That vision had set the course of Moolah's life. To a writer for a wrestling magazine in the early 1960s, Moolah had spoken of Burke with reverence. "Mildred Burke broke my leg once, in Indianapolis," Moolah told *Wrestling Revue*. "She, incidentally, was the greatest of them all. There has never been a better wrestler than Mildred. I doubt that there ever will be." But they had never met in the ring.

After California opened up Burke appealed to Moolah, but Moolah wasn't interested, Burke later said. "The main reason I dislike her—

when California opened up again for women, I had some girls training at the time, and I wrote to Moolah to let her know it was opening
up and I said, 'Moolah, I'd like to work with you. You have everything on that side and I'll have everything on this side and we'll work
together.'" Burke never heard back from the woman who had once
idolized her.

On June 5, 1972, when New York ended its forty-year ban on
women's wrestling, it was Moolah who had the honor of wrestling in
the first woman's match at Madison Square Garden before a crowd of
19,512.

Burke found another avenue that offered the chance of a comeback,
and it did not involve women wrestling women but women taking
on men, the very type of thing that had afforded her the breakthrough
back in the 1930s. It came at a time when women were challenging
men in all walks of life.

By the early 1960s the seeds of a women's equality movement
were taking hold in America, with birth control pills giving women a
measure of sexual freedom and Betty Friedan's *The Feminine Mystique*
providing a manifesto. The idea that women were the "weaker sex"
began to be debated in nearly every forum. It was natural that the
argument would end up in the wrestling ring. "Weaker Sex? Not in
Wrestling—Moolah," read the cover of *Wrestling Revue* in December
1963. Inside, the current women's champion bragged that she was
willing to get into the ring with the current male champion.

Soon letter writers in wrestling magazines were arguing whether
or not women should compete with men in pro mixed matches. The
female writers tended to be in favor of the idea. "I'm a teenage girl—
and I think it's about time men and women can fight the 'Battle of
the Sexes' in the ring," wrote an aspiring female wrestler from Shelby
Gap, Kentucky. "Not allowing men and women to wrestle each other
is just plain discriminatory." A former female pro said she and her sisters

"could cripple any male amateur"; at nineteen, she had dispatched a "real confident" male wrestler with "a tight head scissors for about 5 minutes."

Many men relished the prospect. "If any professional promoters want to pack their houses they have only to stage mixed matches in which the gals would not suffer from too great weight handicaps," a California man wrote to *Ring Wrestling* magazine. Another writer who had seen a mixed match "between a good man wrestler and a good woman grappler in Hamburg recently" noted that the bout was not the least bit indecent. The magazine's editors scoffed. "We do not wish to have anything to do with these affairs of doubtful usefulness and more doubtful propriety." But fans from around the world continued to press for the matches. "Your opposition to mixed matches displays a prudery which was rampant when Victoria was our queen," wrote a man from England. "He who is clean of mind and attentive to skills, to the sinuous movements of the girls, to their speed and adroit demonstrations of the many holds, the many forms of defense, will see only the good points of mixed matches. I have seen a few here in England and they are more thrilling than any one sex fights." The question simply refused to go away. In December 1970, *Ring Wrestling* itself put it on the cover: "Can Gals Beat Men in Pro Mixed Matches?"

In 1972 Congress passed Title IX, which prohibited discrimination in public schools on the basis of sex; the law would eventually do more than anything else to open up high school sports, including wrestling, to girls. The next year, Billie Jean King convincingly beat Bobby Riggs in a tennis match that was billed as "The Battle of the Sexes." As for the battle of the sexes in the wrestling ring, once again Mildred Burke made the breakthough. She had been training her women wrestlers—she called them Millie's Girls—using male opponents. Soon, she was filming her girls in matches against male pros. Joe Wolfe was the cameraman, capturing the matches on Super 8mm film.

In August 1974, *Wrestling Monthly* splashed a picture on its cover of a mixed match between Laura Del Rio, a 150-pounder who was one of Burke's top prospects, and Angel Cortez, a 180-pound male light heavyweight. Inside, a five-page article featured a dozen more photos of the match. Burke's touch could be seen in the "eye-popping" details. Del Rio entered the ring in a bright orange suit and white boots, a brilliant contrast to the coal-black trunks and boots of Cortez. When the bell sounded, the deeply tanned, well-built Del Rio tore into her bigger male opponent. From the outset, she was faster and more aggressive. The article's author surmised that the muscular Cortez figured on treating the match as an exhibition and taking it easy on his attractive female opponent, only to be surprised by a whirling wildcat who wanted to prove a point about women's wrestling. An obviously talented athlete who had been well trained by Burke, Del Rio body-slammed Cortez so hard he bounced off the mat like a rubber ball. She trapped him in a painful body scissors and followed up with Burke's favorite hold, a crooked-leg head scissors that made Cortez wince. For the coup de grâce she applied a "famous new hold" called the tiger claw, which had to be seen to be believed: Del Rio used her powerful legs to force apart Cortez's hamstrings and trap the hapless man upside down in midair. He soon submitted, and the victorious Del Rio bounded up from the mat, her arms raised in triumph. In this charged atmosphere, Millie weighed in with her usual laconic midwestern pragmatism. "I don't know how Laura or any other girl would do in a regular mixed match with commission approval but there is no question Laura and some of my other girls would give a good account of themselves. They might tire out against a seasoned male grappler but before it was over, I'm confident these girls would give the guys a good test."

It was obviously a worked match but that was not the point. Like all of pro wrestling, it was primarily a matter of symbolism and imagery. For the first time in a nationally circulated pro wrestling magazine, a woman could be seen defeating a man in a credible-looking pro mixed match that appeared to be fought on equal terms. "Before this article I would have never believed a woman could beat a man," one reader wrote to *Wrestling Monthly*.

Millie's girls started appearing regularly in mixed-match photos in wrestling magazines, and Burke played up the theme of female empowerment. "There is nothing like a good tussle to liberate a woman," said one of Burke's prettiest trainees, a 118-pound fashion model named Lynn Marie who was photographed wrestling in a bikini. "When you successfully pin a male wrestler in a fair contest, it does more for your sense of self, your identity as an individual, than all the propaganda and parades put together." Burke's best wrestler, a five-foot, three-inch, 150-pound powerhouse named Princess War Star, took time off from winning women's titles in Japan to beat up male pros in the pages of U.S. wrestling magazines.

Burke began marketing her filmed mixed matches to the world and at the same time promoted her Mildred Burke's School of Professional Wrestling—"for girls only." The films emphasized the feminist angle. "Tanya is out to give women's lib a big push—and does she ever," read the catalogue entry for a photo showing a 185-pound woman body-slamming a 200-pound male wrestler. "A brilliant episode in the struggle for equal fights," read the caption on a photo of a "no quarter women's lib bout" where the woman trapped the man in a crooked-leg head scissors. Burke created an ad for her business featuring a cartoon of a shapely female wrestler grappling against a hunk built like Arnold Schwarzenegger. "The Weaker Sex???" the caption asked. The cartoon provided Burke's answer. The smiling woman's powerful legs were wrapped in a tight body scissors around the groaning muscleman's six-pack abs, a female boa crushing a bull.

Ron Fox, one of the male wrestlers who fell victim to Millie's girls, was just a guy who happened by Burke's wrestling school in North

Hollywood in the early 1970s. The door was open because there was no air-conditioning and he could see the female wrestlers working out inside. "I watched a few minutes and left, then came back a few times, and eventually Millie saw me watching and invited me in," Fox said. "There were folding chairs around the wall for family and friends to watch, and I soon made it a habit. Eventually Millie asked if I would like to wrestle a girl in a film. I explained I knew nothing about actually doing the moves, she said no problem, I was to be a 'victim,' anyway."

In the beginning the matches were clean, scientific displays of classic holds, and the wrestlers were outfitted professionally in relatively modest one-piece suits and pro boots. But Mildred Burke knew she was selling much more than wrestling. The ancient sport, as she later wrote, tapped into deep sexual currents. She knew she was playing on the sexual fantasies and fetishes of her customers. "Wrestling has always had strong sex appeal," she wrote. "Fantasies are lived out by fans through the various personages in wrestling. Right and wrong and good and evil meet in primal struggle under the lights. Human beings are sexual beings—all of them. The wrestling game allows all manner of drives and frustration to be vented." And mixed wrestling was gasoline on the fire. The sheer symbolism of the battle of the sexes and the striking contrasts it provided in the wrestling ring—powerful muscle and delicate beauty, savage holds and graceful moves, leather and lace—was a combustible mix that produced an erotic punch. Mildred Burke was working a delicate balance, purveying a strange but alluring mixture of empowerment and exploitation.

In her later films the women began to wrestle in bikinis, or barefoot, and on rare occasions they would lose their tops. Burke created a separate line called Star Films, where women wrestled each other and, occasionally, men, naked. The line to pornography had been crossed. And this would open a floodgate of imitators specializing in "catfight" films that dispensed with any semblance of wrestling and sold only the sex.

Burke's mixed-match films proved extremely popular, and at up to $52 apiece for a single fifteen-minute match the money began to roll in from as far away as Europe, Australia, and Japan. By 1973 she had moved into her own apartment in Van Nuys and was renting space in a new gym in North Hollywood. She named her film business Mildred Burke Productions and continued to try and break back into the arena wrestling business in the United States. But her booking operation remained strictly small-time, shut out by Moolah from any lucrative U.S. markets. The mixed matches never took hold in American arenas—the bouts were banned outside of private gyms—and the excitement they generated in the wrestling magazines soon dissipated. The feminists simply ignored her.

Burke's women were reduced to small-time gigs, such as competing for a $1,000 prize in Modesto. She found the same old problems dealing with male promoters. After she put on an all-women's card in Las Vegas, she said she got death threats from powerful California promoter Roy Shire. When the Olympic Auditorium in Los Angeles stopped using her women, she organized a picket line to protest discrimination and low pay for women wrestlers. "My girls cannot work for $25," she said. "They come back with nothing." She had ten women on the picket line over a three-day period and got a lot publicity. "The girls have got to go to foreign countries to make any money," she told the *Los Angeles Times*. "That's pretty lousy for the country that originated professional girl wrestling." She asked for a minimum of $50 a match.

Jeff Walton, a publicist for the Olympic, later wrote a book in which he claimed that Burke's girls were dropped because they did not perform well. "When I met her, she was the sweet grandma type who coached young ladies on the art of grappling," Walton wrote. "The trouble was that only a few of her girls were any good. So using these ladies and watching their poor ability hurt the draw of girl wrestling in Southern California . . . Mildred at the time was an outstanding athlete but she just couldn't teach many of her girls the difference between a toenail and a toehold." The Olympic went back to using Moolah's wrestlers. The next year, Burke's women found themselves putting on a forty-five-minute wrestling show at the Lion's Club in Long Beach for $250. "The mostly middle-aged and older men who did show up were grinning from ear to ear," the local paper wrote.

She trained Joe's kids, her granddaughter, Wendy, and her grandson, Brian. She matched them against each other and got their pictures into wrestling magazines. She reached out to the women she had known throughout her wrestling career, inviting them to come out to California to train girls or asking them to suggest women who could wrestle for her. Burke even called Byers. The old bitterness between them was gone. They talked about wrestling. And jewelry. "At that time, she still had an especially beautiful nine-carat ring that Billy Wolfe had given her," Burke wrote. "I remembered it well. That is the only diamond object of all those involved in my diamond-studded career in any way whose fate I know."

The writer Joe Jares visited Millie and painted a sad portrait in his colorful book *Whatever Happened to Gorgeous George?* "Time and sedentary habits have softened her muscles and her figure is now more in keeping with the image of a grandmother who can cook a great pot of chili," Jares wrote. He compared the circumstances of Moolah and Burke, the two dominant figures in the history of women's wrestling. Moolah lived on a twenty-five-acre estate in Columbia, South Carolina, while Burke "lives in a modest home in California's San Fernando Valley and works with her son for a soft-water company. On the side she operates Mildred Burke's Private School of Professional Wrestling in North Hollywood. Inside the claustrophobic little gym, which consists of two stores with the separating wall knocked out, there is a photograph hanging on the north wall showing the young Burke flexing her impressive biceps." Jares called Burke's World Wide Women's Wrestling Association "a relatively unsuccessful rival of Moolah's group." Burke's wrestlers barely worked outside of Los Angeles, Japan, and Kentucky. She blamed Moolah and her patron, McMahon. "They don't have any girls who can touch my girls," Burke said. "I represent the years when a wrestler was somebody. I represent the years when the wrestlers got paid the way they should be paid. I represent everything they're trying to tear down."

She complained that Moolah was turning the sport into a farce because she was still wrestling even though she was the same age as Burke, fifty-seven—Moolah was actually about forty-nine at the time. "Really, I don't begrudge the girl wrestling, I really don't," Burke said. "What I begrudge is her keeping mine from wrestling." Burke was reduced now to reliving past glories. For Jares, she reminisced about the Golden Age of Wrestling. She vividly recalled what it had been like to be the champion who had brought glamour to wrestling. She caressed the details in her memory, especially her brilliant white suits and dazzling rhinestone robes. "Now everybody wears white," she said. "It's so common you don't even think about it."

By the late 1970s, Burke had made enough money from her films that she was able to move into a better house and gym, both of them in Encino. Hollywood began to seek her out. She was hired as a technical adviser on two feature productions about women wrestlers. *To Smithereens* was a small independent film based on the wrestling novel by Rosalyn Drexler, who had been a Billy Wolfe prospect in 1950. Burke also worked on *All the Marbles,* a big 1981 Hollywood movie about a female tag team known as the California Dolls. Peter Falk starred as the manager of the Dolls and Robert Aldrich, the director of *The Dirty Dozen,* was in charge behind the camera. It was the most serious and expensive film treatment ever given to women's wrestling and Burke worked on it for months. She trained the actresses in her gym—she worked with the Dolls alone for more than two months—

putting them through their paces with her own wrestlers and teaching them the crooked-leg head scissor and other holds. "Mildred used to tell us, 'Even if you don't get the part, you can go on the Japanese tour,'" said Vicki Frederick, one of the actresses playing the Dolls.

In the movie, Peter Falk plays a morally upstanding version of a Billy Wolfe–type manager who did not sleep with his very attractive Dolls but merely drove them relentlessly toward the women's world tag team title in the film's Rocky-like finale. *All the Marbles* got considerable critical acclaim, though it did less well at the box office, earning $6,468,195.

All the Marbles brought Mildred Burke, now sixty-five, renewed attention. The *Los Angeles Times,* her hometown paper, ran a feature story on her in April 1981. When reporter Alan Greenberg visited, he found Burke seemingly in much better circumstances than Joe Jares had. Greenberg wrote that Burke now weighed 180 but "you wouldn't know it to look at her. It's mostly muscle." In her prime, she said, she had been offered movie roles but had always turned them down. "They wanted to make fun of wrestling," Burke said. "To me, it was terrific. I didn't want to put it down."

Greenberg noted, "Even now, she says, she gets marriage proposals in the mail. She's an outgoing woman with a gentle manner who apologized to a visitor recently for not wearing eye makeup. She's allergic to it." Speaking at her desk under the portrait of herself flexing her biceps and wearing her championship belt, Burke said she had about five hundred wrestlers under contract, and they wrestled throughout the nation and in Canada, Mexico, and Japan. Her thriving mail-order business selling films of mixed matches and women's matches, now using videotape rather than film, grossed about $150,000 a year. She said MGM paid her $3,000 a week for her work on *All the Marbles.* She announced that she had just moved into a $500,000 home and that she owned both a 1980 Lincoln and a Cadillac.

In reality, everything was rented or bought on credit. As in the days with Billy Wolfe, it was still important to project a shimmering image to the outside world.

She told Greenberg that she was still working on her autobiography. It had now been a work in progress for twenty-four years, longer than she had been champion. The title had been changed to *Sex, Muscles, and Diamonds.*

The film based on Drexler's book had appeared in 1980. The title had been changed from *To Smithereens* to *Below the Belt* and it had a limited release. Burke was featured in a bit part as a trainer.

As the 1980s progressed her health began to fail and she eventually had to move in with her son, Joe. She suffered mini-strokes and found walking increasingly difficult. On February 14, 1989, Valentine's Day, she had a massive stroke. Joe found her slumped on her kitchen floor. She died four days later at Northridge Hospital in Los Angeles. The news went out over the AP wire.

> Mildred Burke, the female professional wrestling champion who was as well known for her muscular build as her success in the ring, has died after suffering a stroke. She was 73.
>
> Burke, the women's wrestling champion from 1936 to 1955, attributed much of her 20-year success not just to her strength but to the alligator clutch wrestling hold she said she created.
>
> "She was totally feminine," said her son, Joseph Wolfe of Conoga Park. "More than anything else, she stressed being very feminine and a loving mother."
>
> Best known for her muscular physique, she claimed to have won more than 150 matches against men and more than 5,000 against women. She claimed to have never lost.

"I've had two or three girls say they beat me and I've threatened to take them to court because they never even wrestled me," she said in 1981.

Burke, who stood 5-feet-2-inches tall and weighed 138 pounds in her wrestling prime, had such a well-muscled build that the Los Angeles Police Department once displayed her poster in its offices to shame its officers into staying in shape.

She was buried at Forest Lawn of Hollywood Hills. The name on her tombstone is not the once famous Mildred Burke but the ever obscure Mildred Younker, her final married name and the surname of a man from whom she had been divorced for nearly thirty years.

The title of Burke's autobiography, cowritten with author Trevor James Constable, was changed yet again, to *Wrestling Queen*. The 334-manuscript would be rejected by more than thirty publishers. Constable blamed female editors, who had "strong emotional resentment that anyone as historically large as Millie could ever have lived." He wrote to Joe, "And so it has been, Joe, that your mother's biography has been rejected repeatedly by women, to whose position in the world Millie contributed so much."

The last chapter of the manuscript bore the work's original title, "The Third Fall." She used it to sum up her life and her lifelong battle with Billy Wolfe: "In championship wrestling, it is the third fall that decides the match. My struggle with Billy Wolfe had many elements of a wrestling match, and the Byers bout in Atlanta had left Wolfe and myself on even terms. We were both badly hurt. The Orient tour was the third fall in this bitter conflict. . . . My troupe of professionals had been ably guided through a record-setting tour. This victory in all its completeness gave me the third fall in my long battle with Billy Wolfe."

She struggled to assess the course she had picked for herself when she was nineteen. "Were I to live my life over again, I would certainly still want to be a wrestler," she wrote. "I would not wish to be anything else. Second time around, I would be a lot smarter in directing and controlling my affairs, for my life has been rich in lessons. I truly loved the sport of wrestling, and the acclaim of huge audiences is an addictive thing from which the thrill is never missing. Were I granted a re-run of my life, I would ensure that I would not again subjugate my own emotional and sexual needs to my ambition. Deliberately ignoring and avoiding loving companionship for decades parches the soul."

She mentioned that she once had a fan, a high official in the federal government whose name she did not know, who would send a dozen roses to her dressing room before her matches in Washington. He had contacted her through emissaries but she had declined his invitations to dinner. Now, she wrote, she would like to hear from him again.

She lamented the sad present state of women's wrestling. "What I built up for women in the wrestling game through my own bruises and blood, what I won for females in this ancient and exciting sport, has now been almost totally eroded," she wrote. Restoring the status of women, she argued, would revive the entire sport. "That is what happened in the dirty thirties, when I hit those post-depression rings in the shimmering robes and eye-popping tights. The whole game was uplifted, interest surged into the sport and with it came new fans and new money." She called on the women's movement for support. "In a highly masculine sport like wrestling, I came head on against what is now called male chauvinism," she wrote. "My experience is that this has been blown up out of proportion to its real dimensions and strength. Even in the 1930s, male chauvinism was a paper tiger."

She balanced the bitterness she still felt toward Billy Wolfe with the affection she had experienced from "scores of wonderful men," naming Senator John Bricker and Gorgeous George Wagner, "one of God's noblemen."

Finally, she addressed herself to women like herself. "For the woman who feels herself hemmed in or blocked, perhaps my life can provide an answer. From penniless, pregnant, divorced minor in the depths of the depression, I moved up into the millions and into international fame. This happened because I made up my mind what it was I wanted to do, shut out everything else and thereby focused the power of my subconscious."

She ended as she had begun, with her unconquerable will.

Afterword: Millie's Girls

On December 30, 1985, sophomore America Morris of Clairemont High School in San Diego made national news when she pinned sophomore Russell Cain of Madison High School during a match in the 107-pound weight class. That made Morris the first female high school wrestler to pin a male at the varsity level. Cain said he "froze" after he mistakenly touched Morris's breast. "I didn't know what to do," he said. "I was in dream time." Morris's victory generated stories in the San Diego *Union Tribune,* the Orange County, California, *Register,* the *Los Angeles Times, Sports Illustrated,* and *People* magazine. She also appeared on *The Tonight Show with Johnny Carson,* where a video clip of her match was shown.

Morris was not a freak or a fluke. She turned out to be a harbinger. Title IX, passed while Mildred Burke was releasing her first mixed-match films in the early 1970s, turned out to be the reason. The law mandated equality for girls and boys in high school sports. If the school did not have a wrestling team for girls, the courts ruled, it had to let girls compete with boys. Beginning in the lower weight classes a trickle of girls, then a stream, began turning out for their high school wrestling teams. By 1990 there were 124 girls wrestling on boys' teams; five years later, 804. It led to debate, it led to protests, it led to scoffing, it led to concern about improper touching, it led to lawsuits. And it led to forfeits by boys unwilling to risk their budding manhood against girls on the mat. But the girls, increasingly, made the teams and got to wrestle. And, increasingly, they started to win. Concern about the fragility of girls began to be replaced by concern about the fragility of boys' egos.

By 1999 there were more than 2,361 girls wrestling in high school. That year, Sarah Van Skaik, an Ohio high school senior, put a 160-pound male wrestler in a cradle hold and pinned him, becoming the first girl in state history to qualify for a district tournament. "The place erupted," her coach said. "People were yelling, 'Pin him, pin him.' It took her about ten or fifteen seconds." The next boy to wrestle Van Skaik beat her convincingly.

The next year a sophomore girl in Michigan, Keristen LaBelle, racked up a record of 50–11 in the 103-pound class on her way to becoming the first girl to win a regional title in state history. She beat several boys by pinning their shoulders down with their legs in the air, a hold that left them looking a little like Angel Cortez in the grip of Laura Del Rio. "She was stronger than I predicted," said the boy who eventually beat LaBelle in the state tournament. "She's a worthy opponent, very quick."

Boy wrestlers still prevailed in the great majority of mixed matches, but the improvement and success of the girls stunned everybody. The phenomenon even saw the rise of online chat groups taking on such topics as "pinned by a girl," where beaten boy wrestlers could commiserate. "Lots of guys get beat by girls, but it's usually because she has better technique and agility, not because she's stronger," wrote a boy named Andy. "I know. I've been there." A boy named Sergio said he was simply overpowered. "Last year as a senior I wrestled at about 135 pounds and was pinned pretty quickly by a freshman girl. She was simply too fast and strong for me and really threw me around! Boy was I out of breath! I wasn't depressed or anything, but it really changed my attitude toward girl wrestlers." A boy named G.H. described how his own plan to go easy on a female opponent had gone awry when he tired in the third period and she took control. "I was exhausted and she knew it, but unfortunately her strength remained steady," he wrote. "She was no longer a 'weaker girl,' but an opponent who had me in trouble."

By 2002 the number of female high school wrestlers was up to 3,500. Perhaps the most impressive was 154-pound Samantha Lang of Tualatin High School in Oregon. Trained in judo and a wrestler since elementary school, she was used to competing against males. "I don't know what it is, but I have this strange fascination with beating up on the boys," she said. "Maybe it's a women's power thing. It's one thing to win against girls, but if you can beat the boys, that's even better." At five feet, four inches tall, Lang constantly wrestled boys who towered over her. Her opponents weren't small kids just reaching puberty, but six-footers with bulging muscles. She compensated for her lack of leverage and upper body strength with good position and technique. As a sophomore, she managed to give up nearly twenty pounds in weight and pin two 171-pound boys on her way to finishing fifth in an eight-school varsity tournament. In 2004, her senior year, Lang was 22–2 and expected to qualify for the 160-pound class at the state tournament. But she ended up being disqualified before she could make it through the district tournament. Her offense: jogging during a weigh-in. Her coach saw sexism behind the sanction. "It's unfortunate, but it's going to have to be some sort of gender complaint." In the end, efforts to reinstate her failed.

That year, women's wrestling debuted at the Athens Olympics, in four weight classes: 103, 121, 138, and 158 pounds. Among those wrestling for the United States was Sara McMann, who won a silver medal at 138 pounds. Japan led all nations with two golds, a silver, and a bronze. The island nation had become the women's wrestling powerhouse of the world, thanks in part to the push provided by Mildred Burke's groundbreaking 1954 trip and the forays by her troupe Millie's Girls in later decades. Like Burke, the Japanese women were known for their speed, tenacity, and technical proficiency.

People began speculating about when a girl wrestler would win a boys' state championship. They didn't have to wait long. History was made in Alaska in 2006 when Skyview High sophomore Michaela Hutchison won the 103-pound class at the state 4A tournament. She recorded an escape to win the title match, 1–0, with fifteen seconds left. "I don't look at it as I lost to a girl," said the boy she beat. "I look at it as I lost to a wrestler."

Women's professional wrestling took a somewhat different route, with much zigzagging and backsliding. In the early 1980s the Fabulous Moolah was still champion. It was an indication of everything that was wrong with women's pro wrestling that a sixty-year-old woman stood atop the field. Moolah and a strong young wrestler from Texas named Wendi Richter traded the title back and forth in the mid-1980s in matches staged by Vince McMahon Jr., who had succeeded his father and whose World Wrestling Federation had supplanted the dying NWA. The younger McMahon became the outstanding showman in the history of the business and the most successful wrestling impresario of all time.

In July 1984 Richter ended Moolah's twenty-eight-year title reign in a bout promoted by McMahon at Madison Square Garden that got the most publicity ever for a female wrestling match. The next year, in a perfect reflection of the absurdity of it all Moolah, then sixty-two, won the title back at the first WrestleMania extravaganza staged by McMahon. The proceedings had much to do with show business and little to do with wrestling, with the pop singer Cyndi Lauper acting as Richter's manager. The action got a lot of ink, but that quickly subsided and women's pro wrestling went into a steep decline for more than a decade, even as pro wrestling itself soared with the rise of Hulk Hogan. Moolah lost the title in 1987 and then won it back, briefly, in 1999, again under the auspices of McMahon's organization, which had changed its name to World Wrestling Entertainment to avoid a trademark lawsuit brought by the World Wildlife Foundation.

Moolah's last ring appearances featured Johnnie Mae Young, Billy Wolfe's old ring villain, as Moolah's tag-team partner. Both women were now in their eighties, but they still bounced around the ring with smiles on their faces, relishing the spotlight one more time. They were part of McMahon's unparalleled genius for spectacle and promotion, which took pro wrestling to the greatest financial heights it had ever seen with stars such as the Rock and Triple H as the twentieth century came to a close. The name of the game now is entertainment and wrestling skill is a thing of the past.

Finally, a new female champ arose who could credibly take on the men. Chyna, billed as the Ninth Wonder of the World, began as a valet for Triple H and quickly came into her own as a main attraction. Chyna presented a package of sheer power and intimidation. Entering the ring, she sported the physique of a female body builder encased in the black leather of a dominatrix. At five feet, ten inches tall and 180 pounds, she was big enough to take on even the steroidal males, matching them hold for hold, including a dirty one that they could not match: a driving fist to the groin. On October 17, 1999, she became the first female pro wrestler to win a men's championship belt, defeating Jeff Jarrett to gain the Intercontinental Title. But in a few years she fell out with the McMahons and faded from the scene, reappearing occasionally on reality TV. Men now dominate pro wrestling and the women who enter the ring serve mainly as eye candy.

The world of Mildred Burke had disappeared by the twenty-first century. The Interstate Highway System in the 1950s and '60s took out

Mom's Café, the Park Hotel, and Haft's Acre. The K.P. castle was lost to a fire. The Kuramae Kokugikan Hall in Tokyo was torn down to make way for a new sumo arena. The Atlanta City Auditorium is gone as well, as are most of the arenas and auditoriums where Burke had won her glory. The once mighty National Wrestling Alliance is but a faded memory and the magazines that touted Mildred Burke and Millie's Girls are long defunct. In 1993 there was talk of a television movie about Mildred Burke, "Stranglehold," written by Broadway playwright Ronald Ribman, for the ABC network. Ribman said Burke was "the first and only female wrestler they had in the 1930s, an amazing 5-foot-2, 140-pound woman who believed she was inhabited by the soul of a wrestler who may have lived back among the Greeks in the fifth century B.C." There was a problem finding a lead actress who could play the role. Madonna was said to be under consideration. Like many other projects involving Burke it did not come to pass. Fifteen years later, in posing for her album, *Hard Candy,* Madonna dressed herself as a wrestler from Burke's era, wearing a gold championship belt.

Around the time the Burke movie was under discussion, a veteran newspaper columnist reminisced about what it had been like to work fifty years earlier at the *Minneapolis Times,* a long-dead newspaper. In doing so, she recalled Mildred Burke and her long-gone era.

"Everything about the *Times* seemed larger than life, raffish, ribald, extremely important and fun," wrote Barbara Flanagan. "The paycheck wasn't so much, but there was the glamour of being in a big-city newsroom.

"Glamour? What's that, you may ask? If you'd ever seen wrestler Mildred Burke in the newsroom wearing her diamond-studded World Championship belt and her mink-lined cape, you'd know what I mean."

A few of the new generation of female pro wrestlers invoked the name Mildred Burke, but they were very few indeed. In 2004 the documentarian Ruth Leitman made a critically acclaimed film, titled *Lipstick & Dynamite,* about several of the women wrestlers who had been trained by Billy Wolfe. Leitman tracked down and interviewed Gladys Gillem, Ella Waldek, Ida May Martinez, Penny Banner, the "Great" Johnnie Mae Young and the "Fabulous" Moolah. The women related their hardscrabble lives and their various journeys through the pro wrestling business. They showed that they warranted the film's subtitle, "Piss & Vinegar." They were tough, salty women, adventurers and pioneers, who had loved the limelight and appeared to regret little. They all appeared to hate Billy Wolfe. "Billy Wolfe was a promoter of flesh, not a promoter of wrestling," said Young, who gave a vintage performance in her interview. "He hated me so much. He was so afraid I would beat his wife, Mildred Burke. She really wasn't the great champion she thought she was. And that was the problem. She got to believe her own publicity that she was a champion."

In her autobiography, written fifty years after the fact, the Fabulous Moolah pointed out that Mildred Burke had been arrogant on the one occasion that they had met, in the dressing room after a Burke match. The memory still seemed fresh.

Everyone seemed to have forgotten how it all began, or seemed not to care. Old grudges carried over the decades like long-lost letters finally finding their way home. Burke and Wolfe and Byers appeared in *Lipstick & Dynamite* only as still photographs. Their voices were not heard. But it is fair to say that Mildred Burke would have embraced all of them. Gladys Gillem, Johnnie Mae Young, Nell Stewart, June Byers, Wendi Richter, Chyna, all the high school girls, even the Fabulous Moolah. They were all Millie's girls.

Billy's Girls

Beverly Anderson
Adela Antone
Ada Ash
Barbara Jean Baker
Penny Banner
Gloria Barattini
Mars Bennett
Lillian Bitter
Ruth Boatcallie
Jane Boyer Wolfe
Joyce Bragg
Ethel Brown
Mildred Burke
June Byers
Carol Carota
Bette Carter
Juanita Coffman
Cora Combs
Caroline Copeland
Carol Cook
Rosa DeCarlo
Donna Marie
   Dieckman
Dot Dotson
Belle Drummond
Lillian Ellison

Joyce Ford
Libby Gonzalez
Gladys Gillem
Wilma Gordon
Louise Green
Betty Jo Hawkins
Helen Hild
Mary Alice Hillis
Jean Holland
Ethel Johnson
Lois Johnson
Karen Kellogg
LeeChona LaClaire
Lola Laray
Ann Laverne
Eva Lee
Sherrie Lee
Beverly Lehmer
Lynn Livingston
Terry Majors
Caroline Martin
Ida May Martinez
Frances Minor
Mary Jane Mull
Jo Ann Mulleniex
Ellen Olsen

Vicki Page
Ella Phillips
Betsy Ross
Gloria Shelton
Marilyn Shipman
Anna Slotterbeck
Elvira Snodgrass
Mille Stafford
Ann Stanley
Georgia Steen
Nell Stewart
Shirley Strimple
Therese Theis
Princess Tona Tomah
Violet Viann
Ella Waldek
Bonnie Watson
Betty White
Kathleen Wimbley
Babs Wingo
Mae Weston
Johnnie Mae Young
Sheba Zenni
Olga Zepeda

Millie's Girls

Lynne Black

Pearl Bryant

Deana Cagle

Casey Carr

Cheryl Day

Laura Del Rio

Diane Flanagan

Betty "Panama"
  Franco

Gail Gardner

Sylvia Hackney

Aggie Henry

Yvonne Jennings

Elaine Kay

Karen Kelly

Lola Kiss

Carol Landis

Sarah Lee

Sharon Lee

Lita Marez

Lynn Marie

Beverly Morris

Perla Nieto

Jane O'Brien

Patty O'Hara

Sonya Orellana

Sandy Parker

Marlene Petrilli

Patricia Renee

Rosalyn Royce

Susan Sexton

Jane Shirrel

Rhonda Singh

Susan Smith

Patti Steger

Patty Stevens

Princess War Star

Marie Vagnone

Jackie West

Tanya West

Patty Wiggs

Wendy Wolfe

Acknowledgments

Growing up in the St. Louis suburbs, I would eagerly enter Rexall Drugs to spend what seemed like hours perusing the magazine stands. I was on the lookout for Marvel Comics and glossy depictions of war, movie monsters, and sports heroes. Among the latter were the baseball and football players, the boxers, the body builders, and, lastly, the wrestlers. Growing up in St. Louis also meant catching Sam Muchnick's cheesy but spectacular Saturday morning TV show, *Wrestling at the Chase*, and what little boy in the 1960s wasn't a fan? I marveled at the antics of Dick the Bruiser, Bruno Sammartino, Harley Race, and Cowboy Bob Ellis. Wrestling on TV and the wrestling magazines led me ultimately to Mildred Burke. The front parts of the magazines were packed with stories and photos about the exploits of hugely muscled men, providing an image of masculinity that beckoned a skinny boy worried about ever having biceps. In the backs of the magazines, in tiny ads, a woman showed off her own impressive biceps, touting her school for "girl wrestlers." This was a shock. More than that, the magazines occasionally featured photographs of "Millie's girls" squaring off in the wrestling ring against the muscle men. More often than not the women won these battles of the sexes. This was an even bigger shock. How could this be? Answering that question led me to the forgotten story of Mildred Burke and the golden age of wrestling.

Uncovering that story required all the tools I have developed in thirty years as an investigative reporter and editor. It also required a trip through a long-departed era and a subculture long devoted to secrecy and deception. Luckily, I had an army of guides and supporters to aid my journey.

I would not have embarked at all without the singular example of Laura Hillenbrand's *Seabiscuit* to light my way like the brightest beacon in a dark ocean of lost time. Both Seabiscuit and Mildred Burke rose out of the Great Depression, making their debuts on the national sports scene in the summer of 1937. This seemed to me much more than mere coincidence.

Like Laura Hillenbrand, I turned to the Internet and eBay for primary source material, bidding on and buying a boatload of women's wrestling videos and wrestling magazines like *Wrestling Review* and *Wrestling Monthly*, which returned me to my youth at Rexall.

Exhausting the wonders of the Internet and Google, my search for Mildred Burke began in earnest in the Hesburgh Library at the University of Notre Dame. My guide was the very able George Rugg, curator of the Joyce Sports Research Collection, which numbers among its treasures the records of the women's baseball players immortalized in *A League of Their Own*. George curates the archive left behind by Jack Pfefer, an inimitable and Runyonesque character who was also a glorious packrat that saved every piece of paper that came his way. I went through the Pfefer collection, which entails seventy-five banker's boxes of documents containing more than fifteen thousand letters, thousands of photographs, and primary source material virtually untouched by researchers. The correspondence between Pfefer and Billy Wolfe convinced me that this was a story worth telling. George graciously put his archive at my disposal, cheerfully answered my questions and requests, and arranged for Notre Dame students to aid me, particularly Sara Szakaly.

I tracked Mildred Burke's seventy-year-old son, Joe Wolfe, to a small town in Oregon. Joe granted me permission to use material from his mother's unpublished autobiography and spent hours sharing his own memories and photographs of his mother during her heyday. Joe's daughter, Wendy Koep, also provided stories of her own career as a wrestler for her grandmother. Mildred Burke's manuscript, written with the assistance of Trevor J. Constable, proved to be an invaluable key for unlocking her story and her state of mind. She spent thirty years toiling on the work she variously titled The Third Fall; Sex, Muscles and Diamonds; and, finally, Wrestling Queen. This book you are holding in your hands could not have been written without her labors. Every sentence in my book is my own and I alone am responsible for its conclusions and any errors it contains, but a part of me cannot help but feel that my effort in some small way completes Mildred's own journey.

Also helpful and generous with their memories were Bert Younker, Mildred Burke's third and last husband; Terry Patterson, Nell Stewart's niece; and Jewel Olivas, June Byers's daughter.

Billy Wolfe's relatives greatly aided my search for the truth about Millie and Billy. Especially helpful was Betsy Wolfe Stemple, G. Bill Wolfe's daughter; and her sister, Mickie Johnson, who opened up their homes and hearts to me and showed me their grandfather's surviving business records. Tim Kelly, Billy Wolfe's son by Karen Kellogg, took time to tell me about his own search for his biological father.

My search continued through dusty archives that spanned the country, from College Park, Maryland, to Kansas City to Los Angeles. Especially helpful were Maudine Bennum, corresponding secretary of the Harrison County (Mo.) Genealogical Society in Bethany, Missouri; John Struchtemeyer, district registrar for the Kansas City,

Missouri, school district; Tom Reeder at the Columbus Historical Society; Shirley Harper, records clerk in the civil division at the Franklin County Hall of Justice in Columbus, Ohio; and Jim Hunter, librarian for the Columbus Dispatch.

In the National Archives in College Park, I sought *United States v. National Wrestling Alliance*, Civil Action No. 3-729, which records the efforts of the Justice Department to bring wrestling's illegal monopoly to heel. I benefited from the helpful professionalism of the archives staff. Alas, the main part of the case, FBI File 60-406-0, could not be located. A large piece of this story would be lost but for the efforts of Tim Hornbaker, author of the authoritative *National Wrestling Alliance: The Untold Story of the Monopoly That Strangled Pro Wrestling*. Tim sent me relevant documents, read this work in manuscript and provided helpful suggestions. Weldon T. Johnson, coauthor of another fine examination of the NWA, *Chokehold: Pro Wrestling's Real Mayhem Outside the Ring*, also provided me with quick answers and documents at a time when I needed them most. Steve Johnson, coauthor with Greg Oliver of books on tag teams, villains, and *Benoit: Wrestling with the Horror That Destroyed a Family and Crippled a Sport*, provided encouragement and reasoned judgment, and also read the work in manuscript and offered suggestions and corrections. I value his friendship.

At the Library of Congress, Bruce Martin set me up in one of the world's greatest research facilities and Thomas Mann, reference librarian in the main reading room, kindly showed me what I could do with it.

The professional wrestling world, in the form of the Cauliflower Alley Club, welcomed me with just a pinch of skepticism and an abundance of patience and kindness for which I am forever grateful. Karl Lauer, CAC executive vice president, paved my way into the wrestling community, and Dean Silverstone, the organization's executive director, was also helpful. The best of the wrestling historians generously schooled me in the subject they have turned into their life's work: Tom Burke, who worked his vast network of connections on my behalf; the late Jim Melby, Greg Oliver, Vance Nevada, Scott Teal, Don Luce, and, especially, J Michael Kenyon, who spent hours explaining the sport's nuances to a newcomer. Several wrestling old-timers let me in on what it was like to live through the golden age of the sport: Frankie Cain, Al Mandell, Tommy Fooshee. Ruth Ellen Henry, Terry Milan, Michael Lano, Judo Gene LeBell, and Joseph Svinth also helped with various aspects of the story.

I am grateful to John Capouya, biographer of Gorgeous George. I recommend his fine book, *Gorgeous George: The Outrageous Bad-Boy Wrestler Who Created American Pop Culture.*

I consulted more than forty books but, in addition to those I have already mentioned, five stand out for the authenticity of their prose and the valuable insights they provide into a business that reveals its secrets only with the greatest reluctance: *Fall Guys: The Barnums of Bounce, The Inside Story of the Wrestling Business, America's Most Profitable and Best Organized Professional Sport* by Marcus Griffin; the biography of Lou Thesz, *Hooker: An Authentic Wrestler's Adventures Inside the Bizarre World of Professional Wrestling* by Lou Thesz with Kit Bauman; *Whatever Happened to Gorgeous George: The Blood and Ballyhoo of Professional Wrestling* by Joe Jares; *Catch Wrestling: A Wild and Wooly Look at the Early Days of Pro Wrestling America* by Mark S. Hewitt; and *Ringside: A History of Professional Wrestling in America* by Scott M. Beekman. Anyone who wants to learn more about this strange and wonderful world cannot do better than picking up these books.

I also recommend the work of David Meltzer, who writes the *Wrestling Observer* newsletter, as well as Keith Eliot Greenberg and Michael Mooneyham. In addition to these authors and writers, Steve Yohe produces some of the best and deepest historical wrestling essays at wrestlingclassic.com, legacyofwrestling.com and other sites. Frank Deford, long the star of *Sports Illustrated*'s superlative stable of writers, wrote the definitive newspaper piece on Mildred Burke in 1990 for the now-defunct sports daily *The National*.

The best visual record of that time belongs to Ruth Leitman, director of the highly entertaining documentary *Lipstick and Dynamite, Piss and Vinegar*.

I cannot properly thank the wrestlers themselves who spent hours recounting their days with Billy Wolfe and Mildred Burke: the late Penny Banner, Johnnie Mae Young, Ethel Brown, Barbara Jean Baker, Gloria Barattini, Ruth Boatcallie, Gladys Gillem, Ida May Martinez, Kathleen Wimbley, Sherrie Lee, and Cora Combs. Marie LaVerne, daughter of Ann Laverne, went above and beyond the call of graciousness to provide me with leads, sources, and memories.

I could not have finished without the help and support of colleagues, friends, and family. My former colleagues at *The Miami Herald*—Ed Pope, Joan Fleischman, and Gay Nemeti, were there when I needed them. My current colleagues at *The Washington Post* are the best in the business at investigative reporting and make my job a pleasure every day. Don Graham and Katharine Weymouth, the best newspaper owners alive, provide a home for outstanding journalism and generously allow their employees to pursue book projects on the side. My former boss, former executive editor Len Downie, has always been my professional inspiration. Several *Post* colleagues came through in ways large and small. Marilyn Thompson and Cynthia Boren helped at key moments, as did Will Lester, a friend from the Associated Press. Larry Roberts, my deputy in the *Post*'s investigative unit who helps me carry the load, took time to read portions of the manuscript, and subject them to his keen critical eye. Also offering sage advice were Eric Lieberman, the *Post*'s general counsel, Joel Achenbach, one of the *Post*'s most talented scribes, and Steve Friedman, who is as good a friend as he is a writer.

Vital sustenance also came from my friend Jim McGee; my brother-in-law, Michael Medford; my sister, Sarah Leen; and my other brother-in-law, Bill Marr, who deserves special thanks for doing the design of the photo inserts for this book. And to my brother, Steve Leen, who put me up during my California forays.

Post researcher extraordinaire Alice Crites worked voraciously to find materials that nobody else had, including a lost story in a dead newspaper that remains the only surviving contemporaneous account of the Atlanta match between Mildred Burke and June Byers. My Ohio researcher, Miriam Kahn of MBK Consulting, combed the archives at the Ohio State Historical Society and elsewhere for the records I needed.

My editor at Grove/Atlantic, Joan Bingham, was kind, perspicacious, penetrating, and supportive. Her talented assistant, Alex Littlefield, worked as hard as anybody could to improve on what I submitted.

This book would not exist without my agent, Gail Ross, whose belief in the story spurred me to do it in spite of myself. I will always value her friendship and tenacity. Her extremely able assistant, Howard Yoon, helped shape the project and bring it into fresh focus.

Finally, there is Lynn Medford. My soul mate, my final reader and first editor, everything begins and ends with her.

Notes

A note on sources: As I researched this subject, I occasionally came across material—newspaper clippings, photographs, online postings—that did not have complete publishing information, some dates, mainly page numbers. In cases where this happened, I have attempted to provide enough information to guide more diligent researchers coming behind me. I relied heavily on Mildred Burke's unpublished autobiography, "Sex, Muscles and Diamonds," written with Trevor J. Constable. Reference to this work is abbreviated SMD throughout these notes. I also relied on materials at the Jack Pfefer Wrestling Collection, part of the Reverend Edmund R. Joyce Sports Research Collection in the University Libraries of Notre Dame, which is simply rendered Pfefer Collection in these notes. In addition, the Department of Justice investigation of the NWA, File No. 60-406-0, which is housed at the National Archives and Records Administration in College Park, Maryland, is here rendered as DOJ.

Chapter 1

2   At her peak she earned $50,000 a year: Frank Eck, AP Newsfeatures Sports Editor, "$50,000 Per Keeps Gal Grappler in Groceries," *Boston Globe,* May 5, 1949.

3   When she was starting out: Melville Carico, "Reporter Finds Mildred (Cyclone) Burke Gentle As Breeze," *Roanoke Times,* February 9, 1938.

3   When she drop-kicked: Jim Ogle, "Millie, Gladys Set Record," *Newark-Star Ledger,* July 11, 1940, sports front.

3   "Sure, when I'm on the mat . . .": Omar Garrison, "Who Said It Was a Man's World?" Mirror Enterprises Syndicate, *Lima News,* Ohio, March 20, 1952.

4   body bridges: "Believe It or Not by Ripley," *Zanesville Times Record,* Ohio, August 31, 1940.

4   On the eve of the Atlanta match: Joe Wolfe, personal interview, May 15, 2005.

5   "All eyes of the wrestling world . . .": "Two Title Matches On Friday's Card," *Atlanta Journal,* August 17, 1954.

5   "Most Important Match of the Year . . .": *The Ringsider,* wrestling program of Paul Jones's Atlanta promotion, n.d., Pfefer Collection.

6   a "grudge match": "Burke, Byers Settle Grudge," *Atlanta Journal,* August 20, 1954, p. 15.

6   "She's my prize package . . .": Timothy G. Turner, "Star Female Wrestler Muscular Glamour Girl," *Los Angeles Times,* July 18, 1943, A1.

6   "His diamonds make him shine . . .": Walter Haight, "It Was Different, This Derby Morning," *Washington Post,* May 14, 1950, p. C4.

7   At a time when most wrestlers donned drab black togs: Joe Jares, *Whatever Happened to Gorgeous George?* (New Jersey: Prentice Hall, 1974), p. 58.

7   Her matching white wrestling boots: Mildred Burke, as told to Trevor J. Constable, "Sex, Muscles and Diamonds," unpublished manuscript, with permission of copyright holder Joe Wolfe, pp. 131–132.

8   "Wrestling partakes . . ." Roland Barthes, "The World of Wrestling," *Mythologies,* (New York: Hill and Wang, 1984). Translated by Annette Lavers. Original essay published 1957.

8   Byers in training: Penny Banner with Gerry Hostetler, *Banner Days* (Charlotte: A Flying Mare Publication, 2004) p. 45.

8   "She had a bouncy, elastic quality . . .": Jack Fletcher, "June Byers Tells About My Toughest Bout," *Girl Wrestling: The World's Sexiest Sport,* Spring 1965, pp. 63–68.

Chapter 2

10   Millie Bliss's childhood: 1910 U.S. Census, Haw Creek, Morgan County, Missouri; Bruce E. Bliss, World War I Draft Registration Card, Serial Number 1983, September 11, 1918; U.S. Patent No. 1,311,309, "Two-Part Interlocking Tire," July 29, 1919, and U.S. Patent No. 1,380,522, "Antiskid and Mud Chain," June 7, 1921, Bruce Edward Bliss of Wichita, Kansas, U.S. Patent and Trademark Office, Alexandria, Virginia; Glendale City Directory 1923; Kansas City Directory 1933; Alan Greenberg, "Mildred Burke . . . She Never Met Her Match," *Los Angeles Times,* April 17, 1981, p. D1; SMD, pp. 3–4.

11   She often played with the boys: Jares, *Whatever Happened to Gorgeous George?* p. 52.

11   "When I first menstruated . . .": SMD, p. 4.

12   Three of Mildred's sisters: Mildred Burke promotion sheet prepared by Billy Wolfe, n.d, circa 1948, Pfefer Collection; Gus Schrader, "Wrestling Queen's 3 Sisters Are Ministers," *Cedar Rapids Gazette,* Nov. 2, 1952, p. 20.

12   Millie's dreams: SMD, p. 6.

12   She dropped out: Manual High School transcript of Mildred Bliss, September 5, 1929 to December 4, 1929, Kansas City, Missouri, School District.

12   She and her fifty-five-year-old mother: 1930 U.S. Census, Kansas City, Jackson County, Missouri.

12   "The struggle resulted . . .": SMD, p. 3.

13   on the reservation: Ibid, p. 6;

13   "I would have married anyone . . .": Greenberg, "Mildred Burke . . . She Never Met Her Match," D1.

13   B & S Café: Kansas City Directory 1933.

14   Millie worked 12 hours a day: SMD, pp. 8, 14; Jares, *Whatever Happened to Gorgeous George?* p. 52.

14   watching her first bout: SMD, p. 6.

15   nineteenth century wrestling: Scott M. Beekman, *Ringside: A History of Professional Wrestling in America* (Westport, Connecticut, Praeger Publishers, 2006), p. 20.

15   "When I began to read sports pages . . .": A. J. Liebling, "From Sarah Bernhardt to Yukon Eric," *New Yorker,* November 3, 1954, p. 135.

15   a new form of wrestling: Griffin, *Fall Guys,* p. 19–20; Lou Thesz with Kit Bauman, *Hooker: An Authentic Wrestler's Adventures Inside the Bizarre World of Professional Wrestling* (Seattle: The Wrestling Channel Press, 1995), p. 45.

16   philosophical meditation: Barthes, *Mythologies.*

16   Strangler Lewis: Thesz and Bauman, *Hooker,* pp. 45, 51–53.

17   "Whether Londos was the best wrestler . . .": Liebling, "From Sarah Bernhardt to Yukon Eric," p. 136.

17   ". . . shrill screams reveal how thin is the veneer . . .": Kenneth W. Barr, "Women Spur Wrestlers to Savagery," *Galveston Daily News,* Texas, June 19, 1932.

17   A "well-dressed, genteel" college girl: John C. Meyer, *Wrestling, from Antiquity to Date* (St. Louis: Von Hoffman Press, 1931), p. 50.

17   "Immediately I began fantasizing . . .": SMD, p. 6–7.

18   Atalanta wrestling Peleus on vases: Chalcidian black-figure hydra, ca. 540 B.C., artist unknown, Antikensammlungen, Munich; black-figure

amphora, ca. 500 B.C., artist unknown, Antikensammlungen, Munich; red-figure kylix by Oltos, ca. 500 B.C., Museo Civico Archeologico, Bologna.

18   Marco Polo wrote of another wrestling princess: David P. Willoughby, *The Super Athletes: A Record of the Limits of Human Strength, Speed and Stamina* (New Jersey: A. S. Barnes & Co. Inc., 1970) p. 580. The Tartar princess Aiyaruk, daughter of King Kaidu, of Great Turkey (now Russian Turkestan) received a hundred horses from each man she defeated, and by the year 1280 had acquired a herd of 10,000. Obviously exaggerated.

18   George Hackenschmidt: "Wrestling Ills Blamed on Public by Hacken-schmidt," *New York Journal and American,* April 10, 1938. Hack stood five feet, nine inches, weighed 215 and could lift 269 pounds with one arm.

19   "The erotic component . . .": Aleksander Khromov, "Circus strong-women and female wrestlers in the beginning of the XX century, Part II," the Female Single Combat Club, www.fscclub.com/history/borchihi2-e.shtml, September 30, 2002, p. 3.

19   the first U.S. women's wrestling championship: Alice Williams won the contest sponsored by the *National Police Gazette.*

19   "The action was spirited . . .": William Braucher, "Why Pro Wres-tling Attracts Record-Breaking Crowds, Part Six," Newspaper Enterprise Association, spring 1931.

19   "I beheld this vicious-countenanced woman . . .": Natalie Taylor Carlisle, "A Texan in New York," *Galveston Daily News,* July 14, 1908, p. 9.

20   "Women are not fit . . .": Meyer, *Wrestling,* p. 66.

20   Male middleweight champion Joe Parelli struggled: "Miss Virginia Mercereau Holds Decision Over World's Best Middleweight Matman," *Mansfield News,* Ohio, October 18, 1927, p. 13; "Appleton Loses Claim to Woman Mat Star," *Appleton Post Crescent,* Wisconsin, May 2, 1930.

20   *Ring* articles: Marion Lewis, "Leather and Lingerie," *The Ring,* No-vember 1933, pp. 40–41; Marion Lewis, "Women Wrestlers? Why Not!" *The Ring,* January 1934, pp. 36–37.

20   Then Joe Shaffer walked out: Mildred Shaffer vs. Joseph M. Shaffer, No. 437396, Circuit Court of Jackson County, Missouri, April 5, 1935; SMD, p. 7.

20   They renamed the diner Mom's Café: Kansas City Directory 1934.

21   "Urgent need for money . . ." SMD, p. 9.

Chapter 3

22   Meeting Billy Wolfe: SMD, p. 10.

23   Wolfe birth date: William Harrison Wolfe paid obituary, *Newark Advocate,* Ohio, March 7, 1963, p. 35; The death information at Maple Grove Cemetery in Granville, Ohio, where Billy Wolfe is interred, also indicates he was born July 4, 1896 in Wheaton, Missouri.

24   When Billy was young: 1910 U.S. Census, Phillipsburg City, Phillipsburg Township, Kansas.

24   The Wolfe boys were drafted: Tim Hornbaker, *National Wrestling Alliance: The Untold Story of the Monopoly That Strangled Pro Wrestling* (Canada: ECW Press, 2007) p. 290.

24   he married nineteen-year-old Margaret Johnson: 1930 U.S. Census, Kansas City, Jackson County, Missouri.

24   By 1923 he was described: "Krieger's Opponent Has A Great Record," *Lincoln State Journal,* June 18, 1923, p. 11.

24   Wolfe's bear did not fare so well: "Fisher In Fine Form, Winning A Fast Exhibition," *Chillicothe Constitution-Tribune,* Dec. 18, 1930, p. 6.

24   Wolfe feature story: "Billy Wolfe Is Home Folk," Chillicothe Constitution-Tribune, Jan. 21, 1933.

25   A picture of Wolfe: "Has The Mighty Fallen," *Chillicothe Constitution-Tribune,* March 19, 1934, p. 5.

25   That year Wolfe left his wife: Margaret J. Wolfe vs. William H. Wolfe, No. 426261, Circuit Court of Jackson County, Missouri, Dec. 12, 1933.

25 "Barbara is another example . . .": "Roughers Plan to Please Public in Mat Show Tonight," *Chillicothe Constitution-Tribune,* March 2, 1934, p. 7.

25 She had been mentioned in *Ring* magazine: Lewis, "Leather and Lingerie," pp. 40–41.

25 she defeated a 130-pound male: "Woman Throws Man," Associated Press in *Bismarck Tribune,* November 30, 1932.

26 After Ware and Wolfe appeared: "Mat Fans Are Happy At Last," *Chillicothe Constitution-Tribune,* March 3, 1934, p. 5.

26 The crowd really got its wish: "Big Bad Wolfe Gets A Beating From Audience," *Chillicothe Constitution-Tribune,* March 22, 1934, p. 9.

27 an account told a hundred times: SMD, pp. 12–19.

30 she ran into Gypsy Joe years later: "Gal Grapplers Learn Ropes in Ohio Class," Associated Press in *Galveston News,* October 18, 1951, p. 14.

30 Burke's wrestling ability: SMD, p. 20.

30 Wolfe recounted the story: Edythe Farrell, "Strong Woman Takes All Comers," *National Police Gazette,* December 1940, p. 3.

Chapter 4

33 "He could be likable . . .": SMD, p .22.

33 birth of pro wrestling: Beekman, *Ringside,* pp. 1–33; Gerald W. Morton and George M. O'Brien, *Wrestling to Rasslin: Ancient Sport to American Spectacle* (Bowling Green State University Popular Press, 1985), pp. 3–43.

34 Muldoon's history: Beekman, *Ringside,* pp. 22–26; Meyer, Wrestling, p. 22.

34 catch wrestling: Mark S. Hewitt, *Catch Wrestling: A Wild and Wooly Look at the Early Days of Pro Wrestling in America* (Boulder, Colorado: Paladin Press, 2005).

35   Ed Decker: Morton and O'Brien, *Wrestling to Rasslin,* p. 29.

35   at shows:: Beekman, *Ringside,* p. 39; Thesz and Bauman, *Hooker,* p. 11; Morton and O'Brien, *Wrestling to Rasslin,* p. 31.

35   "The main feature of this show . . .": "Mammoth Carnival Visits Kingston," Kingston, New York, *Daily Freeman,* May 21, 1915, p. 1.

35   Banners adorned the stage: Geraldean Mae McMillin, *Wrestling With Life: The Wisdom and Wit of a Woman Wrestler,* (Rocheport, Missouri: Pebble Publishing, Inc., 1999), p. 52.

36   The civilians in the audience: Mark Hewitt, "Taking On All Comers: A History of the Carnival Athletic Shows," www.1wrestlinglegends.com/columns/hewitt/mne.htm, 2002; Merrill Swanon, "Carny Fights—Bullies, Sweat, Pride," *Minneapolis Tribune,* May 3, 1970.

36   Before she left for the at show: SMD, pp. 23–26.

37   Millie Bliss at the carnival: Ibid, pp. 30–34.

38   Millie later said she lost only one: Jares, *Whatever Happened to Gorgeous George?* p. 52; SMD, p. 65.

38   Joe's earliest memories: Joe Wolfe, personal interview, May 15, 2005.

39   Buck Thompson: Bill Plummer, "Reflections," *Chillicothe Constitution-Tribune,* January 19, 1983, p. 4.

39   "Ligaments popped . . ." SMD, p. 38; She later said her right knee was in a cast for three months: "She Pins 'Em to the Mat," *San Antonio Light,* October 4, 1939, p. 11-b.

40   Burke's account of wrestling giantess: SMD, 45–52.

41   the woman's daughter wrote: "Remember Momma: Mrs. Penny Coyle Recounts Mother's Carnival Matches With Mildred Burke, Weston," *Wrestling Revue,* March 1974, p. 46–47.

42   Life and sex on the carnival circuit: SMD, pp. 39–44, 55–65, 70–71.

43   she approached promoter Gust Karras: Ibid, p. 73.

43   Mildred Burke challenge ad: Want-Ad Wonders, "Woman Wrestling Champion Got First Match Via Want Ads," *Penn Yan Chronicle Express,* New York, December 22, 1949.

43   a very cold night: "Fans Like Savage, Who Uses Toes Hold in Besting Nabors," *Bethany Republican-Clipper,* Feb. 19. 1936, p. 4. Burke had begun wrestling men in Chillicothe the previous month, but it is not clear whether those matches were held in arenas.

44   She repeated the challenge in Leavenworth: SMD, pp. 83–85.

45   she had another match in Bethany: "Miss Burke Vs. Carl Hunter, Match Sort of Steals Show, With Bethany Boy Bashful," *Bethany Republican-Clipper,* April 8, 1936, p. 2.

45   Burke description of "first" match: SMD, pp. 74–82.

47   marriage: William H. Wolfe and Mildred Shaffer, marriage license, Probate Court, Dickinson County, Kansas, April 24, 1936.

47   "There was no question of my being in love . . ." SMD, pp. 66–69.

47   Buck Thompson: Plummer, "Reflections," p. 4.

47   account of Chillicothe match: SMD, pp. 86–92.

48   "I saw stars . . .": Ibid, p. 93.

Chapter 5

50   The show was shabbier than Landes: SMD, p. 99.

51   Mortensen and Ware each claiming championship in Topeka in 1932: Bess Middleton, "Girls, If You Must Pull Her Hair, Just Take Up Professional Wrestling," *Fresno Bee,* July 1, 1937, p. 1; "Barbara Ware And Stote Clash in Mat Headliner," *Lima News,* December 23, 1938, p. 14.

51   *Ring* magazine had touted her: Lewis, "Leather and Lingerie," pp. 40–41.

51   A classic Nordic beauty: "World's Leading Woman Wrestler Retains

Charm And Poise Despite Rigors Of Her Profession," *Washington Times,* April 21, 1937, sports front.

51   One newspaper account: Ibid.

51   She had been trained since childhood: "Behind the Scenes with the Pretty 'Tigress,' "*San Antonio Light,* July 3, 1938, p. 4.

51   When she was seven years old: "Edwards Defeated In Terrific Bout," *Portland Oregonian,* July 18, 1925.

51   she appeared before 31,000 fans: Al Warden, "Feminine Wrestlers Make Big Money," Ogden City, Utah, *Standard-Examiner,* April 20, 1945, p. 8.

52   Wolfe and Chris Jordan: SMD, pp. 100–102.

53   Burke had to agree to lose: Ibid, p. 102.

53   the knowledge was devastating: Ibid, p. 106,

53   Lewis in private "shooting matches": Thesz and Bauman, *Hooker,* p. 41.

53   It also protected him: Ibid. Thesz recounts bouts with Paul Boesch, Primo Carnera, Ruffy Silverstein, Rikidozan, Antonino Rocca and Bruno Sammartino where he resorted to real wrestling to defend himself or prove a point.

53   Double-crossed: Stanislaus Zbyszko doubled-crossed Wayne "Big" Munn in 1925 and Dick Shikat did the honors to Danno O'Mahoney in 1936.

54   "Wrestlers with an honest background . . .": Liebling, "From Sarah Bernhardt to Yukon Eric," p. 135.

54   Gold Dust Trio: Marcus Griffin, *Fall Guys: The Barnums of Bounce, The inside story of the Wrestling Business. America's most profitable and best organized sport* (Chicago: Reilly & Lee Co., 1937) p. 19. Republished by Scott Teal, "Whatever Happened to . . . ?" Hendersonville, Tennessee, 1997.

54   Burke said Mortensen's triumphs: SMD, p. 104.

55   Cora Jurgens: Ibid, pp. 100, 104–106.

55   the huge crowd: "6,200 See Females Wrestle For Title," *Chattanooga Times,* January 29, 1937.

56   "These two otherwise demure misses . . .": Murray Wyche, "Pictures to the Editors," *Life,* Feb. 22, 1937, p. 67.

56   The pictures also made it into *Life:* Ibid.

56   Burke, Seabiscuit and Cinderella Man: "Camera Sports Shots," *Modesto Bee,* Feb. 12, 1937.

56   a sneering reference in the United Press: Henry McLemore, "Grappling Gal Lays Success To Perfection Of Girdle Grip," *Modesto Bee,* Feb. 19, 1937.

56   Burke later said: SMD, p. 111.

56   The local paper supported Burke: "Mildred Thinks She Was Robbed," *Chattanooga Times,* Feb. 12, 1937.

57   They did not wrestle that night: Instead, Burke wrestled Betty Lee, *Chattanooga Times,* Feb. 13, 1937.

57   Burke claimed that she was so angry: SMD, p. 113.

57   "Those who are of the opinion . . .": "Women Grapplers In Feature Bout," *Charleston Gazette,* April 14, 1937, sports front.

57   a record for wrestling in Charleston: "Mortinson Defeats Mildred Burk," *Charleston Gazette,* April 20, 1937.

57   a few weeks before the Charleston match: "Molly's Best not Good Enough, So Says Poet," *Norfolk Ledger-Dispatch,* April 1, 1937.

58   Burke at the time was wrestling in Texas: researcher Don Luce insists Mildred was still out in west Texas, where she had a match against Betty Lee in Amarillo on April 1, 1937.

58   the Charleston paper reported the wrong result: "Mortinson Defeats Mildred Burk," *Charleston Gazette,* April 20, 1937; Correction, *Charleston Gazette,* April 21, 1937, p. 13, provided by Don Luce.

58   Mortensen claim: Warden, "Feminine Wrestlers Make Big Money," p. 8.

JEFF LEEN

58 Burke-Mortensen feud: Tom Burke, telephone interview, April 13, 2008; Burke, WrestlingClassics.com Message Board: Women Wrestlers, August 23, 2007.

58 Mortensen in *Time* magazine: "Strong Sister," *Time,* Nov. 1, 1937.

58 She suffered a major setback: "Women's Wrestling Receives State Ban," United Press in *Fresno Bee,* November 17, 1939, sports front.

59 Mortensen, for all of her physical beauty: "Nick Lutze Saves Mat Program," *Santa Monica Outlook,* May 22, 1937, provided by J Michael Kenyon. A devastating account of Mortensen's match with Betty Lee: "The less said about the female match, the better. They weren't even good actors and the only thing complimentary that could be said is that the bout was well rehearsed. If the fans never see them again it will be too soon, as evidenced by the chorus of boos at the end of the match."

60 Their joint triumph: "Gal Grapplers To Hold Forth Here Tonight," *Fresno Bee,* July 17, 1943, p. 2-B; Ed Orman, "Sports Thinks," *Fresno Bee,* July 26, 1943, p. 2-B.

60 There was talk in 1943 of again matching Burke and Mortensen: Tim Hornbaker, *www.legacyofwrestling.com/Women_Wrestlers.html*; Burke said Wolfe offered Mortensen $50,000 winner-take-all for a rematch in 1943, SMD, p. 115.

60 Mortensen provided the final proof: Warden, "Feminine Wrestlers Make Big Money," p. 8.

60 She retired the next year: Craig Stark, "Former World's Women's Wrestling Champion Now With Carnival Here; Recalls Long Mat Career," *Humboldt Standard,* June 8, 1956, p. 11.

60 "Things just started taking off...": SMD, p. 116.

61 When Mortensen claimed she had beaten Burke: Bob Voight, Sports Editor, *Long Beach Independent,* September 5, 1943, p. 21.

61 "Miss Burke is now on her second tour . . .": "Feminine Wrestlers Appear Here Monday," *Mansfield News-Journal,* April 28, 1937, p. 16.

61 Burke signing for her first match: Dorothy Todd Foster, "Women's Wrestling Champion Still Learning," *Columbus Dispatch,* April 13, 1937, p. 4-b.

62 "Miss Burke always plays the same role . . .": Ernie Harwell, "Queen of the Seize," *Sportfolio,* April 1947, pp. 90–91.

62 Burke won a tournament: "Milly Burke Flattens Her Foe In Hurry," *Ohio State Journal,* April 30, 1937, p. 10.

63 Wolfe said it cost $525: Billy Wolfe letter to Jack Pfefer, August 28, 1937, Pfefer Collection.

63 barnstorming wrestlers often mixed: Meyer, *Wrestling,* p. 22; "Wrestling," *Brooklyn Eagle,* November 14, 1877, p. 2, provided by *Wrestling Perspective, The Thinking Fan's Newsletter,* Paul MacArthur & David Skolnick, 2007, www.wrestlingperspective.com/working/1877/brookeag1114.html.

63 Hackenschmidt was injured: Thesz and Bauman, *Hooker,* pp. 66–67. Thesz maintains that Gotch's people paid $5,000 to a hooker named Ad Santell to injure Hackenschmidt in training before the match.

63 Hack agreed to limp through: Ibid, p. 66.

63 "If ever there was a fraud perpetrated: Meyer, *Wrestling,* p. 34.

64 Another noted wrestling writer: Griffin, *Fall Guys,* p. 64.

64 In 1933 a new trust came together: Ibid, p. 70.

64 Liebling called Curley: Liebling, "From Sarah Bernhardt to Yukon Eric," p. 136.

64 Jack Curley bio: Steve Yohe, "A Jack Curley Bio," www.otherarena .com, 2002; Julius Bromberg, "Old Timers On Parade," *NWA Official Wrestling,* April 1953, pp. 26–28; Curley obituary, *Time,* July 19, 1937;

65 a devastating headline: Al Copland, "Won 0, Lost 22, Marshall Tries Londos Again!" *New York Daily News,* November 19, 1934.

65 "Curley, Mondt and the rest . . .": Griffin, *Fall Guys,* p. 75.

65 When they made their peace: Ibid, p. 70.

65 Jack Pfefer's history: Hornbaker, *National Wrestling Alliance,* pp. 250–253; Griffin, *Fall Guys,* pp.69–74.

65 Parker demolished wrestling's reputation: Thesz and Bauman, *Hooker,* p. 55.; Griffin, *Fall Guys,* pp. 72–73.

66 "Them thiefs is stealin' . . .": Griffin, *Fall Guys,* p. 72.

66 "It was through his own teeth . . .": Toots Mondt letter to I. T. Flatto, November 3, 1938, Pfefer Collection.

66 Londos had allegedly received $70,000: Griffin, *Fall Guys,* p. 77.

66 Shikat conspiracy with Jack Pfefer and Al Haft: Yohe, "A Jack Curley Bio."

66 "Stop him, he's killing me . . .": "Remember the Good Old Days," *Boxing and Wrestling,* July 1952, p. 63.

66 Federal case in Columbus: Griffin, *Fall Guys,* pp. 82–85.

67 experience had shown: William Muldoon flattened the Great John L. Sullivan in 1887 in the first notable mixed match between a wrestler and boxer. Football stars Wayne "Big" Munn and Gus Sonnenberg entered the game and proved to be no match for real wrestlers.

67 John Pesek: Hewitt, *Catch Wrestling,* pp. 162–166.

67 "I have not been writing . . .": J. E. Wray to Jack Pfefer, August 15, 1939, Pfefer Collection.

Chapter 6

68 "three splendid lady wrestlers . . .": Billy Wolfe letter to Jack Pfefer, August 5, 1937, Pfefer Collection.

69 The Very Reverend W. E. R. Morrow: "Pastor Scores Mat Contests Among Women," United Press in *Oakland Tribune,* Nov. 20, 1938, p. 6-S.

69 California ban: "Women's Wrestling Receives State Ban," sports front.

69   Nazi propagandists: "She Pins 'Em to the Mat," *San Antonio Light,* October 4, 1939, p. 11-b.

69   "Wrestling has been bumped . . .": "Women In Game Draw Strangler Lewis's Ire, *Los Angeles Times,* June 25, 1937.

69   "I had nothing against . . ." Thesz and Bauman, *Hooker,* p. 139.

70   "Living in her trailer . . .": "That's No Hooey by R. E. Hooey," *Ohio State Journal,* August 26, 1937, sports front.

70   "I am on the road . . .": Billy Wolfe letter to Jack Pfefer, August 12, 1937, Pfefer Collection.

70   The matches drew: Bill Foley, "The Women Wrestled in '37, and Who Won? The Promoter," *Florida Times-Union,* December 3, 1997, p. 3.

70   Millie floated into Havana: SMD, pp. 151–154.

71   "This was a long way . . .": Ibid.

71   "From a job banging . . .": Byron Hollingsworth, "Women's Mat Champ Here," *Tampa Daily Times,* Nov. 8, 1937.

71   Burke had risen: "Jim Londos Returns To Local Mat Tonight," *Washington Post,* December 9, 1937, p. 21.

71   the women outshined: "Jim Londos Pins Strack; Female Rasslers Steal Spotlight In Armory Bouts," *Cumberland Daily News,* Maryland, December 8, 1937.

72   the sad columns: SMD, pp. 137–140.

73   she saw Wolfe walking: Ibid, p. 145.

73   "That touching bit . . .": Jerry Brondfield, NEA Service sports writer, "Wrestling Has Gone Berserk," *Lowell Sun,* Massachusetts, Jan. 12, 1938, p. 14.

73   after the mud match: John Henry, "Her Place Isn't at Home," *Mobile Times,* Alabama, Jan. 13, 1938.

74   In the newsroom: "In the Press Box with Charles Reilly," *Norfolk Ledger-Dispatch,* February 9, 1938, p. 14.

74   with a female reporter: LeGette Blythe, "Asides," *Charlotte Observer,* February 15, 1938, p. 1.

76   $224 in sound equipment: Billy Wolfe letter to Jack Pfefer, July 26, 1938, Pfefer Collection.

76   The headline after: Emerson Davis, "Kudo Defeats Wahlberg, Mildred Burke Is Loser," *Ohio State Journal,* Nov. 19, 1938.

76   Burke published: Mildred Burke, "My Bloodiest Bout," *National Police Gazette,* September 1946, p. 14.

77   Nichols had her picture: "Champion: Betty Nichols," *Columbus Dispatch,* Dec. 1, 1938.

78   "Betty did not appear . . .": "Mildred Burke Regains Her Lightweight Championship," *Ohio State Journal,* Dec. 2, 1938.

78   Burke later told the Associated Press: Eck, "$50,000 Per Keeps Gal Grappler in Groceries."

78   Burke and Nichols wrestled again: "Mephisto Beaten By Ray Schwarz," *Charleston Gazette,* December 6, 1938.

78   "Wrestling is one of the last . . .": "Babe Myers Replaces Ryan On Mat Card," *Mansfield News-Journal,* February 23, 1939, p. 18.

79   "Every booking brought me new fans . . .": SMD, p. 125.

79   "I didn't want to work in a ten-cent store . . .": Gladys Gillem, personal interview, February 9, 2007.

79   "This is when Billy and Mildred wasn't rich . . .": "Interview with Gladys "Killem" Gillem," *Whatever Happened To . . . ?* Issue #29, Scott Teal, editor and publisher, January 1997, p. 3.

79   he tried Gladys Ryan: "Women Wrestlers to Feature Program At Weekly Show Monday in Armory Hall," *Zanesville Sunday Times-Signal,* February 12, 1939.

79   particularly apt: Killem Gillem has proved popular enough over the

years to became the name of a L.A. punk-fusion band headed by Gillem's grandson, Shawn "Beaver" McCoy.

80   "Miss Burke is a wonderful . . .": "Mildred Burke, Gladys Gilliam To Wrestle on Special Bout At Auditorium Thursday," *Galveston Daily News,* October 1, 1939.

80   a candid locker room scene: Albert Reese, "Here's The Dope," *Galveston Daily News,* October 7, 1939.

80   a reporter in Ohio tried: Al Cline, "Battered Reporter Finds Talk With Woman Wrestler Risky," *Coshocton Tribune,* November 1, 1939, p. 1.

81   Wolfe's voluminous address book: Wolfe address book, provided by Betsy Wolfe Stemple and Mickie Johnson.

81   The first reference to her "white togs": "Women Thrill Armory Fans, Fair Sex Features In Double-Header," *Charleston* (Virginia) *Daily Mail,* December 19, 1939.

81   "Ninety percent of my wrestling . . .": Jares, *Whatever Happened to Gorgeous George?* p. 58.

82   Covering one Burke-Gillem match: "Pesek Is Still Good Matman," *Charleston Daily Mail,* February 4, 1941, p. 13.

82   "Her working garments vary . . .": Farrell, "Strong Woman Takes All Comers," p. 3.

82   "Most state commission rulings . . .": Jares, *Whatever Happened to Gorgeous George?* p. 58.

82   "I'd have some beautiful colored robe . . .": Ibid, p. 58.

83   "Out of her wrestling garb . . .": Farrell, "Strong Woman Takes All Comers," p. 3.

83   wrestling and femininity: SMD, p. 129; Wolfe also had a major influence in transforming women wrestlers into glamour girls. He told the writer Rosalyn Drexler: "In the ring anything goes; like in bed a man wants a woman

to be a bitch in heat, but in the street, in the home, in the restaurants, wherever the public congregates, a man wants a woman to make him proud."

83   One of Burke's favorite coats: SMD, p. 131.

83   "This exciting melody . . .": Ibid, p. 213.

84   "The girls dress backstage . . .": Edythe Farrell, "Lady Wrestlers," *American Mercury*, December 1942, p. 679.

84   a vigorous schedule of self-improvement . . .": "Berneice Schlemmer, "Champion Says Wrestling Fan To get Glamor," United Press in *Ogden Standard-Examiner*, Utah, May 21, 1942.

84   She used weights: SMD, p. 141.

84   "I wouldn't say she was built . . .": Tommy Fooshee, telephone interview, June 29, 2007.

85   body bridges: SMD, pp. 142–143.

85   "Every eye in the place . . .": Lillian Ellison with Larry Platt, *The Fabulous Moolah: First Goddess of the Squared Circle* (New York: HarperCollins, 2002) p. 33.

Chapter 7

86   He asked for Pfefer's forbearance: Billy Wolfe letters to Jack Pfefer, June 26 and June 30, 1940, Pfefer Collection.

87   "The difference between Pfefer's productions and Curley's . . .": Liebling, "From Sarah Bernhardt to Yukon Eric," p. 137.

87   "Jack, as he is affectionately known . . .": Jim Ogle, "The Gals 'Rassle' At Bowl Tonight," *Newark Star-Ledger*, July 10, 1940.

88   Pfefer hygiene: "Classy" Freddie Blassie with Keith Elliot Greenberg, *Listen, You Pencil Neck Geeks* (New York: Pocket Books, 2003), pp. 32–33; Joe Wolfe, personal interview, May 15, 2005.

88   The *Star-Ledger* broke the news: Ogle, "The Gals 'Rassle' At Bowl Tonight."

88   "Jack made a short speech . . .": Jim Ogle, "Millie, Gladys Set Record," *Newark Star-Ledger,* July 11, 1940, sports front.

89   in an article headlined: Willie Ratner, "They Know Their Stuff," *Newark Evening News,* July 11, 1940.

89   "The fans gasped . . .": Ogle, "Millie, Gladys Set Record,"

89   Burke outearned Murphy: Jack Pfefer Account Book, July 10, 1940, Pfefer Collection. Pfefer earned $161.50 on a gate of $1,066.02. It was his largest profit in nearly three months. Wolfe and his wrestlers received $94.70; the ten male wrestlers on the card, including Dropkick Murphy and the Irish Angel, divided $76.

90   There was a blizzard: Jim Ogle, "Beauty Via Milly Burke Shoos Beast From Local Mat," *Newark State Ledger,* July 7, 1940; "Mildred Burke Wins Over Gladys Gillen in Sensational Bout," *Atlantic City Press,* July 10, 1940.

90   "While the male villains . . .": Ogle, "The Gals 'Rassle' At Bowl Tonight."

90   "With Pulchritude on Parade . . .": Jim Ogle, "Burke Beats Acosta In Wild Mat Battle," *Newark Star-Ledger,* July 18, 1940.

90   the return match: "Gillem, Burke In Wild Draw," *Newark Star-Ledger,* August 8, 1940, sports front.

91   As Gillem would say: Gladys Gillem letter to Nat Loubet, January 5, 1965, Pfefer Collection.

91   "Crazy Gladys actually bit me . . .": Charley Gazzello, "The Bare Facts Are Women Do Wrestle Bears In Ring," *Wrestling Monthly,* December 1973. p. 17.

91   wrestlers form a union: "Male Pachyderms Stage Protest Parade," *Newark Star Ledger,* September 25, 1940, sports front.

92 "I ran into Jake . . .": Louis Royal, "Fans Want Pfefer's Mat Cuties," *Daily Advocate,* Aug. 28, 1940, p. 29, Pfefer Collection.

92 With Jack Dempsey: "Whaddayamean, the Weaker Sex?" *Washington Post,* Aug. 29, 1940, p. 19.

92 Burke and Wolfe were now signing: Burke and Wolfe letter to Jack Pfefer, July 23, 1940, Pfefer Collection.

93 fun-loving and adventurous: Gladys Gillem, personal interview, February 9, 2007.

93 Burke turned a blind eye: SMD, p. 68.

93 "We wrestled in Lima . . .": Billy Wolfe letters to Jack Pfefer, August 21 and 22, 1940, Pfefer Collection.

93 "It was the usual blistering . . .": Doc Shaw, "Burke, Corral Beat Rivals on Mat," *San Antonio Light,* Oct. 29, 1940, p. 11-A.

93 blocks of ice: Tommy Fooshee, telephone interview, June 29, 2007.

94 sun tans: Joe Wolfe, personal interview, May 15, 2005.

94 "When Mom was on the road . . .": Ibid.

94 a stable of seven: Billy Wolfe letter to Jack Pfefer, October 18, 1940, Pfefer Collection.

94 the most detailed word portrait: Farrell, "Strong Woman Takes All Comers," p. 3.

95 chaw of seaweed: "Petticoat Pounding Here This Saturday," *Burlington Times-News,* North Carolina, April 10, 1941, p. 16.

95 "Regarding the girls . . .": Al Haft letter to Jack Pfefer, December 2, 1940, Pfefer Collection.

96 "Jack, I really do think . . .": Billy Wolfe letter to Jack Pfefer, October 27, 1940, Pfefer Collection.

96 Pfefer's own attitude: Herbie Freeman letter to Jack Pfefer, April 15, 1957, Pfefer Collection.

Chapter 8

97   "I get letters all the time . . .": Romney Wheeler, "Mildred Burke Claims Women's Grunt Title," Associated Press in *Kingsport Times,* Tennessee, September 7, 1941.

97   When she wrestled in Charleston: "Mountain Girl Rage on Mat," *Charleston Daily Mail,* February 11, 1941.

97   She had grown up one of nine: "Johnnie Mae Young—Sand Springs High School Class of 1941," provided by Ruth Ellen Henry, programs and public information coordinator for the Sand Springs Cultural and Historical Museum, September 2007.

98   She thought she could beat either: Johnnie May Young, telephone interview, May 15, 2007.

98   "She had men's shoes on . . .": Penny Banner, *Lipstick & Dynamite*: *The First Ladies of Wrestling,* DVD, dir. Ruth Leitman (Ruthless Films LLC,

2004;   New York: KOCH Lorber Films LLC, 2005).

98   "She'd play poker . . .": Blassie and Greenberg, *Listen, You Pencil Neck Geeks,* p. 33.

98   She would later make the papers: "Woman Wrestler Held in Robbery," Associated Press, April 30, 1949.

98   Within days of graduating: Burke and Young wrestled on May 27, 1941 in Nashville. Soon Young was pushing Burke to the limit: Oscar Elder, "Miss Young Misses Stunning, Terrific Wrestling Upset," *Washington Post,* October 22, 1942, p. 15.

98   "Mae's rough . . .": Lewis Hensley, "Mildred Burke Risks Title For 500th Time Here Tonight," Abilene, Texas *Reporter-News,* May 14, 1951.

99   "The first lick . . .": Jares, *Whatever Happened to Gorgeous George?* p. 59.

99   "The average American woman . . .": Wheeler, Associated Press in *Kingsport Times,* September 7, 1941.

99   Jolson and Washington dinners: SMD, pp. 128, 155; "Al Jolson Turns Lady Wrestling Fan," *Washington Post*, November 6, 1941, p. 26.

99   "Many wrestlers have been drafted . . .": Al Haft letter to Jack Pfefer, August 30, 1941, Pfefer Collection.

99   Max Clayton predicted: Bernie Kooser, "Pro Wrestling Needs New Drawing Power," *Lowell Sun*, Massachusetts, May 7, 1942.

100   "If the predictions of Mildred . . .": Schlemmer, Champion Says Wrestling Fan To get Glamor."

100   In 1941 three million spectators: Farrell, "Lady Wrestlers," p. 674.

101   "Mildred and I are still poor . . .": Billy Wolfe letter to Jack Pfefer, July 30, 1943; Mildred Burke letter to Jack Pfefer, August 9, 1942; Pfefer Collection.

101   Millie rode troop trains: SMD, pp. 171–173.

101   shows in Nebraska: "Manpower shortage doesn't hurt rassling; women battle," *Nebraska State Journal*, April 2, 1943, p. 13.

101   the annual Associated Press poll: "Miss Callen, Star Swimmer Voted No. 1 In Poll for 1942," *New York Times*, December 17, 1942, p. 47.

101   No female wrestler had ever made the list: Among male wrestlers, only Danno O'Mahoney of Ireland had appeared, receiving three votes for 12th place in 1935, in the entire twelve-year history of the poll. In the poll for best female athlete of the century in 1949, Burke received four votes and tied for 19th place.

101   Her coronation: Farrell, "Lady Wrestlers," p. 678.

102   a slight crack: "Women Wrestlers Banned By State Ring Commission," United Press in *Oakland Tribune*, April 23, 1944, sports front.

102   "Time was . . .": Prescott Sullivan, "Lady Rasslers Coming Back," *Referee and Redhead*, January 23, 1943, p. 4., Pfefer Collection.

103   "She has an offer . . .": "Leone and Swenski to Test Marvel Tonight," *Los Angeles Times*, January 25, 1943, p. 16.

103 "Mildred came to town . . .": Ed Orman, "Sports Thinks," *Fresno Bee,* July 26, 1943, 2-B.

103 Wrestling before her father: Ibid.

103 A *Times* reporter visited: Timothy G. Turner, "Star Female Wrestler Muscular Glamour Girl," *Los Angeles Times,* July 18, 1943, A1.

103 Just a few months earlier: Ed Orman, "Sports Thinks," *Fresno Bee,* July 22, 1943, p. 2-B.

104 The man who stayed with her: Joe Wolfe, telephone interview, June 30, 2007.

104 "We had a promotional and professional . . .": SMD, p. 150.

105 Burke kept a snub-nose .38: Joe Wolfe, personal interview, May 16, 2005.

105 the threat of bandits: SMD, pp. 135–136, 165–169.

105 Mildred and G. Bill at the Los Angeles house: Joe Wolfe, personal interview, June 30, 2007.

106 Gladys Gillem remembers: Gillem, telephone interview, February 9, 2007.

106 Johnnie Mae Young also thought: Young, telephone interview, May 15, 2007.

106 "When he was first assigned . . .": SMD, p. 157.

107 "there was love": Joe Wolfe, telephone interviews, May 15 and 16, 2005.

109 He included a proud note: Billy Wolfe letter to Jack Pfefer, December 28, 1943, Pfefer Collection.

109 The calendars created a stir: "Sports Thinks," *Fresno Bee,* January 4, 1944, p. 3-B; Porter Wittich, "Globe Trotter," *Joplin Globe,* Missouri, January 5, 1946, p. 5; Truman Twill, "They Cut her Down," *Marion Star,* Ohio, December 6, 1946, p. 6.

109   Time magazine: "Queen of the Mat," *Time,* March 27, 1944.

109   Women's wrestling had finally earned: Harold V. Ratliff, "Women Wrestlers Furnish Thrills With Spills," AP Newsfeature in *Galveston News,* March 17, 1944, p. 20.

109   Some promoters even thought: Ibid.

109   Clergymen appeared before Congress: "Women Wrestlers Worry Washington," Associated Press in *Moberly Monitor-Index and Democrat,* Missouri, February 10, 1944, p. 5.

110   The commission resisted: "Sport Thinks, *Fresno Bee,* January 4, 1944, p. 3-B.

110   They were "clever, capable . . .": Alan Ward, "On Second Thought," *Oakland Tribune,* February 25, 1944, p. 17.

110   The Women's council appealed: "Women Protest Women Wrestling," United Press in *San Mateo Times,* April 14, 1944, p. 2.

110   In a letter to the governor: "Women Wrestlers Banned By State Ring Commission," United Press in *Oakland Tribune,* April 23, 1944, sports front.

110   The reporter quoted one: "Ban Is Placed On Female Grapplers," *Modesto Bee,* April 22, 1944, p. 1.

111   Six months later: Ed Herlihy, "Mat Mamas Maul for Millions," *Universal International News,* December 27, 1944.

111   "Mildred Burke, champion lady wrestler . . .": "Sol's Weekly Newsletter," *Ogden Standard-Examiner,* January 8, 1945.

111   "Catch her in a housewifely pose . . .": Mary Jane Brooks, "Mildred Burk Will Knock Your Eye Out—Either way," *Nashville Banner,* January 23, 1945.

111   Another profile: Patty Johnson, "Lady Looks Feminine But Won World Title with Muscles Strong as Iron Bands," *Waterloo Sunday Courier,* Iowa, July 7, 1946, p. 22.

112   The United Press seized on: Helen Ashby, "Mat Champ Looks for Sports Boom," United Press in *Ogden Standard-Examiner,* February 23, 1945, p. 23.

112   Mildred Burke was back in Ogden: Les Goates, "Girl Mat Champion Wins 1,000 Consecutive Bouts," *Ogden Standard-Examiner,* May 24, 1945.

Chapter 9

114   Her $25,000 a year income: "Queen of the Mat," *PIC* magazine, October 24, 1944; Ashby, "Mat Champ Looks for Sports Boom," p. 23; Frank Colley, "Mildred Burke's Rise In Mat Game Reads Like A Story Book," *Hagerstown Morning Herald,* Maryland, November 28, 1945, p. 5.; "Meet Mildred, Mighty Wrestling Queen; Earns $25,000 A Year In Sport," *Bradford Era,* Pennsylvania, February 8, 1946, p. 11.

114   desperation diamonds: SMD, p. 133.

114   "I collect diamonds as a hobby . . .": Johnson, Waterloo, Iowa, *Sunday Courier,* July 7, 1946.

114   Millie wore four rings: "Meet Mildred, Mighty Wrestling Queen," p. 11; Harwell, "Queen of the Seize," p. 90.

115   "Most of my other pieces . . .": SMD, p. 134.

115   outdo Diamond Jim: Interview with Leo B. Whippern, "Lord Carlton," DOJ, March 3, 1955.

115   Sonja Henie movie: Harwell, "Queen of the Seize," p. 90.

115   Inventory of Wolfe's diamonds: Oscar Fraley, "Women Wrestlers Keep Wolfe in Diamonds," United Press in *Syracuse Herald-Journal,* New York, May 9, 1950, p. 24.

116   One writer outstripped his metaphors: Haight, "It Was Different, This Derby Morning," p. C4.

116   Bobby Bruns: Tommy Fooshee, telephone interview, June 29, 2007.

116   Somewhere along the line: Marie Laverne, telephone interview, August 15, 2007.

116   "He couldn't get a good . . .": Gladys Gillem, personal interview, February 10, 2007.

116   "He would never force himself . . .": Barbara Jean Baker, telephone interview, June 30, 2007.

116   Bette Carter: Frank Deford, "Wrestling with the Devil," *National Sports Daily,* July 8, 1990, p. 31.

117   "Any girl that would screw . . .": Johnnie Mae Young, telephone interview, May 15, 2007.

117   Of the women who slept with Wolfe: Johnnie Mae Young, *Lipstick & Dynamite,*

117   "Billy, of course . . .": Ethel Brown, telephone interview, September 19, 2007.

117   Johnnie Mae Young spotted: Young, telephone interview, May 15, 2007.

118   "The first time I attended . . .": Carlton Squires, "Lucky . . . Lovely and Loaded," *Boxing and Wrestling,* November 1954, pp. 42–43, 75–76; *The Ring,* November 1951, pp. 31–32.

118   Wolfe put her in: Lois Deas, "Mildred Burke Inspired Pretty Nell Stewart, Wrestling's Queen," *Raleigh Times,* n.d., circa 1948, Pfefer Collection.

118   "I lent her a black dress . . .": "Interview with Gladys "Killem" Gillem," Scott Teal, pp. 3–4.

118   Gillem disliked Nell: Gladys Gillem, personal interview, February 10, 2007.

118   Wolfe was so enamored: Harlan Beidick, "The Purple Flash wins again

in main event at arena with Mae Young victim," *Lincoln Journal,* Nebraska, July 1, 1944.

118   For Gillem: Gladys Gillem, personal interview, February 10, 2007.

119   Gillem left wrestling: Lew Eskin, "Former Female Wrestling Terror Now A Model Mother and Dignified Business Woman," *Wrestling Revue,* December 1965, pp. 20–24.

119   "I spent ten years . . .": Gladys Gillem letter to Nat Loubet, January 5, 1965, Pfefer Collection.

119   As he had with Burke: "Lucky . . . Lovely and Loaded," *Boxing and Wrestling,* November 1954, p. 76.

119   "the Betty Grable of the mat": *The Ring,* November 1951. p. 31.

119   Billy Wolfe delighted: "Before and After," *Long Beach Independent Press-Telegram,* Jan. 25, 1953.

120   Burke's and Stewart's measurements: Burke's from "World Champion Lady Wrestler," *PIC* magazine, March 5, 1940: 15-inch neck, 13-inch biceps, 20½-inch thigh, 14½-inch calf, 26-inch waist, 31-inch chest expands to 38 inches; Stewart's measurements from *Glance,* May 1951, Pfefer collection.

120   "We're meaner in the ring . . .": Deas, "Mildred Burke Inspired Pretty Nell Stewart, Wrestling's Queen."

120   "Miss Stewart's tactics: "Says Gal Wrestlers Meaner Than Men, Proves It in Ring," *Bismarck Tribune,* May 2, 1949.

121   June Byers's history: Billy Wolfe promotional sheet on June Byers, Pfefer Collection; "Lone Star Lady," *NWA Official Wrestling,* April 1951, pp. 28–31; Carlton Squires, "She's Beautiful but loaded with guts," *Boxing and Wrestling,* August 1954, pp. 50–51, 76–78; "June Byers: The Golden Age's Great Champion," womens-pro-wrestling.com/byers.htm; *Whatever Happened to . . . ?* Issue #2, Scott Teal publisher, 1993, p. 7.

121   The boy: Jewell Olivas, telephone interview, September 21, 2007.

121 "I used to see the lady wrestlers . . .": Scott Baillie, "Diamond Weakness Makes Her a Wrestler," United Press in *Mansfield News-Journal,* July 15, 1950, p. 6;

122 After being spotted by Wolfe: Ibid. Some accounts say Wolfe was not present when Byers wrestled Davis.

122 Johnnie Mae Young trained her: Young, telephone interview, May 15, 2007.

122 Some of the other women: Barbara Jean Baker, telephone interview, June 30, 2007; Gloria Barattini, telephone interview, July 14, 2007; Ethel Brown, telephone interview, September 19, 2007; Ella Waldek, *Lipstick & Dynamite.*

122 "Byers had Champ Burke groggy . . .": "Burke Retains Crown When June Byers Gets Careless," *El Paso Herald,* December 21, 1949.

122 She drank orange juice: Jewell Olivas, telephone interview, September 21, 2007.

122 June dreamed: "She wants to be a promoter," *Boxing and Wrestling,* December 1952, pp. 46–47.

123 Wolfe, Stewart and Byers: Rosalyn Drexler, "A Woman's Place Is on the Mat," *Esquire,* February 1966, pp. 81, 120–127; Johnnie Mae Young, telephone interview, May 15, 2007; Gloria Barattini, telephone interview, July 14, 2007; Ellison and Platt, *The Fabulous Moolah,* p. 45.

124 Gladys Gillem, curious: Gladys Gillem, personal interview, February 10, 2007.

124 Another young wrestler: Former female wrestler granted anonymity.

124 lesbians: SMD, pp. 117–121.

125 "Wolfe's practice for some time . . ." : Ibid, p. 221.

125 Ellison on Wolfe: Ellison and Platt, *The Fabulous Moolah,* pp. 43–52.

125 "a real funny body . . . : Jares, *Whatever Happened to Gorgeous George?* p. 56.

Chapter 10

127   That arrangement alone: Walter Winchell, *On Broadway,* May 22, 1950.

128   "Billy Wolfe was the daddy . . .": Deford, *National Sports Daily,* July 8, 1990, p. 31.

128   Wolfe-Burke marriage outed: *Bradford Era,* February 8, 1946.

128   "Why Billy . . .": "Mildred Burke Not Ready to Forsake Mats for Marriage," *Council Bluffs Nonpareil,* Iowa, December 1, 1946.

128   In a long piece: Harwell, "Queen of the Seize," pp. 87–91.

128   mixed match with G. Bill: "In This Corner, Mildred Burke," ACME Newspictures, NEA Service Inc., October 9, 1947.

128   *Sportfolio* profile: Harwell, "Queen of the Seize," p. 87.

129   "For the first twenty minutes . . .": Barry Pate, "Queen of the Mayhem," *Sportfolio,* December 1948, pp. 121–128.

129   her highest showing yet: "Athlete of 1947 Is Mrs. Zaharias," *New York Times,* January 15, 1948, p. 31.

130   "It has a big advance . . .": Al Haft letters to Jack Pfefer, September 8 and 9, 1948, Pfefer Collection.

130   Gorgeous George: "Gorgeous George, Golden Villain of Wrestling, Dies," *Chicago Tribune,* December 27, 1963; Nat Loubet, "Gorgeous George dead at 48," *Ring Wrestling,* April 1964, pp. 34–36; Joe Jares, "George was Villainous, Gutsy and Gorgeous," *Sports Illustrated,* January 14, 1969, pp. E5–7; *Jares, Whatever Happened to Gorgeous George?* pp. 11–23; Thesz and Bauman, *Hooker,* pp. 98–100; Beekman, *Ringside,* pp. 86–89; Randy Roberts and James Olson, *Winning Is The Only Thing: Sports in America since 1945* (Baltimore: Johns Hopkins University Press, 1989), pp. 99–101; Chad Dell, *The Revenge of Hatpin Mary: Women, Professional Wrestling and Fan Culture in the 1950s* (New York: Peter Lang Publishing, Inc., 2006), pp. 7, 15–18, 65–66. Anyone interested in George should read John Capouya's

Gorgeous George: The Outrageous Bad-Boy Wrestler Who Created American Pop Culture (New York: HarperCollins, 2008).

131   Burke influence on George: SMD, pp. 257–258.

132   Wolfe remained master: Wolfe promotional sheets for Mildred Burke and June Byers, Pfefer Collection.

132   There was at the time: Edwin Pope, telephone interview, June 29, 2007. Ed, an old colleague of mine at the *Miami Herald,* made clear to me that although he heard of payoffs while working in the south in the 1950s, he did not participate in any.

132   Byers and Stewart as Number One contenders: "Da Preen Shots For Another 'Title' In Sexton Tangle," *Washington Post,* June 22, 1947, p. C3; "Girl Stars Head Expo Mat Slate," Portland, Maine, *Sunday Press Telegram and Sunday Press Herald,* July 20, 1947, B3.

133   She and Wolfe sometimes acted: Drexler, "A Woman's Place Is on the Mat," p. 122.

133   For the columnist's benefit: Earl Wilson, Bumpkin on Broadway, "Gentle Hint to Wolfish Guys: Don't Fool With Gal Rasslers," *Galveston News,* February 11, 1950, p. 4.

133   The madcap scene: Haight, "It Was Different, This Derby Morning," p. C4.

134   "Dripping in diamonds . . .": Baillie, "Diamond Weakness Makes Her a Wrestler," p. 6. During the interview Byers estimated she was wearing 35 carats worth $15,000.

135   "As Mahout of the Pulchritudinous . . .": Dan Parker, "Grappling Gals Pay Off for Maestro Billy," King Features Syndicate, n.d., circa 1948, Pfefer Collection.

135   Wolfe got his own: Fraley, "Women Wrestlers Keep Wolfe in Diamonds," p. 24.

135   "Self made Mahout . . .": William Waller, "Women Wrestlers Find Gold in Grunt-and-Groan Business," *St. Louis Globe-Democrat,* May 2, 1950, F-1.

135   "Perhaps the best proof . . .": Sherman Walker, "The Ziegfeld of Wrestling," *Wrestling and TV Sports,* July 1951, pp. 6–8, 57.

137   To her mind: SMD, p. 150.

137   The publicity had another side effect: Jeane Hoffman, "Women Wrestlers—More Brutal Than Men!" *National Police Gazette,* May 1950, pp. 18–19, 29.

137   "I think it is undignified . . .": Waller, "Women Wrestlers Find Gold," p. F-1.

138   The Cleveland ban attempt: Peter Bellamy, "Councilman Burns up, Asks City to Ban Women Rasslers," *Cleveland News,* May 9, 1950, p. 4; "The Brave Alderman And Lady Wrestlers," *Cleveland News,* May 10, 1950; Peter Bellamy, "Lady Rasslers? Jail 'Em, Says Councilman," *Cleveland News,* May 10, 1950; "And In This Corner . . . 'Pal For Gal Rasslers," *Cleveland News,* May 11, 1950, p. 2; Gordon Cobbledick, "Fair Sex Gets Its Way in Mat Game, Too, as Councilmanic Protest Falls Flat," *Cleveland Plain Dealer,* May 12, 1950; Doris Millavec and George Hixon, "Should women wrestlers be banned in Cleveland?" *Cleveland News,* May 23, 1950.

138   By the middle of 1950: Hoffman, "Women Wrestlers—More Brutal Than Men!" p. 18.

138   In July 1950: "Record Crowd Sees Mildred Burke Win Wrestling Match," *Kingsport News,* July 26, 1950.

139   "The women displayed . . .": "Record Crowd Sees Wrestling Card," *Panama City News-Herald,* August 16, 1950, p. 6.

139   she would like to go to Moscow: "Lady Wrestling Champ Puts Body Slam to Red Propaganda," August 13, 1950, the *Long Beach Independent,* p. 33-A

139   the five reliable drawing cards: "World's Only Wrestling Bear To Appear Here Friday Night," *Anniston Star,* Alabama, January 18, 1951, p. 20.

Chapter 11

140   But he was now managing: Walker, "The Ziegfeld of Wrestling," p. 6.

140   In early 1951: "Gal Grapplers Learn Ropes in Ohio Class," p. 14.

141   Al Haft background: Brad Willson, "Wrestling Grows to Big Business in Columbus," *Columbus Dispatch,* February 15, 1953; Al Haft, "Abe Lincoln Started It," *Ohio State Journal,* February 19, 1958; Hornbaker, *National Wrestling Alliance,* pp. 273–275.

141   "To say that the gym . . .": "Rasslers Work Out In Haft's Fine Gym," *NWA Official Wrestling,* April 1952, p. 12.

141   "Some of the best wrestling . . .": Hornbaker, *NWA,* p. 275.

142   The hotel itself: "Park Hotel, Columbus, Ohio: A Complete Description of this New and Modern Hotel," *Columbus Evening Dispatch,* March 23, 1878, p. 1.

142   Each applicant had to: Walker, "The Ziegfeld of Wrestling," pp. 8, 57.

143   Wolfe's training regimen: Mary Joos, "Lady Wrestler's Life Can Be a Merry One, Feminine Reporter Discovers With Envy," *Columbus Star,* February 9, 1952; "So You Want To Be A Lady Wrestler," *NWA Official Wrestling,* December 1952, pp. 14–17; Carleton Squires, "So You Wanna Be A Gal Grappler," *Boxing and Wrestling,* April 1955, pp. 46–47, 74.

143   The place was a plain little: Boatcallie, telephone interview, June 29, 2007.

144   Billy called her: Cora Combs, telephone interview, March 31, 2007.

145   "He was a manipulator . . .": Ida May Martinez, telephone interview, December 12, 2006, and personal interview, January 7, 2007.

145   "He always seemed to have. . .": Ethel Brown, telephone interview, September 19, 2007.

145   They checked into the Park Hotel: Ida May Martinez interviews, January 7 and September 11, 2007.

145   The stories about Young: Joe Wolfe interviews, May 15, 2005, November 9, 2007, March 20, 2008.

145   Another time Young: "Mae Young and Moolah," *Shoot Interviews,* RF Video, September 28, 2006.

146   "All of a sudden . . .": Ida May Martinez, telephone interview, September 11, 2007.

146   "We were all just young kids . . .": Ruth Boatcallie, telephone interview, June 29, 2007.

146   "She was low-key . . .": Ida May Martinez, personal interview, January 7, 2007.

146   "Mildred was more . . .": Gloria Barattini, personal interview, July 14, 2007.

146   "Mildred was a snob . . .": Barbara Jean Baker, telephone interview, June 30, 2007.

146   Ella Waldek: *Lipstick & Dynamite.*

147   Gladys Gillem: Gillem letter to Loubet, January 5, 1965, Pfefer Collection.

147   Johnnie Mae Young insisted: Young, telephone interview, May 15, 2007.

147   "She was beautiful . . .": Ida May Martinez interviews, January 7 and September 11, 2007.

147   One of Wolfe's young recruits: Banner and Hostetler, *Banner Days,* p. 122.

147   "Nell was a beautiful girl . . .": Gloria Barattini, personal interview, July 14, 2007.

148   Byers was not so popular: Author interviews with Gloria Barattini, Ethel Brown, Ida May Martinez and Johnnie Mae Young; Ella Waldek, *Lipstick & Dynamite*

148   Wolfe eventually tired: *Shoot Interviews,* September 28, 2006; Johnnie Mae Young, telephone interview, May 15, 2007.

149   The first black girls: "Wrestling Card Ready for Thursday: First Appearance In This Area for Negro Grapplers," *Chillicothe Constitution-Tribune,* Jan. 5, 1953, p. 2; Kathleen Wimbley, telephone interview, July 4, 2007; Charles A. Smith, "Grappling's Colorful Colored Girls," *Boxing and Wrestling,* February 1953, pp. 54–55, 74; Dan Daniel, "Gal Grapplers Kill Color Line," *Ring Wrestling,* September 1963, pp. 44–45.

149   He asked his white women: Martinez, telephone interview, December 6, 2006.

150   "Billy should get 100 percent . . .": Kathleen Wimbley, telephone interview, July 4, 2007

150   "Billy liked his booze . . ." Baker Jean Baker, telephone interview, June 30, 2007.

150   He used to frequent: Frankie Cain, telephone interview, July 19, 2008.

150   "We used to play poker . . ." Johnnie Mae Young, telephone interview, May 15, 2007.

151   "His orgies . . .": SMD, p. 162.

151   "He was just an ordinary guy . . ." Ruth Boatcallie, telephone interview, June 29, 2007.

151   "They both had erections . . .": Former female wrestler granted anonymity.

151   "Even though Billy had been a wrestler," Blassie and Greenberg, *Listen, You Pencil Neck Geeks,* p. 34.

152   "Ensconced now in the Park Hotel . . .": SMD, p. 150.

152   "A double-cross was . . .": Ibid, pp. 179–181.

153   As she became more wary: SMD, pp. 216, 232–238.

153   Billy with Joe Wolfe: Joe Wolfe, personal interview, May 15, 2005.

155   Bars used wrestling: "Women Wrestlers on Television at the Embassy Room," Embassy Bar, *Elyria Chronicle-Telegram,* Ohio, March 16, 1948, p. 6.

155   TV phenomenon: Frank Eck, "Wrestling Takes Grip On Public Through TV," Associated Press in *Nashua Telegraph,* May 12, 1949., p. 18.

156   Women and TV wrestling: "It Pays to Sponsor Television Corn," *Business Week,* October 7, 1950, pp. 25–26; Dell, *The Revenge of Hatpin Mary:* p. 20; "TV Is Making Rassle Experts Of Weaker Sex," *Ogden Standard-Examiner,* January 6, 1952, p. 10A.

156   Wolfe's surviving records: Wolfe's address book provided by Betsy Wolfe Stemple and Mickie Johnson.

156   "There's no doubt . . .": Roberts and Olson, *Winning Is The Only Thing,* p. 101.

157   Historian William Manchester: Ibid.

157   Others liked what they saw: Ibid.

157   Sayyid Qutb: David Von Drehle, "A Lesson In Hate," *Smithsonian,* February 2006, pp. 96–101; Daniel Brogan, "Al Qaeda's Greeley Roots," *5280,* June/July 2003; the original article by Qutb, "The America I Saw," was published in the Egyptian literary magazine al-Risala, November/December 1951.

158   But it was a weak group: Thesz and Bauman, *Hooker,* p. 53.

159   The NWA: Hornbaker, *National Wrestling Alliance,* p. 19, 22, 25, 26, 135, 196.

159   Some NWA members: Pinkie George letter to Sam Muchnick, 1949, exact date unknown, provided by Tim Hornbaker.

160   The occasion was marked: Stanley Kligfeld, "Golden Groaners: Spruced-Up Wrestlers Bring a New Boom To an Ancient Sport," *Wall Street Journal,* November 26, 1951, p. 1.

161   "People were afraid . . .": Ida May Martinez, telephone interview, May 7, 2007.

Chapter 12

162 Billy Wolfe and Janet Boyer: "Jeanette Wolfe, 18, Adopted Daughter Of Mildred Burke, Dies of Mat Injury," Associated Press in *Washington Post,* July 29, 1951; 163 Because she was under eighteen: "Girl Wrestler Killed In Ring," *Columbus Citizen,* July 28, 1951. p. 1.

163 They were photographed together: *NWA Official Wrestling,* June 1951, p. 36.

163 Janet Boyer death: *Columbus Citizen,* July 28, 1951; "Girl Wrestler to Be Buried In Minneapolis," *Elyria Chronicle Telegram,* July 29, 1951.

164 the autopsy showed: "2 Factors Cited In Mat Fatality," *East Liverpool Review,* Ohio, July 30, 1951, p. 1.

165 "My daughter's death . . .": "Girl Wrestler, 18, Dies When Ring Match Ruptures Stomach," Associated Press in *Waukesha Daily Freeman,* Wisconsin, July 30, 1951, p. 7.

165 "He was going to make her champion . . .": Johnnie Mae Young, *Lipstick & Dynamite.*

165 "We were exonerated . . .": Ella Waldek, *Lipstick & Dynamite.*

165 "That was just something . . .": Joe Wolfe, personal interview, May 15 and 16, 2005.

166 A dozen years after: "Girl Wrestler Killed In Ring," *Wrestling Revue,* June 1963, p. 22–23.

166 Cleveland Councilman: "Cleveland May Ban Female Wrestling, Associated Press, July 31, 1951.

166 "Perhaps we are just old-fashioned . . .": "Lady Wrestlers," *Syracuse Post-Standard,* New York, July 30, 1951.

166 He paid cash for it: Joint Tenancy Grant Deed to Mildred Wolfe, a married woman, and G. Bill Wolfe, a single man, from William H. Wolfe, a married man, Book 37108, Page 400, Los Angeles County, California, July 26, 1951.

167   Burke on G. Bill, house: SMD, pp. 158–160, 182.

168   G. Bill's approach to Billy: Ibid, pp. 160–161.

169   "The lopsided injustice . . .": Ibid, p. 162.

169   "Inconsolable . . .": Ibid, p. 163.

169   hidden vodka bottles: Joe Wolfe, personal interview, May 15, 2006.

169   The car had pulled slightly: SMD, p. 196; Joe Wolfe, personal interview, May 16, 2005.

170   The car wreck: Joe Wolfe, personal interview, May 16, 2005; SMD, pp. 195–205.

171   Mildred had five ribs broken: Billy Wolfe letter to the editor, "Mildred Burke's Muscles Are Rippling Again and She's Still the Champ," *NWA Official Wrestling,* March 1952, p. 46.

171   "The pain was excruciating . . .": SMD, p. 206.

172   Letter to G. Bill: Ibid, p. 164–165.

173   At least one other wrestler: Ruth Boatcallie, telephone interview, June 29, 2007.

Chapter 13

174   Gloria Barattini: *The Ring,* November 1951, p. 32.

174   "One of his favorite sayings . . .": SMD, p. 218.

175   "Although I had a near-perfect body . . .": Ibid, p. 220.

176   "Her wonderful muscles . . .": Wolfe letter, "Mildred Burke's Muscles Are Rippling Again," p. 46.

176   Wolfe pressured her: SMD, p. 207.

176   Despite the turmoil, Wolfe persisted: *NWA Official Wrestling,* January 1953, p. 46.

176 "ruining her gate": Interview with Mildred Burke, DOJ, March 23, 1955.

176 arguing with Billy: SMD, pp. 225–227.

177 prematch publicity session: Earl Flora, "Florascope On Sports," *Ohio State Journal,* Feb. 7, 1952.

180 Wolfe ensured she got the buildup: Joos, *Columbus Star,* February 9, 1952, p. 1.

180 NWA stories: "The Champ Comes Back," *NWA Official Wrestling,* May 1952, p. 19; William Warren, "Crown Princess Nell," *NWA Official Wrestling,* August 1952, p. 4.

181 Burke on Nell: SMD, pp. 222–225.

182 The surviving newspaper accounts: "Mat Champ Turns Back Stewart," *Arkansas Democrat,* March 5, 1952, p. 16; "Burke Keeps Title By Beating Stewart," *Joplin Globe,* Missouri, March 7, 1952; "Burke Defeats Stewart to Keep Her Mat Crown," *Joplin News-Herald,* March 7, 1952; "Mexican Knocks Himself Out—Mildred Burke In Draw," Memphis *Commercial Appeal,* March 11, 1952, p. 21; "Wrestling: Champ Still Reigns," Chattanooga *Daily Times,* March 14, 1952, p. 33; "Burke, Garcia Win Mat Battles Here," *Albuquerque Tribune,* May 6, 1952, p. 14; "Record Mat Crowd Sees Titles Held," *Tucson Daily Citizen,* May 8, 1952, p. 14.

182 "My heart sank . . .": SMD, p. 183.

183 She simply refused: Ibid, p. 184.

183 "They said, 'Okay . . .": Joe Wolfe, telephone interview, November 9, 2007,

183 Burke's account of the fight: SMD, pp. 184–189.

185 Three weeks earlier: "Mildred Burke Teaches Mat Lesson; Jap, Mexican Win," *Abilene Reporter-News,* Texas, August 12, 1952, p. 8-A.

185 "I don't remember the blows . . .": Joe Wolfe interviews, May 15, 2005 and November 9, 2007.

185 She said they finally: SMD, p. 188.

186 "What dissuaded me . . .": Ibid, p. 193.

187 "The cancer lie . . .": Ibid, p. 191–192.

187 NWA rejection: Burke interview, DOJ investigation, March 23, 1955, p. 4.

187 The California beating finally gave her: SMD, p. 230.

187 She hired lawyers and a private detective: James L. Moats Detective Service report to Mildred Burke, December 8, 1952.

188 Billy Wolfe lined up a new driver: Sworn consent of Margaret E. Williams for her son, Bert Leroy Younker, to travel and accompany Mildred Burke on her wrestling tours as driver, County of Los Angeles, State of California, December 11, 1952. Since Younker was not yet eighteen, his mother also consented to Burke serving as his temporary guardian.

188 *Boxing and Wrestling* magazine: "Gal Grappler Ratings," *Boxing and Wrestling,* November 1952, p. 77.

188 "Beauteous Nell Stewart . . .": "It Was A Great Year," *NWA Official Wrestling,* December 1952, p. 24.

188 Mildred's earnings: Ed Orman, "Sport Thinks," *Fresno Bee,* July 22, 1943, p. 2-B.

189 Nature Boy Buddy Rogers: Herman Dutch Rohde aka "Buddy Rogers" letter to Jack Pfefer, December 27, 1948, Pfefer Collection.

189 Wolfe grossed $250,000: Walker, "The Ziegfeld of Wrestling," p. 6.

189 Wolfe's yearly revenue: Wolfe's Attractions, Inc., "Records of Commissions, Started Clean Slate After Outcome of Court Receivership," Sept. 23, 1953, ledger provided by Betsy Wolfe Stemple and Mickie Johnson.

189 "The true tally . . .": SMD, pp. 240–241.

189 As expenses mounted: Western Union telegrams from Mildred Burke to Jack Pfefer, at 11:39 p.m., December 20, 1952, and at 12:26 a.m., December 31, 1952, Pfefer Collection.

Chapter 14

191   Mildred Burke's account of the divorce: SMD, pp. 230–239.

192   Instead of challenging him: William H. Wolfe vs. Mildred Bliss Wolfe, December 30, 1952, Circuit Court, Hickory County, Missouri.

193   "In my mood . . .": SMD, p. 231.

193   She was still a draw: " Dave Feldman, "Record Crowd Sees Burke Win, Rossi Fume," *Tucson Daily Citizen,* January 8, 1953, p. 24;

194   NWA meeting: Minutes of special meeting of the National Wrestling Alliance, St. Louis, January 11, 1953, DOJ investigation; Burke interview, DOJ investigation, March 23, 1955, pp. 1–2.

194 He immediately agreed: SMD, pp. 245–246.

195   "Another problem faces us . . .": "Speech Made by NWA President Sam Muchnick—January 12, 1953 at a Special Meeting in St. Louis," Tim Hornbaker, legacyofwrestling.com. Stanley Disney, the Justice Department attorney who led the investigation of the NWA, later wrote that one of the "objectionable features" of the organization was that he "understood the members had agreed Billy Wolfe should have a monopoly on women wrestling," Memorandum, Stanley E. Disney to James M. McGrath, DOJ, June 30, 1955.

195   Haft warning: Ted Thye interview, DOJ investigation, June 8 and 9, 1955, p. 12.

195   Attractions, Inc. financing: Notes, all dated February 1, 1953, entered as Exhibits A, B, C and D in the Attractions, Inc., receivership proceeding, Curtis H. Porter, George R. Hedges, et al, vs. Attractions, Inc., No. 188139, Court of Common Pleas, Franklin County, Ohio.

196   She delivered the $30,000: SMD, p. 245; "Mildred Burke Gets Two New Managers," INS, *Lima News,* Jan. 30, 1953; Sam Muchnick letter to Eddie Quinn, January 27, 1973. provided by Tim Hornbaker.

197   Thesz was a "hooker": Thesz and Bauman, *Hooker,* p. 14.

197   Thesz rule: Ibid, p. 139; "Minutes of National Wrestling Alliance Convention, September 4-5-6, 1953," Chicago, DOJ investigation.

197   Still, he had posed: "Louis Thesz, Mildred Burke Defend Mat Crowns Tonight," *Galveston News,* May 31, 1951, p. 33.

197   Wolfe was granted a divorce: Wolfe vs. Wolfe, Divorce Decree No. 481, February 12, 1953, Circuit Court, Hickory County, Missouri.

197   He made sure: "Mildred Burke, Billy Wolfe split," Associated Press in *Lima News,* February 23, 1953, p. 13.

198   Burke wrestled black challenger Babs Wingo: Gai Ingham Berlage, "Robinson's Legacy: Black Woman and Negro Baseball," anthologized in *The Cooperstown Symposium on Baseball and American Culture 1997: Jackie Robinson,* edited by Peter M. Rutkoff, introduction by Alvin L. Hall (North Carolina: McFarland, 2000) p. 132.

199   Wolfe was putting his house in order: Joint Tenancy Grant Deed, G. Bill Wolfe, a single man, and Mildred Wolfe, a married woman, grantors, Book 42168, Page 53-54, March 4, 1953, Los Angeles County, California; Warranty Deed, G. Bill Wolfe, unmarried, to William H. Wolfe, Volume 1730, Page 280, March 4, 1953, Franklin County, Ohio; Articles of Incorporation, Girl Wrestling Enterprises, Inc., No. 232396, March 4, 1953, Office of the Secretary of State, Columbus, Ohio.

199   To add insult to injury: G. Bill Wolfe and DeAlva E. Byers, marriage certificate, March 23, 1953, Probate Court, Franklin County, Ohio.

199   "Billy always had the girlfriends . . .": Kathleen Wimbley, telephone interview, July 4, 2007.

199   G. Bill and June took up residence: address given on application for marriage license, March 18, 1953, Probate Court, Franklin County, Ohio.

199   "Mildred and those attorneys . . .": Ida May Martinez, telephone interview, January 7, 2007.

200   "So now there will be two . . .": "Girl Wrestlers Form New Combine," *NWA Official Wrestling,* April 1953, p. 7-8.

200   full-scale war: *NWA Official Wrestling,* May 1953, p. 8 and 30; picture of Wolfe and Stewart with *NWA* editor Ned Brown at Stork Club, p. 32.

201   Jack Pfefer's records: Rogers letter to Pfefer, Pfefer Collection.

201   Burke began to offer contracts: Burke interview, DOJ investigation, March 23, 1955, p. 2.

201   "I just didn't like hopping around . . .": Ida May Martinez, personal interview, January 7, 2007.

201   "She just told me . . .": Cora Combs interview, February 14, 2006, provided by Greg Oliver.

201   The signs had been in the air: Stanley Weston, "News of the Mat World," *The Ring,* December 1950, p. 30; Nat Loubet, "News of the Mat World," *The Ring,* February 1953, p. 34.

201   "Billy handled all the business . . .": SMD, p. 240.

202   And then a move was made: Dave Feldman, "Doubletalk," *Tucson Daily Citizen,* March 17, 1953, p. 15.

203   The Baltimore tournament: "Women's Mat Tourney Set," *Baltimore Sun,* April 12, 1953; SMD, p. 228.

203   she applied her own hand: Jesse A. Linthicum, "June Byers Winds World Mat Title For Women In Coliseum," *Baltimore Sun,* April 15, 1953.

204   Billy Wolfe had planted: Al Mayer, "Byers Wins Title Tournament," *NWA Official Wrestling,* June 1953, pp. 12–13, 46.

204   Burke took a kind of victory: SMD, p. 229.

204   "She called everybody . . ." Ida May Martinez, telephone interview, May 7, 2007.

205   Stewart later said: Banner and Hostetler, *Banner Days,* p. 122.

205   Wolfe-Stewart marriage: Date from William H. Wolfe vs. Verdie N. Wolfe, No. 77555, September 7, 1954, Court of Common Pleas, Franklin County, Ohio.

205   "June Byers is the lady champion . . .": "Rogers, Stewart TV Champions," *NWA Official Wrestling,* August 1953, pp. 14–15.

206   Inside the magazine: *NWA Official Wrestling,* June 1953, pp. 12–13, 46.

206   Burke was incensed: Burke interview, DOJ investigation, March 23, 1955, p. 3.

206   "Billy would call . . .": Ethel Brown, telephone interview, September 19, 2007.

206   To counteract this problem: SMD, p. 252; Burke interview, DOJ investigation, March 23, 1955, p. 2.

207   As the business worsened: SMD, pp. 253, 255.

207   McGuirk told her: SMD, p. 253; Burke interview, DOJ investigation, March 23, 1955, p. 3.

207   Wolfe efforts were less successful: Nat Loubet, "News of the Mat World," *The Ring,* June 1953, p. 26; "What? Another World's Woman Wrestling Champion?" *Boxing and Wrestling,* August 1953, pp. 52–53, 79–80.

208   Byers on *What's My Line?:* "Professional Wrestler," *What's My Line?* Episode 168, Season Four, August 16. 1953, www.tv.com.

208   The next day, Mildred Burke's partners: Curtis H. Porter, George R. Hedges, Jr., James L. Moats, and Florence E. Stauch, and all of Columbus, Ohio, vs. Attractions, Inc., No. 188139, Court of Common Pleas, Franklin County, Ohio.

209   As her business came crashing down: "Mildred Burke, Martinelli Win Matches Before 3,600," *Tucson Daily Citizen,* August 20, 1953, p. 27.

209   "Before my lawyers knew . . .": SMD, p. 247.

209   Wolfe clearly had planted: "Mildred Burke in $30,000 default, Wolfe to Run Ex-Wife's Agency, *Ohio State Journal,* Aug. 21. 1953.

210   Wolfe wasted no time: Billy Wolfe letter to "Mr. Wrestling Promoter," August 20, 1953, Pfefer Collection.

210   Burke responded: Mildred Burke letter to "Dear Friend," August 26, 1953, Pfefer Collection.

211   Combs statement: Cora Combs "To Whom It May Concern," August 29, 1953, Pfefer Collection.

212   Burke reached out: SMD, pp. 249–250.

212   Bob Barton bio: Bicker & Eckler LLP web site, www.bricker.com/FirmInformation/History.asp.

213   Another deal was brokered: "Minutes of the National Wrestling Alliance Convention, September 4-5-6 1953," Chicago, DOJ investigation.

213   Scene at NWA meeting: SMD, pp. 250–252.

213   In November 1953: Mildred Burke letter to "Dear Alliance Member," November 4, 1953, Pfefer Collection.

214   Burke had had enough: Mildred Burke letter to "Wrestling Promoter," November 25, 1953, provided by Tim Hornbaker.

Chapter 15

215   Burke had to sell her diamonds: SMD, pp. 260–261.

215   "Mom ended up almost destitute . . ." Joe Wolfe, personal interview, May 15, 2005.

215   Visiting with Gorgeous George: SMD, p. 259.

215   A wire she sent to Jack Pfefer: Mildred Burke Western Union telegram to Jack Pfefer, n.d., Pfefer Collection.

215   Sam Menacker canceled: Burke interview, DOJ investigation, March 23, 1955, p. 4.

216   Byers showed off the belt: A.C. Becker Jr., "Bruises Mix With Money," *Galveston News*, February 13, 1954, p. 14.

216   G. Bill Wolfe: Author interviews with Ida May Martinez, Gloria Barattini, Kathleen Wimbley, Johnnie Mae Young, Joe Wolfe.

216   Burke was redoubling: SMD, p. 260; Burke interview, DOJ investigation, March 23, 1955, p. 4.

217   "The title was master key . . .": SMD, p. 242.

217   Despite Wolfe's machinations: Dave Feldman, "Off The Cuff,: *Tucson Daily Citizen,* September 22, 1953, p. 13; "Mildred Burke Stakes World Mat Title Against Millie Stafford," *Kingsport Times,* September 30, 1953, p. 11.

217   In Tampa, she drew only: "Tampa, Florida: 1943–1957," *Rasslin Results* (Hendersonville, Tennessee: Scott Teal, 1996). Burke drew 4,371 for a match against Mae Weston on Oct. 17, 1949.

217   Paul Bowser: Burke interview, DOJ investigation, March 23, 1955, p. 4.

217   Wolfe's business was hurting: "Gorgeous George to Wrestle Red Berry in Main-Go Tonight," *Joplin Globe,* March 24, 1954, p. 2B.

218   "It is not our intention . . .": "Queen of the Mat World: We Clear Up the Controversial Gal Grappling Situation," *Boxing and Wrestling,* March 1954, pp. 44–45, 76–77.

218   Wolfe could not afford: Wolfe's Attractions, Inc., commissions ledger, provided by Betsy Wolfe Stemple and Mickie Johnson.

218   He was still a master: "The Wild Cats of Billy Wolfe," *Boxing and Wrestling* magazine, June 1954, p. 76.

219   Nell going to Hollywood: A.C. Becker Jr., "Li'l Nell Is Scared," *Galveston News,* July 30, 1954.

219   "She was in love with him . . .": Ida May Martinez, telephone interview, January 7, 2007.

220   Wolfe retained a special fondness: Billy Wolfe letter to Jack Pfefer, January 19, 1962, Pfefer Collection.

220 Stewart, however, did not feel the same way: Terry Patterson, telephone interview, June 6, 2007.

220 LeeChona LaClaire's history: Joe R. Mills, "LeeChona And Terrible Tessie Tangle For Nell's Gold Belt," *Columbus Star,* August 25, 1956, p. 4.

221 Luttrall and McIntyre had: Herbie Freeman letter to Jack Pfefer, August 24, 1954, Pfefer Collection.

221 "If Billy Wolfe wanted . . .": SMD, p. 263.

222 "However, Mildred is a screwball . . .": Freeman letter, Pfefer Collection.

222 Burke gives a more detailed account: SMD, pp. 265–266.

223 "He forced her to take this match . . .": Bert Younker, telephone interview, August 21, 2006.

223 "Strongly influencing my decision . . .": SMD, p. 267.

223 Byers went into serious training: Banner and Hostetler, *Banner Days,* pp. 43–45.

224 There had not been such a match: There is no agreement over when the last shooting match for a championship took place. Some say all the matches back to and including the Gotch-Hackenschmidt match of 1908 were fixed. Most experts agree that the Stecher-Lewis and Stecher-Caddock matches had the character of shooting matches; Lou Thesz in *Hooker* (p. 46) says Stecher and Lewis had a shooting match in 1921, won by Lewis, but other sources disagree. Mark Hewitt in *Catch Wrestling* (p. 179) says Stecher and John Pesek had a shooting match in Los Angeles on Oct. 6, 1926, won by Pesek. The arguments will go on.

224 The leading heel: Johnnie Mae Young, telephone interview, May 15, 2007.

225 "She hadn't been able to train . . .": Joe Wolfe, personal interview, May 15, 2005

225 Bert Younker left the locker room: SMD, pp. 271–272.

226   Even though the occasion: The match may not have received coverage for two reasons. First, the wrestling business was in general decline due, many felt, to overexposure on television. Second, another of the periodic and damaging exposés about wrestling being fixed had recently appeared: Herman Hickman, "Rasslin' Was My Act," *Saturday Evening Post,* February 6, 1954, pp. 20–21, 101–102.

227   Burke on shooting vs. working: Ibid, pp. 34–36, 177–178.

226–234   Description of the match: SMD, pp. 273–280; "Mildred Burke's Epic Struggle with June Byers for the Ladies Championship," Burke letter to *Aggressive Women,* a British magazine, 1970, www.proladywrestlers.com/Home_Page/Memory_Land/Mildre . . . /mildred_burke.htm, accessed April 12, 2001; June Byers Gets 'Moral' Victory Over Miss Burke, Associated Press in *Tampa Times,* Aug. 21, 1954; Billy Wolfe telegram to Joe "Toots" Mondt, 5:56 a.m., Aug. 21, 1954, Pfefer Collection; author interviews with Joe Wolfe, Bert Younker, Johnnie Mae Young, and Gloria Barattini; Mildred Burke interview, DOJ investigation, March 23, 1955, p. 4.

234   Herbie Freeman account: Freeman letter to Jack Pfefer, August 24, 1954, Pfefer Collection.

234   "June Byers won the one fall . . .": Wolfe telegram to Mondt.

235   Two days after the match: "Claim World Wrestling Title For June Byers," *Columbus Citizen,* August 22, 1954.

235   "Well, now you know . . .": Pat Schnee, "Wrestling Fan Clubs," *Wrestling World,* September 1954, p. 27.

236   "Tremendous plans and programs . . .": SMD, p. 282.

236   "A newspaper report about the match . . .": "Florida Recognizes June Byers is Champion of the World," *The Sportscaster,* Tampa Official Souvenir Wrestling Program, Aug. 24, 1954.

237   "There are many persons . . .": "Champ Byers, Stafford Go In Mat Bout," *Abilene Reporter News,* Texas, December 12, 1954, p. 4-D.

237   Byers gave a highly embellished account: Jack Fletcher, "June Byers

Tells About My Toughest Bout," *Girl Wrestling: The World's Sexiest Sport,*
Spring 1965, pp. 63–68.

238   His records do not show: Attractions, Inc. commissions ledger provided by Betsy Wolfe Stemple and Mickie Johnson.

238   Robbery of June and G. Bill: "Robbers Beat Gal Wrestlers," Interna-
tional News Service in *San Antonio Light,* October 24, 1954, p. 6-D; "4 Thugs
Throw 2 Gal Rasslers For 20G Loss," United Press, October 23, 1954, Pfefer
Collection; "Lady Wrestler, Companions Lose $40,000 to Holduppers,"
Associated Press in *Ada Evening News,* Oklahoma, October 23, 1954, p. 1.

239   The debate over who was the better wrestler: Steve Sank, "Mildred
Burke Greatest Champ," *Ring Wrestling,* July 1963, pp. 12–13, 65; "Con-
troversy Big on Women Wrestlers," *Ring Wrestling,* August 1964, Pfefer
Collection, pp. 5, 57.

240   Billy Wolfe's opinion: Brock Jones, "Nell Stewart Returns to Ring
in Top Shape," *Columbus Star,* July 13, 1957, p. 6; Emerson Davis, "Wrestling Periscope," *The Wrestler,* published by Al Haft Sports, October 29,
1960, p. 3.

Chapter 16

241   "I am going to stay home . . .": Burke letter to Jack Pfefer, Nov. 1,
1954, Pfefer Collection.

241   He had been stunned: Bert Younker, telephone interview, August 21,
2006.

242   Burke's account of Japan: SMD, pp. 283–305.

245   "Mildred was hard to work with . . .": Ruth Boatcallie, telephone
interview, June 29, 2007.

245   Burke and Young: SMD, pp. 206–308.

245   Mildred Burke had given a lasting boost: Mitsuru Uehira, "Girls in

the Orient," *Wrestling Life,* March 1955, p. 8; "Girl Wrestling In Japan Magnetic After Weak Start," *Ring Wrestling,* July 1972, pp. 22–25; "The Phantom of the Ring: Lipstick, Dynamite and Glowworms, Part 6," *Pro Wrestling Digest,* April 1, 2008, www.prowrestlingdigest.com.

246   "Despite my bad knee . . .": SMD, p. 318.

246   The Japan triumph did little: Burke interview, DOJ investigation, March 23, 1955, p. 5.

246   Al Karasick: "Memo: Recommendation for Criminal Prosecution," DOJ investigation, August 25, 1955, p. 30. In the end, the Justice Department opted for a civil settlement rather than a criminal prosecution.

246   Burke was dead broke: Mildred Burke letter to Joseph "Toots" Mondt, March 9, 1955, Pfefer Collection.

247   Justice Department investigation: Burke interview, DOJ, March 23, 1955, pp. 1–5.

248   She tried to reestablish herself: Bill Newman, business manager of International Women Wrestlers, Inc., letter to "Dear Friend," June 14, 1955, Pfefer Collection.

248   "Lou Thesz is ten years older . . .": Jack Fiske, "Muscular Mildred Burke Owns 'Hall of Form' Here," *San Francisco Chronicle,* July 3, 1955; Hank Hollingsworth, "Sports Merry-Go-Round," *Long Beach Press-Telegram,* July 19 and July 21, 1955, p. A13 and A15.

248   Billy Wolfe outrage: Wolfe postcard to Sam Muchnick, July 11, 1955, DOJ, provided by Weldon Johnson.

249   Burke's last match: Ty Cobb, "Record Crowd Sees Mildred Burke Retain Title," Reno, Nevada *State Journal,* July 19, 1955.

249   One last burst: Hollingsworth, *Long Beach Press-Telegram,* July 19, 1955.

249   Justice Department investigation: Memo from Stanley E. Disney to James M. McGrath, "Telephone Call from Mildred Burke," DOJ, September 26, 1955.

250   "a little bit of an embarrassment . . .": Joe Wolfe, personal interview, May 16, 2005.

250   "If anyone met me . . .": SMD, p. 320.

250   Bankruptcy: In the Matter of Mildred Younker, Bankruptcy No. 5851, U.S. District Court for the Southern District of California, filed Feb. 17, 1958. In a filing, Burke said her net income was $59 a week.

250   When *Ring Wrestling* caught up: John Greensmith, "Mildred Burke . . . The Greatest of All the Women Wrestlers," *Ring Wrestling,* n.d., pp. 11–13, Pfefer Collection.

251   They divorced in 1962: Bert Younker, telephone interview, August 21, 2006.

251   Mildred again became close to Joe: Joe Wolfe, personal interview, May 16, 2005.

251   She kept her hand in wrestling: Gordon Grant, "Ex-Grappler Wrestles With Story of 19-Year Mat Career," *Los Angeles Times,* April, 29, 1962, p. SF6; Classified ad for "Girl Wrestlers," July 16, 1962, p. D2.

251   "I am divorced . . .": Burke letter to Jack Pfefer, October 13, 1962, Pfefer Collection.

252   That year she got a job: Burke letter to "Friend," July 20, 1962, Pfefer Collection.

252   "I got many a chuckle . . .": SMD, p. 322.

252   Joe bought her a small chili parlor: Joe Wolfe, personal interview, May 15, 2005.

Chapter 17

253   "We are now in the midst . . .": National Wrestling Alliance Bulletin No. 2, November 1, 1954, Sam Muchnick, DOJ investigation, "Recommendation for Criminal Prosecution," August 25, 1955, p. 27.

253 Wolfe finalized his divorce: William H. Wolfe vs. Verdie N. Wolfe, No. 77555, September 7, 1954, Court of Common Pleas, Franklin County, Ohio.

254 G. Bill in rehab: Sherrie Lee, telephone interview, March 31, 2007.

254 G. Bill joined Alcoholics Anonymous: Mickie Johnson, personal interview, October 27, 2006.

254 Byers divorced G. Bill: DeAlva E. Wolfe vs. G. Bill Wolfe, No. 82443, February 4, 1956, Court of Common Pleas, Franklin County, Ohio.

254 Ross had left a girls' home: Mickie Johnson, personal interview, October 27, 2006.

254 "Grand Vizier of Gal Wrestling . . .": Squires, "So You Wanna Be A Gal Grappler," p. 74.

254 LeeChona LaClaire: Joe R. Mills, "LeeChona LaClaire Latest Winner In Wrestling and Wedding Ring Go," *Columbus Star,* September 15, 1956.

255 A few days after the *Star* story: Sherrie Lee, telephone interview, March 31, 2007.

255 LaClaire was found in default: William H. Wolfe v. Ana Lee Wolfe, No. 84927, July 17, 1956, Court of Common Pleas, Franklin County, Ohio.

255 The Justice Department settled: Consent Decree, *United States vs. National Wrestling Alliance,* Civil Action No. 3-729, U.S. District Court, Southern District of Iowa, October 15, 1956. Although the attorney in charge of the case argued for a criminal prosecution, the department decided to handle the clear violations of law with a far less punitive civil remedy. Tim Hornbaker, author the definitive history of the NWA, believes powerful members of Congress with ties to NWA promoters might have intervened to tip the scales.

255 Wolfe was interviewed: Jimmy Breslin, NEA correspondent, "Ant-Trust Suit Filed Against Wrestling Group," *Kingsport News,* October 21, 1956, p. 7.

256   He had lost money: Attractions, Inc., financial records.

256   Joyce Bragg: Brock Jones, "Wrestleress Joyce Something to Brag About," *Columbus Star,* April 13, 1957, p. 6.

256   Laray was found in default: William H. Wolfe vs. Gladys Reynolds Wolfe, No. 87824, April 5, 1957, Court of Common Pleas, Franklin County, Ohio.

256   "I needed a way to support . . .": Lola Laray, G.L.O.R.Y. Legend of The Ring, www.glorywrestling.com/gg/LolaLaRay/LL.asp

256   Nell returned to Wolfe: Billy Wolfe letter to Jack Pfefer, July 11, 1957, Pfefer Collection; Jones, "Wrestleress Joyce," p. 6..

257   "I am working with . . .": Billy Wolfe letter to Jack Pfefer, December 1, 1957, Pfefer Collection.

258   A friend visited: Frankie Cain, telephone interview, July 19, 2008.

258   Wolfe was conciliatory: Billy Wolfe letter to Jack Pfefer, February 27, 1958, Pfefer Collection.

258   "Beating Nell . . .": Thomas Drake, "LeeChona LaClaire, West Virginia Wildcat," *Boxing Illustrated-Wrestling News,* May 1960, p. 49.

258   LaClaire returned: Steve Bulkley, "Larrupin' LeeChona To Defend Championship," *Columbus Star,* February 6, 1960, p. 14.

258   He tried to argue: Ibid.

258   When he wrote to Penny Banner: Banner and Hostetler, *Banner Days,* p. 183.

259   Someone finally reported him: FBI Report of interview with professional wrestler, name redacted, June 1, 1960, DOJ, and FBI Airtel, June 1, 1960, Bufile 60-4630, "National Wrestling Alliance, Antitrust," both provided by Weldon Johnson.

259   Karen Kellogg's history: "Billy Wolfe's New Sensation," Billy Wolfe letter to Stanley Weston, Dec. 31, 1961, published in *Wrestling Revue,* Pfefer Collection.

259 "He said they couldn't marry . . .": Sherrie Lee, telephone interview, March 31, 2007.

259 the old promotional magic: "Wolfe letter to Stanley Weston; John Auble, Jr., "Great As Mildred? Karen Kellogg Seen As Lady Wrestling Champ By Wolfe . . .", *Hartley Eastern Review*, Ohio, March 8, 1962, p. 7.

260 "The note you put in . . .": Billy Wolfe letter to Jack Pfefer, July 9, 1962, Pfefer Collection.

260 His tax return: 1961 return provided by Betsey Wolfe Stemple and Mickie Johnson.

260 Wolfe coronated Kellogg: "Dazzling Karen Kellogg Wins World Mat Title," *Bluefield Daily Telegraph*, Virginia, November 4, 1962, p. 10; Stanley Weston, "Coronation In Bluefield," *Wrestling Revue*, April 1963, p. 17–19, 64.

260 He had been fighting the flu: "Billy Wolfe," unsigned obituary written by Betsy Ross in *Ring Wrestling*, July 1963, p. 47.

261 "I am very sorry . . .": Al Haft letter to Jack Pfefer, April 16, 1963, Pfefer Collection.

261 "The year was 1937 . . .": Tom Keys, *Columbus Citizen-Journal*, March 11, 1963.

261 G. Bill bore no resemblance: Mickie Johnson, personal interview, October 27, 2006.

262 He suddenly grabbed: Ibid.

262 G. Bill obit: "Deaths And Funerals, G. Bill Wolfe," *Newark Advocate*, Ohio, August 10, 1964.

262 G. Bill's estate: "Court News, Estates Valued," *Newark Advocate*, April 7, 1965.

262 "Billy was her salvation . . .": Mickie Johnson, personal interview, October 27, 2006.

262 Nell's final days: Ida May Martinez, telephone interviews, May 7 and September 11, 2007.

262 Stewart funeral arrangements: Ibid.

263 She talked in every interview: "Wrestling's Appeal? Cash, Says Byers," *Minneapolis Tribune,* n.d., circa 1955, Pfefer Collection; Johnny Hopkins, "The Way I See It," *Calgary Herald,* n.d., circa 1955, Pfefer Collection; Hy Todd, "How Byers Got to be Champion," *Boxing Illustrated and Wrestling News,* October 1959, pp. 42–45, 63; Shirley Walsh, "Woman Wrestler Keeps Life Busy," *Calgary Herald,* September 28, 1961, p. 39.

263 "She was going down . . .": Jewell Olivas, telephone interview, September 2, 2007.

263 In the 1980s she hocked: Ibid.

263 When she died in 1998: DeAlva Snyder paid obituary in the *Houston Chronicle,* July 23, 1998.

263 The child was given up for adoption: Tim Kelly, telephone interview, January 15, 2007.

263 A DNA test: Marie Laverne, telephone interview, August 15, 2007.

Chapter 18

265 Her circumstances were humble: Frankie Goodman, "Boxing Biz," *Van Nuys News,* September 29, 1968.

265 In Japan, the WWWWA belt: "The Phantom of the Ring: Lipstick, Dynamite and Glowworms, Part 6," *Pro Wrestling Digest,* April 1, 2008, www.prowrestlingdigest.com.

265 "I now have my own gym . . .": Mildred Burke letter to Jack Pfefer, Dec. 17, 1968, Pfefer Collection.

266 Moolah promoted her own: Jares, *Whatever Happened to Gorgeous George?* pp. 49–50.

266 In the view of some wrestling purists: Author interviews with Penny Banner, Ida May Martinez, and Joe Wolfe.

266   Burke was home watching: John Hall, "How Red the Rose," *Los Angeles Times,* May 15, 1968, p. C3.

266   They had met only once: Ellison and Platt, *The Fabulous Moolah,* p.33.

266   "Mildred Burke broke my leg . . .": "Weaker Sex? Not in Wrestling—Moolah," *Wrestling Revue,* December 1963.

266   "The main reason I dislike her . . .": Jares, *Whatever Happened to Gorgeous George?* p. 50.

267   "I'm a teenage girl . . .": Deena Childers, *Ring Wrestling,* December 1970, p. 54.

267   A former female pro said: J.P, "Male Amateur Wouldn't Stand A Chance," *Wrestling Revue,* n.d., 1965, p. 6, Pfefer Collection.

268   "If any professional promoters . . .": Harvey Stimber, "Urges Playing Up Mixed Matches," *Ring Wrestling,* August 1968, p. 40.

268   The magazine's editors scoffed: RW Mat Mail, *Ring Wrestling,* August 1968, p. 50; Nat Loubet, " 'No Mixed Matches' Policy Of Ring Wrestling Stands," *Ring Wrestling,* February 1972, p. 16.

268   Another writer who had seen: John Ludecke, "Wants Mixed Matches," *Ring Wrestling,* February 1972, p. 58.

268   But fans from around the world: *Ring Wrestling,* February 1972. p. 67.

268   She had been training her women: Mike Goodman, "School For Groaners: The Wild, Wonderful World of Professional Wrestling," *Los Angeles Times,* March 4, 1973, p. SF A1.

268   Joe Wolfe was the cameraman: Joe Wolfe, personal interview, May 15, 2005.

269   battle of the sexes in the ring: Jane Beverly, "Laura Del Rio Proves Point Against 180-Pound Male Rival," *Wrestling Monthly,* August 1974, pp. 21–25.

269   Reaction to mixed match: "War Star Up to Pin Male in 3rd Fall, Gal Pros Test Guys on W. Coast," *Wrestling Revue,* October 1974, p. 18–22;

Eave Rhomas, "Finally Convinced," *Wrestling Monthly,* November 1974, p. 6; "These Girls Will Do Anything to Reach Stardom," *Wrestling Revue,* November 1974, p. 16–18; Larry L. Kuhnle, "Mixed Match Mania," *Wrestling Monthly,* February 1975.

270   Burke created an ad: Mildred Burke's School of Professional Wrestling, *Wrestling Revue,* June 1973, pp. 62–63.

270   "There is nothing like a good tussle . . .": Don Wilkins, "Like Topsy, Girls Amateur Wrestling in America Just Grows and Grows," *Wrestling Monthly,* March 1974, pp. 17–21.

270   Ron Fox: Internet posting, "My Mixed Wrestling Career, Part 1," March 23, 2007, blog.360.yahoo.com.

271   "Wrestling has always had . . .": SMD, p. 122.

272   She named her film business: Notice of doing business as the World Wide Women's Wrestling Association and Mildred Burke Productions, Mildred (Burke) Younker, filed with the County Clerk of Los Angeles County, No. 73-25103, September 28, 1973.

272   Burke's women were reduced: "Women Will Wrestle For $1,000 Prize," *Modesto Bee,* June 25, 1973.

272   After she put on an all-woman's card: "Miller Protests Action Of Mat Czar," *Modesto Bee,* June 20, 1973, p. B-1.

272   "My girls cannot work . . .": "Women Wrestlers Claim Discrimination," *Pasadena Star-News,* May 24, 1973, p. 21; Mike Goodman, "Girl Wrestlers to Picket," *Los Angeles Times,* May 22, 1973, p. SF6.

272   "When I met her . . .": Jeff Walton with Scott Walton, *Richmond 9-5171: A Wrestling Story* (Los Angeles: J.W. Enterprises, 2004), p. 78.

273   "The mostly middle-aged . . .": Patricia de Luna, "Lunching Lions roar, relish spicy sport," *Long Beach Independent and Press-Telegram,* January 14, 1974, p. B-5.

273   Burke even called Byers: SMD, p. 281.

273   The writer Joe Jares visited: Jares, *Whatever Happened to Gorgeous George?* pp. 49–65.

274   "Mildred used to tell us . . .": Bob Thomas, "Star Watch: Vicki Frederick and 'All the Marbles,' " Associated Press, Oct. 12, 1981.

275   *Times* interview: Alan Greenberg, "Mildred Burke . . . She Never Met Her Match," *Los Angeles Times,* April 17, 1981, p. D1.

276   Joe found her: Joe Wolfe, personal interview, May 16, 2005.

277   Constable blamed: Trevor J. Constable letter to Joe Wolfe, March 9, 1989.

277   The last chapter: SMD, pp. 316–334.

Epilogue

281   Cain said he froze: "Historic Pin," *Sports Illustrated,* January 27, 1986; Ron Arias, "An unblushing California schoolgirl handles groping boys with takedowns, not putdowns," *People,* March 10, 1986.

282   Statistics on female high school wrestlers from the National Federation of State High School Associations. Observers have noted several advantages girl wrestlers have over boys, including greater flexibility, lower centers of gravity, a tendency to favor technique over strength and greater stamina against boys who exerted themselves too quickly. Plus, the girls wrestled without fear of humiliation.

282   "The place erupted . . .": Mark Schmetzer, "Girl wrestler pins spot in district tournament," *Cincinnati Enquirer,* February 24, 1999.

282   "She was stronger . . .": David Goricki, "Williamston's Simmons perfect," *Detroit News,* March 10, 2000.

283   Samantha Lang: Doug Binder, "Taking A Gender-Neutral Position At Tualatin High," *Portland Oregonian,* January 31, 2002; Cliff Pfenning, "Women's Wrestling: A 'Gold' Opportunity," *Portland Tribune,* February 13,

2004; Cliff Pfenning, "The Scramble for Standings Begins," *Portland Tribune,* February 17, 2004.

284   History was made: Ron Wilmot, "Michaela Hutchison steals tourney thunder," *Anchorage Daily News,* February 6, 2006; "A girl is a state champion among boys," Female Single Combat Club, www.fssc.com.

286   movie talk: Kevin Kelly, "Art Brings Ribman's 'Dream' to Life," *Boston Globe,* January 31, 1993, B25.

286   she recalled Mildred Burke: Barbara Flanagan, "The Flanagan Memo," *Minneapolis Star Tribune,* August 3, 1992, P. 2B.